Tabletop Game Design for Video Game Designers

Tabletop Game Design for Video Game Designers

Ethan Ham

Routledge
Taylor & Francis Group

LONDON AND NEW YORK

First published 2016 by Focal Press

Published 2017 by Routledge
2 Park Square, Milton Park, Abingdon, Oxon OX14 4RN
711 Third Avenue, New York, NY 10017

Routledge is an imprint of the Taylor & Francis Group, an informa business

Library of Congress Cataloging-in-Publication Data
Ham, Ethan.
    Tabletop game design for video game designers / Ethan Ham.
       pages cm
    Includes index.
    1. Computer games—Programming.   2. Computer games—Design.   3. Storyboards.   I. Title.
       QA76.76.C672H35155 2015
       794.8'1526—dc23
       2014040388

ISBN: 978-0-415-62701-6 (pbk)
ISBN: 978-1-315-72612-0 (ebk)

Typeset in Myriad Pro
by ApexCoVantage, LLC

Cover Image: The Last of Us ©2013/™ SCEA. Created and developed by Naughty Dog.

Contents

Dedication

For Bryce, Connor, & Jacob. I am looking forward to the many family game nights to come.

Thank You

Thank you to all the people who have contributed over the years to my growth as a game player, game maker, game teacher, and (now) game writer. In particular, I would like to thank:

My students, for inspiring me to write this book.

My father, for the games he taught me to play, especially *Chess* and *Go*. And for giving me R.C. Bell's *Boardgame Book*, which (along with *Rules of Play*) sparked the idea for including playable games in this volume.

Mr. Sherman, who was my math teacher and dungeon master in junior high school and introduced me to pencil & paper roleplaying games.

The folks I roleplayed with in high school in Mississippi: Scott Hellard, Joe Hudson, Richard Hudson, Lee Parkel.

The folks I roleplayed with during my college years: the UCSC cohort of Jamey Harvey, David Lee, Dean Lee, and Eric Lee and my fellow Santa Cruz High School alums Kevin Cooke, Curtis Erhart, and Dana Gier.

Karen Rosenbaum and Benjamin Rosenbaum for TIC camp, where I learned to program in order to teach programming.

The folks I roleplayed with post-college: David Ackert, Jamey Harvey (again), and Benjamin Rosenbaum (again).

The folks at Books That Work, where I learned to become a professional programmer—especially Marc Goldstein, Dianne Jacob, and Benjamin Rosenbaum (again).

The folks at Digital Addiction: Walter Carter, Paul Dennen, Jamey Harvey (again), Matt Hulan, Lee Moyer, John Mueller, Leslie Power, Howard Rosen, and Benjamin Rosenbaum (again).

Gordon Walton, Tony Van, and the other folks at Maxis and Electronic Arts.

Bart Massey for his mentorship and providing me the opportunity to teach my first game design course.

The Railroad Street Youth Project and the Egremont Free Library for your game nights.

The individuals and companies who allowed me to include their games within these pages: Chrisbo I.P. Holdings for *Cathedral*, Dominique Ehrhard & Gigamic for *Marrakech*, James Ernest for *Button Men* and Lee Moyer (again) & Jeff Lewis for the *Sanctum* and *Button Men* artwork, Dr. Reiner Knizia for *Shoot-Out*, Jeremiah Lee (game design) and Kwanchai Moriya (artwork) for *Zombie in my Pocket*, Adam P. McIver for *Coin Age*, and John Yianni for *Hive*.

The game designers who contributed essays to this book: Greg Costikyan, Liz England, James Ernest (again), Raph Koster, Stone Librande, James Moore, Sarah Northway, and John Yianni (again).

Arne Meyer, Eric Monacelli, Josh Scherr, and the other folks at Naughty Dog for their generosity in providing the book's cover image.

My editor, Sean Connelly, Caitlin Murphy, Denise Power, Sioned Jones, and the rest of the team at Focal Press for all your hard work in making this book a reality.

Benjamin Rosenbaum (again) and Ian Schreiber for their invaluable comments and contributions to the book.

And finally, my wife Janet, for both her patience and feedback.

Support for this book was provided by a PSC-CUNY Award, jointly funded by The Professional Staff Congress and The City University of New York.

CHAPTER ONE

Getting Started

INTRODUCTION

This is book about game design. It is intended for people who want to make games and are looking for a book that can provide not only conceptual tools for defining and analyzing games, but also practical guidance in the craft of making them. It does so by having the reader focus on tabletop games. As this chapter explains, working with tabletop games is an ideal way to develop game design skills that are as applicable in the digital realm as they are on the tabletop.

The learning objectives for this chapter are:

1 Gain an understanding of the book's goals and scope.

2 Learn how playing and creating tabletop games is useful to video game developers.

3 Develop the ability to effectively read and comprehend the rules to a tabletop game.

Welcome to the Fun Mines

Game design is a young academic discipline. Game design teachers (the author included) are still learning how to pass on its best practices—and, indeed, what exactly *are* the best practices. Because of this, it is all too common for game design instruction to root itself in the analysis of games and their structures. That is useful information, to be sure, yet on its own it can maroon students and leave them unsure of how to bridge the gap between understanding games and actually making them. The goal of this book is to guide you to actually making games. It does this through short, highly focused design exercises that will take you step-by-step towards being a skilled practitioner of game design.

If you are reading these words, you are probably someone who loves to play games. Part of this book's ambition is to help you discover that you also love creating games. Towards that end, it is important to understand that being a consumer of games is different from being a creator of games. A love of playing games does not necessarily translate into a love of making games any more than a love of eating equates to a love of cooking. It is true that most game professionals enter the industry because they find games irresistible, but only a fraction of game players will find that they enjoy creating games. Playing a game is a diversion. We play games to socialize, to procrastinate, and to submerge ourselves into a fantasy existence. Game development is not a diversion. Making a game takes great perseverance, organization, and intellectual sweat. The characteristics of people drawn to the profession can be the very traits that prevent them from succeeding at it.

The hope is that you will find this book's lessons in game design compelling and will be drawn into the discipline. To build upon what you learn within these pages, you will need to continue making and playtesting your own games, find ways to meet and share ideas with other game designers, and work your way into the industry. Even if game design proves to be less appealing than you had hoped, the book's lessons can still serve to make you a better player of games and might even introduce you to types of games that you find exciting and fun.

Why Tabletop Games?

How can tabletop games make you a better video game designer? Tabletop and video games share numerous traits, and many of the design lessons that are learned by making and playing tabletop games can be applied to video games.

What is Game Design?

"Game design" is an ambiguous term. Within the professional game industry it is understood to refer to the creation of a game's rules. The wider world, however, often associates "design" with making visuals and non-game professionals tend to mistake a game designer for a game artist. Even some schools offering undergraduate and graduate degrees in game development mislabel their game art degrees as "game design." For example, the Academy of Art University describes its Game Design BFA as providing "a well-rounded education in the arts with an emphasis on understanding and applying techniques including 3D modeling, animation and lighting in video game production" (Academy of Art University 2012).

Bernard Suits, who wrote *The Grasshopper* (an early and groundbreaking game studies book), uses the term "gamewright" in place of game designer. The suggestion that a game designer's role is akin to that of a playwright is apt. Both professions are responsible for creating content whose finished form is typically realized by others—actors in the case of plays, and players in the case of games.

However, gamewright as a word has never gained much usage, so game designer is the designation we use, despite the confusion it engenders.

The video game of *Tetris* has at least as much in common with the tabletop game of *Cathedral* (figure 1.1) as it does with a console game like *Mass Effect*. Likewise, it is entirely reasonable to view tabletop miniatures games as being more closely related to real time strategy video games than to *Chess*.

Certainly there are ways in which tabletop games and video games differ, yet this can be just as illuminating. Learning how to translate a video game's real-time action onto the tabletop imparts a deeper understanding of the structure of video games (and gives you a valuable technique for video game prototyping).

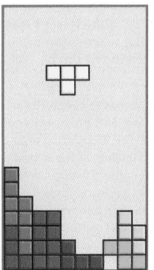

Figure 1.1 *Tetris* screenshot (left) and *Cathedral* (right).

Video games have the ability to hide their game mechanics. In fact, deducing a game's underlying algorithms is often the central player experience. For example, the iPhone version of *Jetpack Joyride* provides no directions regarding how the game works—players learn how to control the jetpack (and what they should collide with and what they should avoid) through trial and error. In contrast, playing a tabletop game typically involves the players understanding every game mechanic in detail. This is because tabletop games require the players to manually determine the effect of their actions. In essence, players take on the role of a "game engine" (see sidebar on page 6).

The rules for *Marrakech* (page 10) detail the precise way in which players are allowed to move their pieces because the players are responsible for making sure that it is done in accordance with the game's rules. As game designer Mike Pondsmith puts it:

> Trying to understand the nature of a gameplay experience directly from a video game is akin to trying to understand an internal combustion engine while it's running at 60mph! A tabletop game allows you to break down all the components of the game and see how all sections (mechanics, rules, characterization, player risk/reward structures, psychological paradigms) interrelate.
>
> (in Novak 2012, 186)

Just as a video game artist is well-advised to learn to draw well using pencil and paper, a video game designer should learn to create tabletop games. In both situations, a lot of the lessons learned in the physical medium can be applied in the digital realm—and being able to work in an analog medium (i.e., outside of a computer) can be useful for brainstorming and developing ideas.

Creating tabletop games is simpler than creating video games. Video games require programming, and programming is a detail-oriented pursuit that can all too easily absorb the focus of an entire development team (especially when there is a looming deadline) at the cost of neglecting the game's design. Because of this, professional game development projects sometimes begin by modeling parts of the game in tabletop form. This kind of paper prototype allows quick experimentation and easy, but dramatic, changes to the design prior to translating the gameplay into its final computer-based form.

There is a level of investment (time, money, effort) that programming requires. Once a game mechanic is implemented on a computer, the development team will have a natural hesitation to radically change or abandon it. (For a similar reason, it is best to avoid creating beautiful physical components for a tabletop game while its game design is still in flux.)

If your main desire is to make video games, you may be tempted to jump straight into making paper prototypes of video games (the topic of the book's final chapter) and not bother learning how to make games that are truly intended for tabletop play. However, developing a skill in making tabletop games is time well spent. Tabletop games can be evaluated on their own merits; either they are fun and balanced or they are not. Paper prototyping is a tricky undertaking and it is best to hone your tabletop design skills on their own terms before trying to apply them to modeling games intended for another medium.

Reading Rules

If you are like most people, you dislike reading rulebooks. Trying to make sense of a game's directions can be unsettling. Learning how to play a game often requires you to plow on through reading the rulebook, even though

Getting Into the Game

Most of the games referenced in the book can be found listed in the ludography, pages 300–303. An effort has been made to reference games that are easily and freely available for the reader to play. When this is the case, the game's title is printed in *blue text* as a way of letting you know that you can directly experience the game being described in the text.

In particular, whenever it is practical, the games that are included within the pages of this book are used to illustrate the book's concepts. These games are *Button Men* (page 184), *Cathedral* (page 188), *Coin Age* (following page 210), *Hive* (page 46), *Hut* (page 137), *Marrakech* (page 10), *Shoot-Out* (page 61), *Shoot-Out's* Core (page 70), *Sprouts* (page 158), *Tabletop Billiards* (page 29), *Three Musketeers* (page 249), *The Tower* (page 25), *Ultimate Tic-Tac-Toe* (page 177), *The Ultimatum Game* (page 224), *Yut Nori* (page 204), and *Zombie in my Pocket* (page 114).

All the other games whose titles are in *blue text* can be found by visiting the book's accompanying website at www.funmines.com/games. You are strongly encouraged to try your hand at playing all these games. Doing so will allow you to more fully understand the game design issues being discussed in the text and will broaden your knowledge of games and gameplay.

Game Engines

A game engine is the part of the software that executes a video game's core functionality. The engine takes in the players' actions and the various automated activities in the game, determines the outcomes, and updates the game world and its presentation to the player. Many game developers choose to use game engines developed by third parties (such as the Unity game engine)—so much so that the term "game engine" is often treated as being synonymous with these ready-made "middleware" development tools.

you only partly understand the parts that you have read so far. The experience is made worse if you have played relatively few tabletop games. The more games you know, the more likely it is that a game mechanic you encounter in the rulebook will be similar to something you have played before.

You do not need to enjoy reading rules, but you do need to seek out and value the experience. Learning new games extends your knowledge and provides raw material from which to draw inspiration. More profoundly, the process of puzzling out a game's mechanics exercises your sense of how a game is constructed and balanced. As you read a rulebook, your game designer mind is constantly trying to jump ahead and figure out how the entire game plays. Whether your preliminary guesses about the gameplay prove correct or not, you are (in a way) practicing designing a game. Occasionally, a new game will provide design experience in a more literal way. If you play many tabletop games, you will undoubtedly come across rules that are ambiguous, missing some detail, or are simply unbalanced to the point of being unenjoyable. These occasions call upon you to come up with your own chunk of design to fix the problem.

Video game players have the luxury of learning to play a new game through tutorials that introduce the game's mechanics in bite-sized, easily digested pieces. If your game experience has been predominantly playing video games, the following proposed method for learning new tabletop games may be helpful to you. You could certainly just dive into a new tabletop game and start playing (reading the rulebook as you go along), or favor the more painless method of having someone who knows the game teach it to you. However, for the reasons outlined above, a more structured and hands-on approach can be valuable to your growth as a game designer.

When sitting down to learn a new game, plan to read through the rules at least two times. During the first reading, do not worry too much about understanding every detail. The primary goal of the first reading is to understand the game in broad strokes. The second reading is where you are hoping to gain a solid understanding of the game. Even then, it is not unusual to need to flip through the rulebook a third time, trying to resolve some confusing aspect of the game.

At a certain point, you have learned all you can from simply reading the rules and the next step is to start playing the game. This is your opportunity to explain the rules to the other players—you may be surprised by how much you can learn through the process of teaching. When teaching a game to a group of people, it is easy to overwhelm them with all the details. You may want to outline the rules in broad strokes before starting the game, and then fill in the details as you play. You will likely find yourself returning to the rulebook to look up specific details throughout the game.

The first time you play a game, expectations should be low. The first game is like the first pancake—it can be half-cooked, malformed, and generally pales in comparison to what follows. When you play a game for the first time, you will likely have to play without being able to form a larger strategy or even fully understand the implications of the choices you are making. You may even realize late in the game that you have misunderstood the rules all along and that the entire play session was "pointless." For game players, the first game (like the first pancake) is an investment in the second one. Players put up with the clunky, slightly unpleasant first game in hopes that the later games will justify the effort. For a game designer, the first game is worthwhile in itself as a learning experience, even if the second game is never played (or the play experience does not improve with repetition).

To summarize, the suggested process for learning a new tabletop game is:

1. Read the rulebook at least two times. Doing so is a good exercise in itself for game designers.
2. Explain the rules to the people you are playing with. Clarifying the mechanics for others is the best way to clarify them for yourself.
3. Play the game for the first time. At this point you are probably still absorbing the rules and gaining an understanding of the game's system.
4. Play the game a second time. This is the point at which you can reasonably expect to start playing the game properly.

Why Read Rules?

1. **Game design is communication.** When you were an infant, you understood language before you could speak it yourself. Similarly, you learned to read before you could learn how to write. The same holds true for rulebooks. Before you can become skilled at writing rules, you need to be skilled at reading them.
2. **A tabletop game *is* its rules.** The board and playing pieces are the physical implementation, but the rules are what makes a game a game. You want to study game design? The rules *are* the design.
3. **Rulebooks are design documents.** Video game designers need to write game design documents in order to provide programmers with a blueprint for building the game. Becoming skilled at writing tabletop rules will help prepare you for writing video game design documents. In fact, if you can write a good rulebook, your game design documents will probably be outstanding. Rulebooks are more difficult to write than game design documents because they need to be polished and comprehensible to a wide spectrum of readers. In contrast, video game design documents are internal and for the development team. Whenever the document is unclear, the team members can simply ask the designer for an explanation (as opposed to having to puzzle it out for themselves).

EXERCISE Playing *Marrakech*

Marrakech is a light-hearted game designed by Dominique Ehrhard. Players take on the role of merchants who are trying to dominate the rug market through the placement of their color-coded rugs.

The game is included in this book and can be played by photocopying and cutting out the board and pieces on pages that follow page 13 (or, if you prefer, simply cut out the pages themselves).

Alternatively, you could construct a copy of the board and game pieces yourself. Doing so is good practice for prototyping your own games (a subject that is covered Chapter 3). If you do make your own board, be sure to include the arrows on the edges. At a glance they seem merely decorative, but they also serve the practical purpose of indicating how pieces move upon reaching the edge of the board.

Figure 1.2 The retail version of *Marrakech* by Dominique Ehrhard, ® & © Gigamic 2007, www.gigamic.com.

The rules are on page 10—you will need to read them before proceeding with this exercise.

Having read the rules, did you find them confusing in any way? In particular, did you find the rules for a two-player game a bit ambiguous:

> *Each player receives twenty-four rugs (twelve each of two different colors). The rugs should be mixed together into a stack and then played in order.*

For the two-player version of the game, the rules do not explicitly state whether each player's set of two rug colors are treated as being identical for the purposes of calculating a payment. However, the fact that the rugs are played in order suggests that each player's two colors are treated as being distinct and non-contiguous.

How would having contiguity determined by ownership (instead of by color) affect the game? How might the difference change the choices players are motivated to make?

What happens if a player does not have enough Dirham to pay the penalty for landing on an opponent's rug? The rules included in this book do not address that situation. How would you choose to handle it?

The rulebook for the first edition of the game was also silent on the matter. However, it was updated in later printings to specify that a player who does not have sufficient funds should pay as much as possible, and is then eliminated from the game. The eliminated player's rugs become neutral; no payment is made by opponents landing upon them. However, there are other ways that a game designer might choose to handle the situation. Zoch, a German company that publishes *Marrakech* under the name *Suleika*, opted to have a bankrupted player pay as much as possible and then remain in the game without owing any debt. Which version do you prefer (and why)?

Round up some people to play *Marrakech* with you. Try playing the basic rules as well as the variant that is described at the end of the rules. If you have trouble finding people to play with, you can play the game against yourself. To do so, set up the game for a four-person game, then take each player's turn. Playing against yourself in this manner is good practice for solo playtesting your own games (see page 76) and is

Variations

A game variant is a modification to an existing game. The result is recognizably related to the original game, but has changed in a way that creates new gameplay possibilities. A common *Monopoly* variant is to set aside all the money paid in taxes and fees and reward it to whoever lands on Free Parking. Thousands of variants exist for *Chess*. A popular one is *Chess960* in which the starting positions of the pieces are semi-randomized so that the game does not favor a player who has memorized the standard openings.

This paper cut-out version of the game is being provided by kind permission of the game's publisher, Gigamic (en.gigamic.com). Their retail version greatly enhances the aesthetic experience of playing the game by having cloth rugs and wooden game pieces.

worth trying, even if you can find people to play with.

Having played the game, did you discover anything about it that you did not foresee when you originally read the rules? What affect did the variant have on the gameplay? Which version of the rules do you prefer and why?

Marrakech

The rug market in Marrakech is on tenterhooks: the best salesperson will soon be named. Lay out your rugs, amass your fortune, and perhaps you will be that lucky rug merchant.

Players:

■ Two to four players

Required Materials:

■ Game board
■ Four sets of fifteen rugs
■ Twenty silver "one" Dirham coins and twenty gold "five" Dirham coins
■ Game piece representing Assam the market owner
■ Customized 6-sided die

Pre-Game Preparation:

■ Cut out the game board, rugs, and coins (the pages that follow page 13).
■ Locate a game piece to represent Assam. The game piece must allow easy determination of what direction Assam is facing. A *Chess* knight works well.
■ Modify a 6-sided die so that it has the following values on its sides: 1, 2, 2, 3, 3, 4. An easy way to accomplish this is to cover the sides with masking tape on which the custom values are written.

Object of the Game:

■ Have the largest fortune when the game concludes. A player's fortune is calculated by adding together the amount of money owned and the number of the player's rugs' halves that are visible on the board.

Setup:

- Place the game piece representing Assam on the board's center square (see figure 1.3). He should face one of the square's four sides (which side does not matter).
- Give each player thirty Dirhams: five silver "one" pieces and five gold "five" pieces.
- Assign rug colors to the players. The number of rugs each player receives is based upon the number of people playing the game:
  Two players: Each player receives twenty-four rugs (twelve each of two different colors). The rugs should be mixed together into a stack and then played in order.
  Three players: Each receives fifteen rugs of the same color.
  Four players: Each receives twelve rugs of the same color.
- Decide who takes the first turn. Play moves in a clockwise direction.

Taking a Turn:

- A player's turn consists of the following actions:
  1. Rotate Assam (if desired).
  2. Throw the die.
  3. Move Assam.
  4. Pay an opponent (if necessary).
  5. Place a rug.

1) Rotate Assam

- The player chooses the direction Assam faces **_prior to throwing the die_**.
- Assam's direction can be left unchanged or turned 90 degrees left or right—he cannot be turned 180 degrees (see figure 1.3).

2) Throw the die

- See "pre-game preparation" above for details regarding the die's customized values.

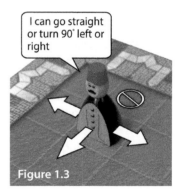

I can go straight or turn 90° left or right

Figure 1.3

3) Move Assam

- The player moves Assam a number of squares equal to the die's value.
- Assam moves in a straight line (not diagonally) in the direction determined in step 1 above.
- If Assam moves off the board, he turns around by following the arrow on the edge of the board, rotating to face the new direction of travel. The movement along an arrow is "free" and does not use up one of the die's movement points. (see figure 1.4).

4) Pay an opponent (if necessary):

■ If Assam ends his move on an opponent's rug, the player moving him must make a payment to the rug's owner.

■ The amount owed is one Dirham for the square that Assam landed upon plus one Dirham for each orthogonally contiguous square (see sidebar on page 13) covered by a rug of the same color. This means, that for each half rug that is part of the uninterrupted shared-color group that Assam landed upon, one Dirham is owed to the rugs' owner (see figure 1.5).

■ The player makes no payment if Assam ends his move on an empty square or on one of the player's own rugs.

5) Place a rug:

■ After moving Assam and paying the owner of the rug Assam landed upon (if necessary), the player lays a rug on a square next to where Assam landed.

■ The rug must cover one of the squares orthogonally adjacent to the square Assam is occupying (see Figure 1.6). Placing a rug so that it is only diagonally adjacent to Assam's square is not allowed.

■ The rug may be placed upon:
   ■ Two empty squares.
   ■ An empty square and half a rug of any color.
   ■ Two halves of two different rugs of any color (see Figure 1.7).

■ A rug may *not* be placed upon:
   ■ An entire single rug.
   ■ Under Assam.

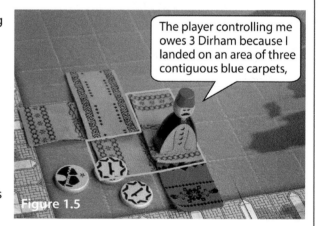

When I reach the green edge of the board, I follow the white path. I rotate to follow the direction of travel. This movement does not count against the number of spaces I am moving.

Figure 1.4

The player controlling me owes 3 Dirham because I landed on an area of three contiguous blue carpets,

Figure 1.5

Ending the Game:

- The game ends once the last rug is laid.
- Players earn one point for each rug half that they have visible and for each Dirham owned.
- The player with the most points wins the game. In the case of a tie, the player with the most Dirhams wins.

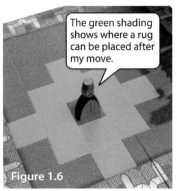

The green shading shows where a rug can be placed after my move.

Figure 1.6

It's okay to cover two different rugs, but not both halves of a single rug.

Figure 1.7

Variant:

- Players take the following actions in order each turn:
  1. Throw the die.
  2. Move Assam.
  3. Pay an opponent (if necessary).
  4. Place a rug.
  5. Rotate Assam.
- The next player must move Assam in the direction the previous player set in the variant's step 5.

® & © Gigamic 2007
Creator: Dominique Ehrhard
www.gigamic.com

Orthogonal and Contiguous

Game spaces are "orthogonal" if they are at right angles (i.e., not diagonal) to one another. "Contiguous" refers to a group of game spaces that share a particular trait and are not separated from one another. See the sidebar on page 157 for a more detailed explanation of contiguity.

In *Marrakech*, when you land on a square occupied by another player's rug, you have to pay your opponent a number of Dirham equal to the number of orthogonally connected squares that are contiguous in terms of their rug color.

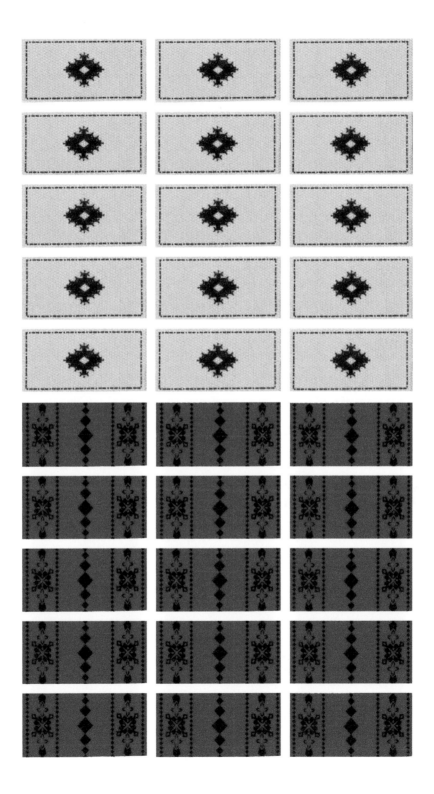

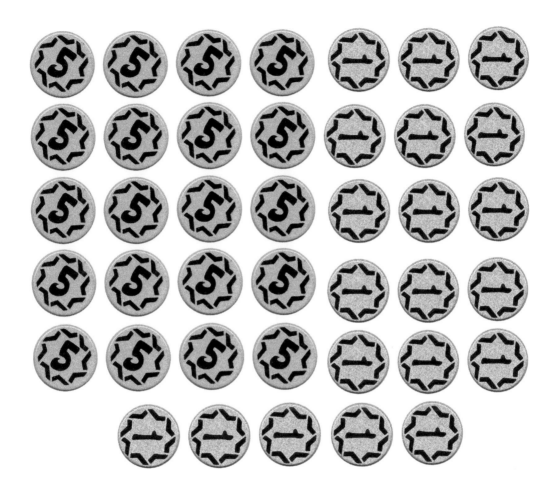

® & © Gigamic 2007
Creator: Dominique Ehrhard
www.gigamic.com

Dominique Ehrhard

Dominique Ehrhard is a French artist and the designer of dozens of tabletop games. After graduating from the University of Strasbourg, Ehrhard spent several years teaching painting in Morocco (perhaps the memory of his time in the country inspired him to create *Marrakech*). Upon returning to France, he collaborated with the CLAC artist collective in the city of Nancy and worked as a scenographer for l'Ensemble Artistique d'Alsace. Since setting up his own art studio on the banks of the Loire, Ehrhard has devoted himself to painting and exhibiting regularly in galleries both in France and abroad. He also continues to write and illustrate children's books as well as develop games.

Photo 1.1 Courtesy of Dominique Ehrhard, used with permission.

Ehrhard's first game, *Snarps*, was published in 1990. Since then, he has published more than fifty games with European and American game companies including Amigo, Asmodee, Fantasy Flight Games, Games Work, Gigamic, Goldsieber, Haba, Hasbro, Interlude, Jumbo, Kosmos, Milton Bradley, Nathan, Piatnik, Ravensburger, Schmidt, Tilsit, Winning Moves, and Ystari.

In 2005, the Musée Français de la Carte à Jouer (the Museum of Playing Cards) devoted a large exhibit to exploring the relationship between Ehrhard's paintings and games. For the occasion, twenty-five of Ehrhard's paintings were published in the form of a special-edition card game, *Via Vitae*.

Game Literacy

As you read this book you will find that in addition to the games included within its pages, *Chess* and *Monopoly* are frequently referenced. If you do not already know how to play *Chess*, you should learn it as part of the basic game literacy that every game designer should possess.

Chess is a highly regarded game, *Monopoly* is less so. Still, *Monopoly* is a useful touchstone game because of its widespread popularity. And to give *Monopoly* its due, it is an early implementor of the trading, bidding, and set collecting mechanics that are often considered hallmarks of the contemporary tabletop "Eurogames" (see page 19).

Even the most creative people borrow ideas. Doing so is almost inevitable. But the broader your knowledge is, the more your appropriation can be subtle, interesting, and targeted. If your knowledge is shallow, then you will find yourself overly influenced by the few works you know. In the case of tabletop games, inexperienced game designers tend to find themselves making games that resemble the few games they know. If you have mainly played *Monopoly*, then you are likely to create a game that (like *Monopoly*) involves moving pieces around the periphery of the board.

Patent-Mine is an independently produced educational game that aims to both raise awareness about African American inventors and teach how the patenting process works. While the game's topics have little in common with *Monopoly*'s real estate theme, *Patent-Mine*'s board (figure 1.8) clearly shows its influence.

Figure 1.8 *Patent-Mine*. Used with permission of Ernest & Yolanda Green.

The games included in this book and on the accompanying website (www.funmines.com) can provide a good start towards developing a game literacy. If you are serious about games, do not limit yourself to just these games. Seek out as much diverse game playing experience as possible. Visit the website's resource section (www.funmines.com/resources) to find places where you can learn about and purchase games.

You may find the Games For Change / ESI Design's "The 100 Games Everyone Should Play" (www.funmines.com/games-to-play) useful in helping you prioritize what games you should play. The list presents one hundred games (video games, parlor games, playground games, and a few sports) that were nominated and voted upon by game developers and academics as being important, influential, or simply fun to play.

BoardGameGeek's game ratings (www.boardgamegeek.com/browse/boardgame) are also worth reviewing. BoardGameGeek's ranked list is based on game ratings provided by the site's community of users. The list is restricted to tabletop games and has a bias towards recently released games that appeal to hardcore gamers.

Both of these lists can steer you towards games that are worth taking the time to play—but keep in mind that there is plenty of room for disagreement about what games are truly the greatest. *Tic-Tac-Toe*, for example, is fifty-sixth on the Games for Change / ESI Design list, but ranked last (9,080th out of 9,080 games at the time of this writing) on BoardGameGeek's list.

The Top Twenty Games

Games for Change and ESI Design's Top 20 Games

(* indicates a video game)

1. *Chess*
2. *The Settlers of Catan*
3. *Portal**
4. *Dungeons & Dragons*
5. *Tetris**
6. *Go*
7. *Sid Meier's Civilization**
8. *SimCity**
9. *Pandemic*
10. *Super Mario Bros.**
11. *Magic: The Gathering*
12. *Hide-and-Seek*
13. *Minecraft**
14. *Pac-Man**
15. *Carcassonne*
16. *The Legend of Zelda: Ocarina of Time**
17. *Rock Paper Scissors*
18. *Capture the Flag*
19. *Grim Fandango**
20. *Katamari Damacy**

EXERCISE Making a List

What criteria do you think should be used when determining what are the best games? Using your own criteria, put together a ranked list of what you consider to be the top ten games you have played. Once you have your list, compare it to the top twenty (according to Games for Change and ESI Design) in the sidebar.

Are there any games that made it onto both lists? Does the Games For Change/ESI Design top ten include any game that you have played, but did not include in your own list? If so, why do you think you did not rank it as highly?

Boardgames Without Bankruptcy

Acquiring tabletop games can quickly become a prohibitively expensive pastime. If you are interested in a game, but find it hard to justify the cost of purchasing it, you may want to see if it is available as a web browser game or a smartphone app.

Pandemic is a well-regarded game; it is #9 on the Games for Change list and ranked #48 on BoardGameGeek (at the time of this writing). The physical game has a list price of $39.99, but it can be purchased on an iPhone or iPad for $6.99 (one fifth the price).

Computer-based versions of tabletop games will not only save you money, but they will also provide you with the ability to play against computer-controlled opponents. The games tend to be much speedier as well; you do not need to manually set up the board or move game pieces around as you play (and computer-opponents will not spend time taking bathroom breaks or agonizing over their moves). Artificial opponents are a major benefit for anyone who has trouble finding the time to play a game or people to play with.

BoardGameGeek has a blog (boardgamegeek.com/blog/164) dedicated to keeping abreast of tabletop games being released on iOS and (to a lesser extent) Android devices.

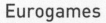

Eurogames

by Greg Costikyan

In this essay, Greg Costikyan explains what is meant by the term "Eurogame." In the 1990s these kinds of tabletop games were mainly a product of Germany and they were often referred to as "German games." As the style of game grew in popularity and designers beyond the borders of Germany began adopting it, the category's term was broadened to Eurogame. Today, these games are so widespread and prevalent that simply referring to them as "contemporary tabletop games" would be entirely justifiable.

The Eurogame is so called because the instances to which most gamers are exposed were first published in Germany. Paradoxically, however, the game style owes its origins to games published by the American conglomerate, 3M, in the 1960s—the fabled 3M games, in which Sid Sackson and Alex Randolph, acknowledged by Eurogame designers as the inspiration of their form, came to prominence.

Eurogamers prize strategic depth; if you listen to Eurogamers talk, again and again you will hear the phrase "interesting choices." They expect games that provide a limited number of options each time the player has an opportunity to act, but which make deciding among those options interesting, and non-trivial. If the best option is obvious, there's really no choice at all; but for the choice to be meaningful, there must be ramifications expanding from it. Choosing one option closes off some avenues and opens others. This requires a system of sufficient complexity, with a degree of uncertainty in terms of outcome—and yet, perhaps paradoxically, Eurogamers dislike games where "uncertainty of outcome" depends on random factors.

This dislike of randomness applies only to randomness that can dictate outcomes; that is, a Eurogame would never contain something like a wargame's Combat Results Table. But randomness is commonly used in Eurogames as a way of providing variability in outcome, or to break symmetry to ensure that players have different objectives or strategies; Eurogamers accept this, so long as random elements either expose all players to the same opportunities and disadvantages, or else confer no strong advantage on any single player. As an example, distribution of cards at the beginning of play does not confer a strong advantage on any player, so long as all cards are of equivalent power, but do "break symmetry" by giving players' different starting vantages.

In general, however, to a Eurogamer a game that can be won "by luck" is hardly worth playing, and suitable only for children.

Eurogames are strongly shaped by their market; they are mass-market products in Germany, after all, if relegated to hobbyists in North America. An ideal Eurogame is played in an hour or less and supports between three and six players. It has a low level of complexity by the standards of the wargame, but somewhat more than is typical of the American mass market game (most of which are marketed primarily to children). Ideally, it is accessible to fairly young players—many Eurogames are played by families together—but rewards the intellectual maturity that older players bring to bear, and the evolution of deeper strategic thinking by younger players.

The Eurogamer prizes clever simplicity; while he will not flinch at a degree of complexity, he admires a game that creates strategic depth with a minimal investment in learning the rules.

By and large, Eurogamers find games that pit players too directly against one another disturbing. Instead, the ideal game is one in which people injure or aid each other only at the margins, where each is building toward a win, perhaps competing for resources but not stabbing each other in the back. They prefer positive sum games, not zero sum games. Only one player can win, of course, and win conditions are necessary to motivate play, but winning should come from strategizing more efficiently, not crushing your opponents.

Eurogamers enjoy novelty. They consider themselves followers of an artistic form, and often know the names of the game designers whose work they enjoy, looking forward to new works from these "spieleautoren." They typically have large game collections.

Eurogamers enjoy the themes of the games they play, though they know the actual gameplay is divorced from the theme, that the theme is a mere marketing appendage on what is at heart an abstract strategy game. They view games as more than their mechanics, but as objets d'art, products whose art style, component value, and graphic design affect and inform the experience of play. Just as digital game players have problems divorcing an understanding of mechanics from the visuals to which they are exposed, a Eurogamer's judgment of a title may be as much informed by its production values as its actual gameplay.

Used with permission and excerpted from *Tabletop: Analog Game Design*, Greg Costikyan and Drew Davidson et al. 2011. Available for download at www.etc.cmu.edu/etcpress/content/tabletop-analog-game-design

CHAPTER TWO

Foundations

INTRODUCTION

Many of the terms used to describe and analyze games are loose in terms of having a precise and widely accepted definition. Game studies is still a young discipline, and its terminology may one day solidify. In the meantime, this chapter presents definitions for how this book uses a number of game terms. It is important to understand these definitions (especially "game state" and "game mechanic") in order to fully absorb the chapters that follow.

The learning objectives for this chapter are:

1 Define the book's usage of "game state," "game mechanic," "algorithm," and "gameplay."

2 Understand the relationship between game mechanics, dynamics, and player experience.

3 Demonstrate an ability to analyze a game's mechanics and game state.

What is a Game?

What is a game? This seems like a simple question, but it is one that game scholars (and game developers who care to join in on the fun) have grappled with many times without coming up with a thoroughly convincing definition.

It is all too easy to put forth a definition that initially seems promising, but ends up conflicting (when examined more closely) with our common-sense understanding of what a game entails. For example, one game studies book uses knife fights and *World of Warcraft* to illustrate its definition of what does and does not constitute a game (Burgun 2012, 14–15). That would seem reasonable enough except the book argues that a knife fight to the death is a game and *World of Warcraft* is not.

Your intuitive understanding of what constitutes a game will serve you as well as (if not better than) any fixed definition. That said, the quixotic task of attempting to define "game" can help you explore your own assumptions about what a game is or should be.

Salen and Zimmerman's *Rules of Play* (2004, 79) and Juul's "The Game, the Player, the World" (2003, www.jesperjuul.net/text/gameplayerworld) both provide excellent overviews of the various definitions that have been put forth by game studies academics. A heated discussion among game developers about what is and is not a game can be found in the replies to game designer Raph Koster's blog posting, "Two cultures and games" (www.raphkoster.com/2012/07/06/two-cultures-and-games). If this topic strikes your fancy, you might want to read through the various definitions put forth and, perhaps, even try to formulate your own.

Game State

Most video games are made up of a number of different sections such as a main menu, a load/save game screen, the game itself, a character upgrade screen, and so forth. Typically, each of these sections has its own user interface and its own way of working that is different from the other areas of the game. Sometimes game programmers refer to these varying areas of the software as "game states." The game can only be in a single state at a time and the computer program can be thought of as shifting gears as it changes from one state to another. This usage of "state" refers to the concept of finite-state machines (which is covered in Chapter 14).

When game designers use the term "game state," they are referring to something entirely different. For a game designer, a game state is a snapshot of the current situation in the game (whether it is a tabletop or video game). A game state includes all the information necessary to recreate that particular moment in the game—it is what the players (or the computer program) would need to know if the game were to be saved and reconvened at a later time. The game state changes every time a player takes an action or the computer program changes something in the game's world. With each state change, the game has shifted a bit and attentive players reevaluate their standing in the game and the strategies they are employing.

The ease with which a game state can be altered can have a major impact on the experience of playing the game. When the players' actions have only a minimal impact on the game state, the game can feel plodding. When players can easily make major changes to the game state, winning may feel a bit arbitrary.

Monopoly's game state includes how much money each player holds, who owns what property, which properties (if any) are mortgaged, the buildings on the board, the location of each player's token, the cards remaining in the Community Chest and Chance card decks, and whether anyone is holding the "Get Out of Jail Free" card.

Tabletop games typically track most of their game state information through their physical components. *Monopoly* players do not need to remember which properties they own because they can simply refer to the deed cards they are holding. Some aspects of the state, for example, whose turn it is, might not be deducible from the game's physical components alone. This sort of game state information could be called the "invisible game state." In addition to tracking whose turn it is, *Monopoly*'s invisible game state also notes whether that player has already rolled any doubles (rolling three doubles in a row results in a jail term). *Chess*'s invisible game state includes whether the players are able to castle if it is not clear from the position of the pieces (e.g., if a king was moved and returned to his home square). The distinction between visible and invisible game state is less relevant for video games because the computer typically tracks all aspects of the game state whether or not they are visible to the player.

The Tower

Reiner Knizia describes this game in his classic book, *Dice Games Properly Explained* (Knizia 2010, 49).

The counters used in the game can be coins, slips of paper, poker chips, packets of sugar, or anything else that is convenient. Knizia suggests using beer coasters if the game is played in a bar. The exact number of counters does not matter and the length of the game can be adjusted by using more or fewer of them. The counters should be pooled in the center of the table. If desired, they can be stacked into the eponymous "tower."

Players:

■ Two to six players

Required Materials:

■ Three 6-sided dice (alternatively, you could use the dice simulator at www.funmines.com/dice-simulator)
■ Approximately five counters per player

Object of the Game:

■ Avoid being the last player holding counters.

Setup:

■ Each player is assigned a number from 1 to 6. When three or fewer are playing, each player is assigned multiple numbers: 1–3 and 4–6 for a two-person game and 1–2, 3–4, and 5–6 for a three-person game.
■ A four-person game will have two unassigned numbers (5 and 6) and a five-person game will have one unassigned number (6).

Rules:

1. Players take turns rolling the three dice.
2. Each player (not just the current player) whose number comes up on one of the dice takes a counter.
3. In a four-person game, 5 and 6 are ignored when rolled because they are not assigned to a player. Likewise, in a five-person game, a 6 is ignored when rolled.
4. A player may end up taking more than one counter in a single roll if the player's number comes up on more than one die (or if the player is assigned multiple numbers, of which more than one was rolled).
5. After all the counters have been taken from the tower, the game's rules change. Now, players return counters to the tower when their numbers are rolled.
6. The game ends when all the players except one have returned their counters. The one remaining player possessing counters loses the game. In situations in which the last roll results in all the remaining counters being returned to the tower, a player returning two counters loses the game. If no one was returning more than one counter, then everyone who returned a counter loses.

EXERCISE The State of *The Tower*

What would you need to remember if you wanted stop a game of *The Tower*, put away the pieces, and later pick up where you left off? In other words, what is the information that forms its game state?

Does the information included in the game state change at different points during a player's turn? If you are a spectator who joined the game mid-play, what parts of the game state are not knowable simply by looking at the game's physical components (i.e., what parts of the game state are invisible)?

As you may recall, the rules for *Marrakech* (as printed in this book on page 10) did not describe how to handle a player becoming bankrupt. Similarly, *The Tower* has a situation that is not addressed in the game's rules, but may or may not arise during the course of a game. Can you spot it? The answer is at the end of the chapter on page 40.

Mechanics

A game's mechanics are the set of processes and actions by which it proceeds from the opening moves to its conclusion. Mechanics can change the game state, change what choices are available to players, or change the workings of another mechanic. For example, *Tetris*'s mechanics for moving and rotating the falling pieces cause the game state to change. *Chess*'s mechanic of putting a king into check limits that king's owner to actions that get the king out of check. The removal of the last counter in *The Tower* causes the removal mechanic itself to change from taking counters to returning them.

Jetpack Joyride's mechanics offer another example of one game mechanic changing the workings of another. Whenever the player's avatar collides with a rainbow box, its movement mechanic changes. For example, the avatar might switch from the default jetpack that moves upwards when the mouse button is pressed and held, to using a "profit bird" that requires repeated clicking to flap the bird's wings and move upwards.

Tic-Tac-Toe has only one mechanic: taking turns placing x's and o's. Most games are not that streamlined and even a relatively simple game will generally involve

Figure 2.1 *Jetpack Joyride* default jetpack (left) and profit bird (right).

several mechanics. For example, *The Tower*'s main game mechanics could be summarized as:

1. Generate three random numbers (a player rolls the dice). Players take counters if their assigned number matches one of the rolled dice.
2. If all counters have been removed from the tower, change mechanic #1 so that players now return counters to the tower.
3. Pass the dice to the next player.

It might seem that the first item in the list should be two separate mechanics: a dice-rolling mechanic and a counter-taking mechanic. However, the movement of counters simply updates the game's physical components to reflect the game state change that was caused by the dice roll. The same could be said of the roll & move mechanic in *Monopoly* or the transfer of Dirham in *Marrakech* upon landing on an opponent's rug.

There is no settled definition of what is meant by "game mechanics." This section presents how the term is used in this book, but readers should be aware that other game designers and academics imbue the term with differing shades of meaning. A good survey of the various definitions that have been given for "game mechanic" can be found at www.gamestudies.org/0802/articles/sicart.

In regard to *The Tower*'s third mechanic (passing the dice to the next player), it is worth noting that it does not really matter who rolls the dice because the result applies equally to all players. This mechanic could be eliminated (the same person could roll the dice the entire game) without changing the outcome of the game in any way. Passing the dice is more of a social mechanic than a game mechanic. It gives the players the illusion of having an impact on the game.

One might think the same could be said of a die roll in any game—that the inherent randomness makes it meaningless who rolls it. However, the difference between the die roll in *Marrakech* and the dice roll in *The Tower* is that rolls in *Marrakech* only affect the current turn's player (even if another player does the rolling) while rolls in *The Tower* can affect any player in the game; no distinction is made regarding whose turn it is.

The three mechanics listed above occur over and over again in *The Tower* as the players take their turns—what would be called a "game loop" in a video game. In addition to these ongoing mechanics, *The Tower* has mechanics for initializing the game ("each player is assigned a number," etc.) and for determining when it is over ("when all the players except one have returned their counters"). Game designer and teacher Ian Schreiber describes these as play mechanics, setup mechanics, and resolution mechanics.

Tabletop Billiards

This two-player game comes from Walter Joris's *100 Strategic Games for Pen and Paper*. It is a simple abstract game that is intended to evoke billiards.

Players:

- Two players

Required Materials:

- Six playing pieces, three for each player. *Go* pieces, pawns, or coins work well
- Four by three grid to use as a game board

Initial Setup:

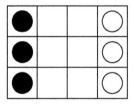

Figure 2.2

Object of the Game:

- Be the first player to move all three pieces into the three spaces that the opponent initially occupied.

Piece Movement:

1. Players take turns moving.
2. A move consists of sliding one piece in a straight line (diagonally or orthogonally) until the piece encounters the edge of the board or another piece.
3. After encountering a wall or another playing piece, the piece in motion must "bounce" which involves a 90 degree turn to either the left or right (the player can select the direction if both are possible). The piece's movement then continues until it encounters a wall or another piece, at which point it comes to rest.
4. If a piece ends its movement on the opponent's home row (i.e., the opposite side of the board from where the piece started the game), then it cannot be moved again.
5. Players must make a move if one is possible. If no move is possible, then the player's turn is passed and the opponent moves again.

Example Illegal Moves:

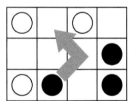

Illegal: the bounce must be 90 degrees.

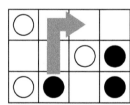

Illegal: a piece's movement must include a bounce.

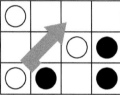

Illegal: a bounce cannot happen on the point between squares.

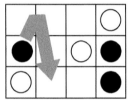

Illegal: the piece must bounce off the edge of the board or another piece.

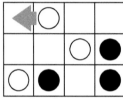

Illegal: after bouncing, a piece cannot stop prior to reaching the edge of the board or another piece.

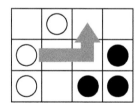

Illegal: pieces cannot move after ending a move on the opponent's home row.

Figure 2.3

Example Game:

Note, the player's choice is forced in move six: there is only one legal move (and a player must move whenever possible).

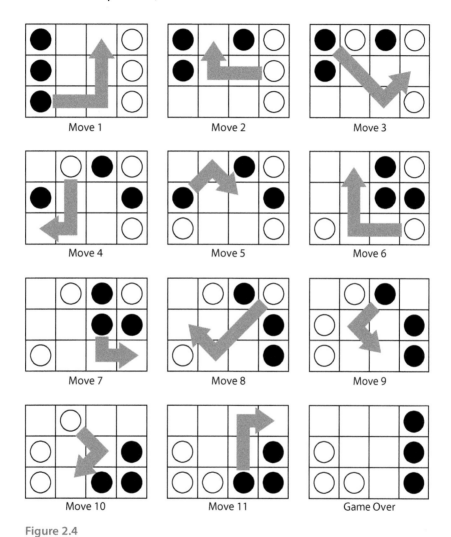

Figure 2.4

System Mechanics

A game mechanic can be an action that a player has some control over, or it can be a system-driven mechanic that is automatically triggered either by another mechanic or a particular game state.

As discussed earlier (regarding the dice rolling in *The Tower*) some mechanics that seem player-driven on the surface, actually involve no player decision making. When a mechanic does not involve player decision making, it is a system mechanic.

In sports, the most important system-driven mechanics are usually enforced by physical limitations and the clockwork of the universe. A billiard ball's ricochet around a pool table is dictated by the laws of physics. A player's action determines the ball's path, but only in the sense that the player is giving the universe some kinetic force to work with. Providing the correct kinetic force is the expertise required by the sport.

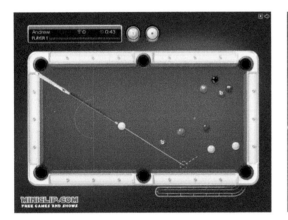 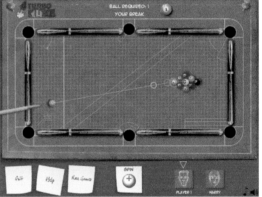

Figure 2.5a and 2.5b *Deluxe Pool* (left), *Blueprint Billiards* (right).

One might think that a billiards video game is also enforced by the universe since the game is programmed to model the universe's physics. However, the programmed physics in a computer billiards game is a simulation and it has limitations that do not exist in the real world. For example, *Deluxe Pool* (figure 2.5a, left) does not allow the player to put spin on the cue ball—an important and basic billiards technique. *Blueprint Billiards* (figure 2.5b, right) does allow the player to put spin on the cue ball, but is still limited in how much reality it presents. No matter how the cue ball is hit in *Blueprint Billiards* (or *Deluxe Pool*) it never leaves the surface of the table, so it is not possible to expertly do a jump shot or to clumsily shoot the ball off the table altogether.

Video games that simulate some aspect of the world *always* simplify what they are modeling. Game designers and programmers must pick and choose which aspects of real-life are part of the gameplay. An additional wrinkle in how games model reality is that the game's world may not function exactly as intended. In the real-world, shooting a cue ball at a ninety degree angle to a bumper has a predictable effect, it will bounce straight back. However, a video game might have a bug (see sidebar) in its collision detection algorithm and instead of bouncing off the bumper, a virtual cue ball might pass straight through the bumper and disappear from the video game entirely.

Where sports typically have their system-driven mechanics enforced by the universe and video games have their system-driven mechanics enforced by the programmers' computer code, tabletop games typically require the players themselves to enforce the system-driven mechanics. Players are usually required to update the game state for everything that happens, so what is a system-driven mechanic and what is a player-initiated mechanic can be unclear and require some analysis.

It is more obvious in video games which mechanics are system-driven because the computer is able to handle the game state changes autonomously and does not require a player to intervene. *Jetpack Joyride* includes both player-driven and system-driven mechanics. For example, the player controls the movement of the avatar (the player's character) on the Y-axis (up & down), but the system controls the avatar's movement on the X-axis (to the right).

> Bugs are errors in a computer program's design or coding that cause it to malfunction or work in unintended ways.

Dynamics

"Dynamics" refers to the patterns of play that are re-enforced and encouraged by a game's mechanics. Dynamics grow out of the ways in which players can affect the game state in support of their in-game goals.

Marrakech's Dirham payment mechanic creates a dynamic in which players tend to group their rugs together in order to accumulate as many Dirham as possible. Additionally, that payment mechanic, together with the movement mechanics, creates a tendency for rugs to steadily fill the entire board (rather than, for example, stacking up in one corner of it) because players want to avoid landing on other players' rugs and tend to move towards safer, less rug-covered areas (which are then populated with a rug via the post-move rug placement mechanic).

A game's dynamics can give rise to player strategies, but a strategy and a dynamic are not one and the same. Dynamics are the aspects of the game that drive its characteristic lines of play and the typical ways that the game unfolds. A strategy is a player's specific plan for developing her position in the game. If a player wants to take advantage of the game's dynamics (which is usually a wise thing to do), then her strategy will probably result in a conventional and characteristic set of choices.

For example, the mechanics of *Chess* has a dynamic in which the games tend to start out steady and focused on pawn development and gain momentum as the board clears and the moves become more sweeping and powerful. There is no rule that a player must begin with pawns (if there were, then it would be a mechanic rather than a dynamic), but most players choose to do so.

The closer a player's choices align with the game's dynamic, the more specifically planned those choices need to be in order to be considered a strategy (as opposed to simply playing the game the way it is sensible to play). Creating contiguous rug groups in *Marrakech* is such a basic part of the game—so tied to the game's dynamics—that it would not be considered a strategy. A more specific plan to focus rug development in the corners, however, would be considered a strategy because, while arguably beneficial, it is not a default line of play.

Mechanics give rise to dynamics which in turn shape the players' choices and experiences (see the sidebar on MDA). Designers sometimes start with an interesting mechanic and see what sort of dynamics and play experience grow out of it. However, it is often useful to work from the other end of the equation and start with a goal for the player experience, choose some dynamics that encourage that experience, and then craft mechanics that drive those dynamics.

The MDA Framework

Mechanics-Dynamics-Aesthetics (MDA) is a way of examining games. It was conceived and written about by game developers Robin Hunicke, Marc LeBlanc, and Robert Zubek (see www.funmines.com/mda). MDA advocates a player-centric approach to game development in which designers focus on the experience they wish to provide for players and then work towards creating mechanics that support it.

The MDA framework takes its name from the idea that Mechanics create Dynamics that provide the game's Aesthetics. In this context "aesthetics" does not refer to a game's visuals. Instead, it is meant to convey the player experience of game—such as being challenged, existing within a story, socializing with friends, or exploring the unknown. The framework's authors suggest that game designers tend to view games from the standpoint of mechanics, whereas players tend to view games from the standpoint of aesthetics.

Implicit in the MDA structure is an idea that creating a game is a second-order design problem in which the developers are not directly creating the player's experience (Zimmerman 2003). Instead, game developers create a system of mechanics which in turn creates an experience that may or may not be the one which the designer wishes to give or the player wishes to receive. This is what makes game design so difficult. As Ian Schreiber explains, "Design is not just a matter of coming up with a 'Great Idea' for a game; it is about coming up with a set of rules that will implement that idea, when two-thirds of the final product (the Dynamics and Aesthetics) are not under our direct control" (Schreiber, *Mechanics and Dynamics* 2009).

MDA is an influential idea and it is important for game designers to know about (especially if they are working in an academic setting).

Algorithms

An algorithm is a series of steps for accomplishing a calculation or task. If you have cooked from a cookbook or followed directions to a friend's house, then you have used an algorithm. A good algorithm is clear, detailed, and unambiguous.

Algorithms are used extensively in both tabletop and video games. For example, the rules to *The Tower* (page 25) include a step-by-step algorithmic process for determining who lost the game:

> The game ends when all the players except one have returned their counters. The one remaining player possessing counters loses the game. In situations in which the last roll results in all the remaining counters being returned to the tower, a player returning two counters loses the game. If no one was returning more than one counter, then everyone who returned a counter loses.

Flowcharts (which are covered in more detail in Chapter 13) are an especially effective way of presenting an algorithm. Capturing an algorithm in flowchart form helps ensure the process has been rigorously thought through. Flowcharts have a visual clarity that can help make a complicated process easier to understand.

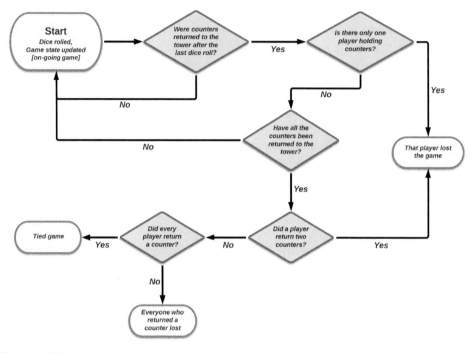

Figure 2.6 *The Tower*'s end game.

Figure 2.6 is a flowchart of the algorithm for determining whether a game of *The Tower* is over and, if so, who lost (note, the flowchart does not diagram the game's entire set of mechanics, just the algorithm for its conclusion).

Rules for tabletop games are frequently algorithmic in order to describe the mechanics in a way that (we hope) is clear and unambiguous. However, it is not entirely correct to say that an algorithm *is* a mechanic. In the same way that driving directions describe a trip but are not the trip itself, algorithms can describe a game mechanic but they are not the mechanic itself.

This distinction is less clear for a video game, however. Video game mechanics are usually algorithms that have been translated into a programming language that the computer program can execute. So for a video game, an algorithm can be more accurately equated with a mechanic.

Chris Crawford's book *Balance of Power* (see www.funmines.com/balance-of-power) is filled with algorithms that detail the inner workings of his game of the same name. For example, the game determines a government's power by rounding down the result of this calculation (Crawford 1986, 32):

$$\text{Government Power} = \frac{(2 * \text{Soldiers} * \text{Total Weapons})}{(\text{Soldiers} + \text{Total Weapons})} + \text{Intervention Power}$$

What sort of game dynamic does this algorithm create? To make things simpler, let us assume there is zero Intervention Power (which is a measure of military power provided by any intervening superpower troops). What is the power of the government if it has five soldiers and one weapon? How about if it has one soldier and ten weapons? Both situations result in a power of 1 (rounded down). The algorithm is designed to reward players who do not overly specialize in acquiring soldiers or acquiring weapons. Crawford explains:

> Suppose, for example, that we have a country like China that has lots of soldiers but not many weapons. Suppose that the values for China are 100 soldiers and a total of 2 weapons. This would yield a total power of 3. Now comes the good part. Suppose that the Chinese added one more soldier; how would that increase their power? Well, if you try the equation with 101 soldiers and 2 total weapons, you still get a total power of only 3. Now suppose that the Chinese added one more weapon instead of one more soldier; then their military power would jump up to 5. The moral of this equation is that you need a proper balance between soldiers and weapons. If you have too many of either, it doesn't hurt you, but you just don't get much benefit from the additional resource.
>
> (Crawford 1986, 32)

Gameplay

If you were getting ready to play *Monopoly* and discovered that all the player pieces were missing, what would you do? You might decide to substitute an assortment of objects for the pieces (maybe a thumbtack, a penny, and a 4-sided die). What if you were also missing the play money? Perhaps you quickly mint your own play money by cutting slips of paper and marking them with denominations? What if you discover that the property deed cards are missing as well? (You really need to take better care of your games.) You might solve the problem by having the banker track property ownership and mortgaging on a pad of paper.

Creating substitute player pieces and play money are cosmetic changes. They alter the game physically, but they do not modify how players interact with it. In contrast, having one player (the banker) track property ownership does change how players interact with the game's system of mechanics, even if it does not actually change the mechanics themselves in any fundamental way. What is changed by centralizing the property bookkeeping is *Monopoly*'s "gameplay."

Gameplay describes the ways in which players can view the game state and access the mechanics. Beautiful artwork may make the game playing experience more pleasurable, but insofar as it is decorative, artwork is not part of the gameplay. The fact that players have unique identifiers (shoe, car, dog, top hat, etc.) to mark their position on a *Monopoly* board is part of the gameplay, but the identifiers themselves could be changed without impacting game play so long as the change does not affect the way in which players view the game state or access the mechanics that change it. Likewise, if the sound of a car in a video game is just atmospheric, it is not part of the gameplay. However, if the car sound communicates something about the game state (e.g., a car is approaching you from behind), then it is part of the gameplay.

What constitutes gameplay can be subjective; it is possible for something to be part of the gameplay for one player and not for another. For example, someone playing a fantasy-themed video game might become cautious upon encountering a corridor smeared with blood and strewn with skulls. Another player may proceed blithely on, treating the gore as artistic atmosphere. The first player is experiencing the gore as part of the gameplay, the second player is not.

Gameplay can exist in the absence of any actual functionality or even designer intention. During the early 1980s the author spent countless quarters on the arcade game *Battlezone* trying to reach a volcano in the distant background. Rumors described the wondrous things contained inside the volcano. However, the volcano was simply a visual flourish added in due to a programmer's whimsy and had no presence in the game state or mechanics (Kent 2001, 121).

Gameplay has been criticized as being a useless word that does nothing that could not be accomplished by simply using the word "game." After all, bookread is not a word, so why bother with the slightly awkward word gameplay? Rather than say, "This game has good gameplay, but sucky graphics," we could just say, "This is a good game, but it has sucky graphics" (Kierkegaard 2007).

Gameplay exists as a word because it describes an aspect of games that is unique to the medium: the players' interaction with the game's system. Books are experienced linearly, so there is no need for a word to describe the experience of traversing a book's narrative as separate from the linear work itself. Gameplay is more analogous to "screenplay" than it is to the made up word "bookread." If we admire the dialogue in an otherwise bad movie, we have the words to say, "The screenplay was good, but the movie itself was pretty bad." If "screenplay" (or its synonyms) did not exist, we would be limited to saying something along the lines of, "That was a good movie, but its acting, directing, editing, and cinematography were bad." Rather than being able to actively discuss the screenplay, we would be reduced to trying to describe that particular aspect of the movie by subtracting everything else. Likewise, the word gameplay allows us to directly discuss a particular aspect of games.

Summary

A *game state* consists of the information required to recreate a particular moment in a game.

Mechanics are the processes that can cause the game state to change.

System mechanics are mechanics that do not involve player decision making.

Dynamics are the player behaviors that are reinforced and encouraged by a game's mechanics.

Algorithms are step-by-step processes.

Gameplay describes the way in which players interact with a game's system. It is the players' interface for viewing the game state and their methods for changing it.

EXERCISE *Marrakech*'s State and Mechanics

This exercise asks you to analyze *Marrakech* in order to create a list of its mechanics and to determine what information constitutes its game state.

Keep in mind that mechanics are processes that 1) change the game state, 2) change what choices are available to players, or 3) change the workings of another mechanic. The game state is the information that needs to be remembered in order to temporarily suspend a game and reconvene it later.

For example, here is how *The Tower*'s mechanics and game states could be summed up:

The Tower's Mechanics

1. Generate 3 random numbers (a player rolls the dice). Players take counters if their assigned number matches one of the rolled dice.

2. If all counters have been removed from the tower, change mechanic #1 so that players now return counters to the tower.
3. Pass the dice to the next player.

The Tower's Game State Information

1. The number(s) assigned to each player.
2. How many counters are held by each player.
3. How many counters are in the tower.
4. Whether players are removing or returning counters.
5. Whose turn it is to roll the dice.

"The state of *The Tower*" exercise on page 27 asked whether the information included in the game state changes at different points in a player's turn. A turn in *The Tower* consists of three steps: roll the dice, transfer counters, pass the dice on to the next player. Since the dice dictate the movement of the counters (there is no player discretion in the matter), the counters' game state can be thought of as updating automatically after a dice roll. The fact that the players have not yet physically moved the counters means that the physical component's representation of the game state is out of date. That is, the physical movement of the counters is a case of the game's components catching up with the change in game state.

The game state of *The Tower* does not need to include information about a player's turn in-progress. When you determine the game state of *Marrakech* however, you will need to include some information regarding the status of a partially completed turn.

Answer to "The State of *The Tower*" Exercise (page 27)

Step two in the rules does not specify how to handle the situation in which there are fewer counters remaining in the tower than there are players whose numbers have been rolled. How would you handle that situation if it arose in a game?

CHAPTER THREE

Creating Tabletop Games

INTRODUCTION

Matt Leacock, designer of the award-winning *Pandemic* tabletop game, advises aspiring game designers to, "Find a spark, Keep it simple, Keep it raw, Find the core game" (Leacock, "Cooperation and Engagement," 2008). That advice describes this chapter's lessons in a nutshell.

The learning objectives for this chapter are:

1 Examine ways of generating ideas for games.

2 Ease into game designing by modifying existing games.

3 Understand what constitutes a core mechanic and a game pillar.

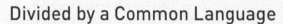

Divided by a Common Language

The tabletop and video game industries have a number of terms that they bestow with meanings that are just different enough to cause confusion.

In a video game company, "game development" refers to the entire process of creating a new game and a "game developer" is anyone involved in making it. In contrast, tabletop "game development" refers to a specific late stage in the creation of the game and a "game developer" is a person involved in that stage. Tabletop game developer Dale Yu explains it as such:

> Game development is one of the final steps that a board game must go through prior to publication . . . In the development stage, the designer's final game submission is prepared to ready it for market by the developer. Rough edges are smoothed over, and the rules are tweaked to ensure a good game experience. Usually, the main ideas and mechanics of a game are unchanged through development—though just about anything is fair game to be modified if the change will result in a better game.
>
> When my family members or other non-gamers ask what I do as a developer, I explain it this way: "Think of my job as being similar to that of a book editor, except that I work with board games instead of books. I take the prototype (manuscript) from the game designer (author), and then go over everything with a fine-toothed comb. My goal is to make sure that the published version is the best possible game for the company that will publish it."
>
> (Yu 2011, 74)

The video game development process (i.e., the entire creation of the game) is sometimes divided into "pre-production" and "production" phases. Pre-production is where ideas are generated, concepts are explored, and software tools and techniques are tested. Production is where work begins on what will eventually be the finished game: programmers write the code, artists create the artwork, and game designers flesh out design and revise it as necessary. In practice, pre-production does not truly cease once production begins. Most games are created using "iterative development" which involves many cycles of playtesting, evaluation, and re-design.

In tabletop games, "prototyping" encompasses the entire process of creating the game up until the point it takes its final form. Prototyping a tabletop game is analogous to "developing" a video game. Tabletop prototyping, however, is not typically divided into pre-production and production phases—if anything, production would refer to the actual manufacturing of the game's final form.

In the video game industry, the act of "prototyping" suggests creating something discardable in order to explore game mechanics, programming techniques, or possible approaches to art and interface design. For some companies, however, a "prototype" simply refers to an early version of the video game—something that may undergo major changes, but is intended to evolve into the actual final product.

This book's usage of the terms "game development" and "game developer" conforms to that of the video game industry. The book's use of "prototyping" varies and is dependent on whether a tabletop game or a video game is being discussed. In the case of a tabletop game, prototyping will refer to the process of designing and creating the game. In the case of video games, prototyping will refer to the creation of something that is not part of the game itself, but rather something that is used to explore or test concepts for the game.

EXERCISE Expanding *Hive*

Before examining the process of prototyping and playtesting a game, let us start by having you do a bit of game development using whatever approach comes naturally to you. As you work on your design, be conscious of your choices and what you think worked and did not work so that you can compare them to the formal process that is presented later in this chapter and the following one (which deals with playtesting).

Rather than having you design an entire game from scratch, this exercise asks you to create an expansion to an existing game, *Hive*.

Hive is a tile-laying game that evokes the gameplay of *Chess* while at the same time being very much its own game. The game involves trying to surround the opponent's Queen Bee piece while protecting one's own. To do so, players put a variety of insects, each with their own unique movement abilities, into play. The rules to *Hive* are on page 46 and

Figure 3.1 *Hive*, courtesy Gen42 Games, www.gen42.com.

the pieces are on the page that follows page 50. It should be noted that while the game is certainly playable using paper cut-out pieces, a much improved play experience can be had with the physical tiles that come in the retail game (see figure 3.1).

Hive lends itself to expansion by way of adding new insect types to the game. In fact, the publisher has Mosquito, Ladybug, and Pillbug pieces that can be added on to the core set of Beetles, Grasshoppers, Soldier Ants, Spiders, and Queen Bees. In addition to these official add-ons, the BoardGameGeek community have come up with several unofficial add-on insects, as well as rule variations (see www.funmines.com/hive for details).

Your task is to come up with a new insect type that expands the core game by adding some interesting gameplay with its unique power or movement. Work on your expansion design until you are fully satisfied with it and consider it "done."

Hive

A game buzzing with possibilities
© 2010 Gen42 Games
www.gen42.com
Author: John Yianni

The Object of *Hive*

The object of the game is to totally surround your opponent's Queen Bee while at the same time trying to stop your opponent from doing the same to you. The pieces surrounding the Queen Bee can be made up of a mixture of both your pieces and your opponent's. The first player to surround the opponent's Queen Bee wins (see figure 3.2).

Figure 3.2 The Queen Bee is surrounded.

Preparation

Cut out the hexagonal pieces that follow these rules. The players each take all eleven pieces of one color and place them face up and within easy reach.

Playing the Game

Play begins with one player placing a piece from her hand in the center of the table and the next player joining one of his own pieces to it, edge-to-edge (see figure 3.3). Players then take turns to either place or move any one of their pieces.

Figure 3.3 Edge-to-edge connections.

Placing

A new piece can be introduced into the game at any time. However, with the exception of the first piece placed by each player, pieces may not be placed next to a piece of the opponent's color (see Figure 3.4).

It is possible to win the game without placing all your pieces, but once a piece has been placed, it cannot be removed from the game.

Figure 3.4 Legal placement (left), illegal placement (right).

The Hive

The pieces in play define the playing surface, known as the Hive.

Placing your Queen Bee

Your Queen Bee can be placed at any time from your first to your fourth turn. You must place your Queen Bee on your fourth turn if you have not placed it before.

Figure 3.5 The Queen Bee.

Moving

Once your Queen Bee has been placed (but not before), you can decide whether to use each subsequent turn to place another tile or to move one of the pieces that has already been placed. Each creature has its own way of moving about the Hive and it is possible to move pieces to a position where they touch one or more of your opponent's tiles.

NB: All pieces must always touch at least one other piece. If a piece is the only connection between two parts of the Hive, it may not be moved. (See "One Hive Rule" below.)

The Creatures

Queen Bee

The Queen Bee can move only one space per turn. Even though it is restricted in this way, if moved at the right time it can severely disrupt your opponent's plans.

From this position (figure 3.6) the black Queen Bee is able to move into one of four spaces.

Queen Bee   Figure 3.6

Beetle

The Beetle, like the Queen Bee, moves only one space per turn. Unlike any other creature though, it can also move on top of the Hive.

From this position (figure 3.7), the white Beetle is able to move into one of four positions.

A piece with a beetle on top of it is unable to move and for the purposes of the placing rules above, the stack takes on the color of the Beetle. The Beetle can move from tile to tile across the top of the Hive. It can also drop into spaces that are surrounded and therefore not accessible to most other creatures. (See "Freedom to Move" below.)

Beetle   Figure 3.7

The only way to block a Beetle that is on top of the Hive is to move another Beetle on top of it. All four Beetles can be stacked on top of each other.

NB: When it is first placed, the Beetle is placed in the same way as all the other pieces. It cannot be placed directly on top of the Hive, even though it can be moved there later.

Grasshopper

The Grasshopper does not move around the outside of the Hive like the other

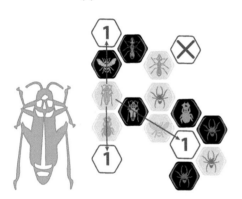

creatures. Instead, it jumps from its space over any number of pieces (but at least one) to the next unoccupied space along a straight row of joined pieces.

This gives it the advantage of being able to fill in a space that is surrounded by other tiles.

From this position (figure 3.8), the white Grasshopper can jump to one of three spaces. NB: It cannot jump across the gap to the space marked x.

Grasshopper   Figure 3.8

Spider

The Spider moves three spaces per turn—no more, no less. It must move in a direct path and cannot backtrack on itself. It may only move around pieces that it is in direct contact with on each step of its move and it may not move across to a piece that it is not in direct contact with.

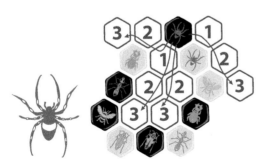

From this position (figure 3.9), the black Spider can move into one of four spaces but is unable to move to the position on its left marked 2 on its first step.

Spider   Figure 3.9

Soldier Ant

The Soldier Ant can move from its position to any other position around the Hive provided the "One Hive Rule" and "Freedom to Move" restrictions (detailed below) are adhered to. The Ant's movement ability makes it one of the most valuable pieces.

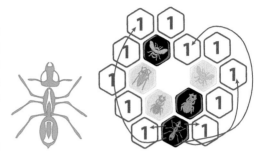

Soldier Ant   Figure 3.10

In this situation (figure 3.10), the Ant can be moved into one of eleven positions but is unable to move into the position in the center of the Hive (see "Freedom to Move" below).

Restrictions

One Hive Rule

The pieces in play must be linked at all times. At no time can you leave a piece stranded (not joined to the Hive) or separate the Hive in two.

Moving the black Ant in figure 3.11 would result In the Hive being split in two.

Figure 3.11

Use this rule to your advantage by moving your pieces to strategic positions around the Hive, leaving your opponent's key pieces unable to move.

Moving the black Queen Bee in figure 3.12 to a position where it re-links the Hive is also an illegal move, as the Hive is left unlinked while the piece is in transit.

Freedom to Move

Figure 3.12

The creatures can only move in a sliding movement. If a piece is surrounded to the point that it can no longer physically slide out of its position, it may not be moved. The only exceptions are the Grasshopper, which can jump into or out of a space, and the Beetle, which can climb up or down.

Similarly, no piece may move into a space that it cannot physically slide into (Figures 3.13a and 3.13c).

NB: When first introduced to the game, a piece may be placed into a space that is surrounded as long as it does not violate any of the placing rules, in particular the rule

Figure 3.13a, 3.13b, 3.13c

about pieces not being allowed to touch pieces of the other color when they are first placed.

Unable to Move or Place

If a player can neither place a new piece nor move an existing piece, the turn passes to her opponent who then takes his turn again. The game continues in this way until the player is able to move or place one of her pieces, or until the game is lost with the surrounding of her Queen Bee.

The End of the Game

The game ends as soon as one Queen Bee is completely surrounded by pieces of any color. The person whose Queen Bee is surrounded loses the game, unless the last piece to surround his Queen Bee also completes the surrounding of the other Queen Bee. In that case the game is drawn. A draw may also be agreed if both players are in a position where they are forced to move the same two pieces over and over again, without any possibility of the stalemate being resolved.

Photo 3.1 John Yianni

John Yianni

John Yianni has been a full-time board games designer since 2005. In addition to designing the award winning game *Hive*, Yianni has designed and published other games including *Army Of Frogs*, *Logan Stones*, and *Junkyard Races*. Yianni runs his own publishing company, Gen42 Games, that have a distribution network reaching twenty-five countries around the world. His company is based in the United Kingdom where he lives with his wife and three children.

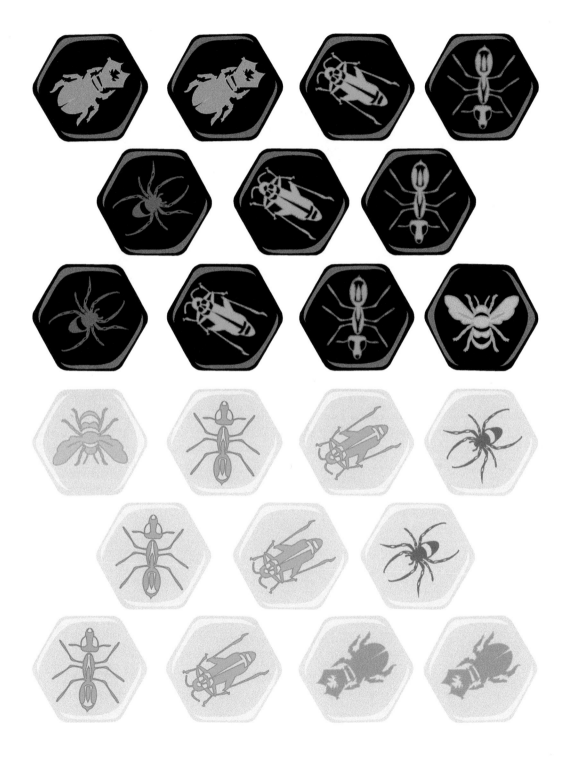

Ideation

How did you go about creating your *Hive* expansion? Most designers would start with ideation. Ideation is a slightly goofy term for the process of coming up with ideas. Brainstorming and ideation are often (mis)used interchangeably, but strictly speaking brainstorming is a particular technique for coming up with ideas whereas ideation refers to the process in general rather than a specific practice.

In coming up with the idea for your *Hive* expansion you may have started by thinking about possible insects and how their traits might translate into a game mechanic. Or perhaps you came up with a mechanic and then tried to think of an insect that it could be associated with. Or maybe you approached the problem in an entirely different way?

An interesting mechanic or an engaging theme are common starting points. Here are some ways of sparking that initial idea and getting the ball rolling:

■ Use a standard game component or convention in a unique way. *TAMSK* is a game that uses sand-timers as game pieces. When a player moves one of the sand-timer/pieces, it is turned over. If a piece's sand runs out, it is lost and removed from the game. Similarly, *Duell* and *Button Men* use dice as game pieces. *OctoDad* (created by a group of DePaul University game students) has the player controlling an anthropomorphized octopus. Tasks that are typically effortless to execute in a video game (such as walking across the room) become a challenge because the player must control the octopus like a puppet, moving each tentacle individually.

■ Take inspiration from a non-standard game piece. Game designer Stone Librande created a game for his children based on a desire to do something with a two-foot tall statue of a Godzilla-like creature. The PlayStation 2 game *Surfing H3O* came with a tiny surfboard that could be snapped on to the PS2 controller's dual joysticks, creating a custom controller for the game's virtual surfboard (unfortunately, the game was widely considered horrible despite its fun add-on).

■ Think of something in an existing game that bothers you and make a new game that does it better. Make sure you are not just making a variant or an obvious clone. Rather, try to make something substantially different that is inspired by what peeves you.

- Take something you particularly like in a game and create a game that does it even better. Again, while you are taking inspiration from another game, you want to end up with something original and distinct.
- Take a "toy" and make it into a game. If you find yourself playing with something and creating informal goals to direct that play, see if you can formalize the activity into a game. For example, the author created a game that was inspired by trying to create towers out of the random wooden blocks that his infant son would hand to him.
- Along the lines of starting with a theme, start with a narrative you want the player to experience or a backstory or game world that you think would be fun to play in.
- Start with market research: identify an underserved market need and create a game to take advantage of that opportunity.
- Start with something you observe in real life that has interesting decisions or interactions that could serve as game mechanics.
- And so on. There are probably an infinite number of starting points or sources of inspiration for game projects.

Most important of all, keep a journal of the ideas (or half-ideas) you have for games. When you feel uninspired, refer back to your journal. Do not limit yourself to thinking about your ideas individually, consider how they might be combined in ways that lead to something exciting and original.

Ideas Come in all Shapes and Sizes

by John Yianni

New ideas are never a problem for me, I see games in most everything I look at. Ideas come in all shape and sizes; some come through sights, objects, some even in conversation. Once you align yourself with the idea of becoming a game designer, ideas just seem to crawl out of the woodwork.

I keep a journal. Whenever I have a new idea or a progression of an old idea I just jot it down, making sure I include the date. Knowing when I had an idea is quite important in my opinion. Some ideas will become part of another game or may progress to become a completely different game. Like *Logan Stones*, which started out as a game about scarabs. That's why it's good to date them so you can trace the idea back if need be. Most of the ideas in my journal may never become published games, but that's okay, I enjoy the

process of coming up with an idea and working through to an end. Even if it will never go beyond that, the process most always teaches me something. I would encourage any budding games designer to have a journal of ideas to draw from. Keep it with you wherever you go. You never know when or where that next big idea will come from and it is good to be prepared.

My biggest idea, the one that has sustained my business and given me the opportunity to be a full-time game designer, is *Hive*.

Hive came to me many years ago, whilst watching a film. The main characters of the film were two old friends that met daily in a park to play *Chess*. They would come together, each bringing one half of the board and half the pieces. I don't remember the name of the film, but I do remember what inspired me. Looking at the unused empty spaces on their Chessboard, I wondered, "Could I design a game that had no need of a board, but still kept the essence of what makes *Chess* so appealing?" I set off to design and make the game using thick cardstock as the pieces. The game was made up of squares (still thinking Chessboard) with symbols of Rats, Dragons, Stones, Kings, and Pigs. The moves of some of *Hive's* pieces can be seen in this early version. For example, *Hive's* Ant moves in the same way as the Rat. However, some pieces had movement abilities that were dropped from the game. For example, the Pig pushed pieces around and the Stone was a blocking piece. My thinking was to have a limited set of pieces to keep the game as portable as possible, so elimination of your opponent's pieces (like you do in *Chess*) was not an option. Instead, the object of the game was to surround an opposing piece (in this case the king) using pieces that all moved in different ways.

Because the game was board-less, I quickly realized that the pieces all needed to be connected to one another at all times, (the "One Hive Rule") but unlike *Hive*, this original idea started with a set-up position (still in the *Chess* mindset).

After making the prototype and working out a basic set of rules I set upon a friend to try it out. (Another piece of advice: playtest, playtest, and above all, playtest). At this point, the game played okay, but was in no way brilliant and was much less fun than I would have liked. I decided that it was not worth pursuing and I put it away never to be played or seen for years. Some eighteen years later, whilst working on something else, I drew a hex shape and for some strange reason, the game came flooding back. I knew instinctively that I was onto something with the different shape of piece. The movement possibilities were multiplied, the pieces could now move in six directions instead of only four and the limitations vanished with that eureka moment.

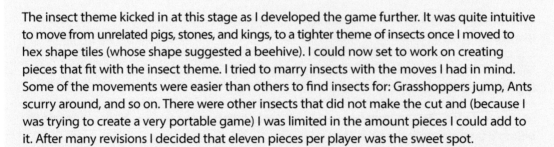

The insect theme kicked in at this stage as I developed the game further. It was quite intuitive to move from unrelated pigs, stones, and kings, to a tighter theme of insects once I moved to hex shape tiles (whose shape suggested a beehive). I could now set to work on creating pieces that fit with the insect theme. I tried to marry insects with the moves I had in mind. Some of the movements were easier than others to find insects for: Grasshoppers jump, Ants scurry around, and so on. There were other insects that did not make the cut and (because I was trying to create a very portable game) I was limited in the amount pieces I could add to it. After many revisions I decided that eleven pieces per player was the sweet spot.

My day job at the time was a qualified carpenter. I was working mostly on big sites and house conversions and, though I enjoyed my job, I found that the game was starting to consume my every thought. I would spend most of my free time and my lunch times drawing hex shapes onto pieces of plasterboard, working out the rules, and making plywood prototypes of the pieces to playtest. Playtesting was still a matter of family and friends, but I was much more excited about the possibilities and focused on getting the game right. After many configurations, piece changes, and playtests, I was happy.

I started looking for *Chess* clubs that I could take the game to and get some outside feedback. I came across Finchley Games Club, a board-games club in North London where people go to play different board and card games. They were very pleasant on the phone when I asked if I could bring along a game to playtest. So I went along that Thursday with prototype in hand and with hopes that they would like the game and give me some positive feedback. This was the first time I had ever seen the inside of a board-games club. I had no idea that such places existed. I was amazed to see grown men huddled around all manner of fantastic looking games. I introduced myself and handed over my prototype to the two founding members. They ordered some beers from the bar and they promptly sat down to play. After a few games they turned to me and said, with a smile "We hate you." I thought that they would play it once and say something like, "It's okay, but don't give up the day job." What I did not expect was their total disgust at their inability to find anything to criticize about the game. "This game is really very good," they went on to say. "We don't like to playtest a game without finding something wrong with it. But this is good, very good. You should get this published." Wow, what a response!

With only a few minor rule clarifications the game was ready. Now the hard part began. While I was developing the idea, I had in mind that I wanted a quality product that would last a lifetime. I wanted it to be a valued family game. So I set about finding manufacturers that could produce the game using similar material to very high quality *Mah-jong* or *Domino* pieces. The problem with this was the astronomical cost of tooling and the minimum production runs. Undeterred I decided to use the next best thing, a material

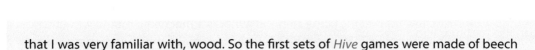

that I was very familiar with, wood. So the first sets of *Hive* games were made of beech wood and mostly by hand.

Here's another bit of advice and I cannot stress this enough: If you are going the self-publishing route, don't spend your life savings on a product that you don't really know if people are willing to buy. It may be a fantastic game, but if people are not willing to pay money for it, it's a failure and you will regret it. Start off small. Once you know the game is selling then you can move on to bigger and better things. We started off with a run of 1,000 wooden games, made with the help of family and friends, and tested the market with these.

With the recent success of crowd funding sites like Kickstarter, there are now other ways to see if a game will be a viable project without spending any money on it, and if you decide to look for a publisher for your game, though this can be difficult, it's a lot less risky. I would advise you take a visit to one of the big toy fairs, like New York or Nuremberg, and make sure you set up meetings beforehand.

Hive is our most successful game and has expanded to include different versions of the game, including a pocket version. Over the years *Hive* has seen many changes and with each we have improved the production and the packaging. To date, *Hive* has won many awards; has been programmed for iOS, Android and Xbox; has had a strategy book written about it; and has sold over 200,000 copies in twenty-five countries and eleven languages. With the addition of the three expansions for the game, the Mosquito, Ladybug, and Pillbug, it goes without saying that *Hive* is successful and here to stay.

Aesthetics

Using the approach described in the Mechanics-Dynamics-Aesthetic framework (page 34), game designer Ian Schreiber suggests that a game's core aesthetic can be a starting point for generating game ideas (Schreiber, *The Early Stages of the Design Process* 2009). He suggests you think about:

- What do you want the players to feel?
- How do you want the players to react?
- What should the play experience be like?

The idea is to work backwards from the player experience (or "aesthetic") you would like your game to provide and figure out a set of mechanics that will support it. For example, you might want the players to experience unstructured interactions and politicking among themselves. What kinds of game dynamics lend themselves to that sort of play? Trading, temporary player alliances, and information sharing are possibilities that might come to mind. What is a mechanic that would encourage a trading dynamic? One possibility would be a mechanic that requires players to collect sets of game elements (such as the property color sets in *Monopoly*). In order for this mechanic to drive exciting play, the value of the trading items must not be static. Perhaps, their usefulness would vary based upon a particular player's situation, so that one player might value a particular item more highly than the others do.

Hive was inspired by a desire to provide a particular aesthetic. As John Yianni describes in his essay (pages 52–55), he wanted to create a *Chess*-like dynamic that could be played without a board. That dynamic remained elusive until Yianni hit upon using hexagonal pieces. That shape allowed for a variety of movement possibilities and a slow, but steady, surrounding of the Queen Bee that evokes (but does not duplicate) *Chess*'s assortment of pieces and the slow, but steady, drive to checkmate the king.

One of my own games started with an aesthetic. The inspiration for the game came from playing with my one-year old son, Bryce. When we played with wooden blocks, it would take the form of him handing blocks to me one at a time. I found myself stacking them and striving to create ever more elaborate and unstable structures—to see how far I could go without having the tower collapse. When I decided to formalize this play activity into a game, my goal was to capture the experience of creating wild, tottering towers. In order to have that dynamic, the game's mechanics must either reward precarious block placement or require it. Better to reward than to enforce, I decided, because allowing players to choose when to be conservative and when to be risk-taking would lead to more interesting play. In this way, the rules for this particular game have grown out of wanting to motivate a particular kind of player behavior.

EXERCISE The Best Game Ever!

Ian Schreiber suggests that game designers think about the best experience they have ever had playing a game and try to identify what game mechanics led to it (Schreiber, *The Early Stages of the Design Process* 2009). This exercise asks you to follow Schreiber's suggestion and reflect on what it is that you value most in your game playing experiences:

1. What was the best experience you have had playing a video game? In what ways did the game's dynamics and mechanics help create it?
2. What was the best experience you had playing a tabletop game? In what ways did the game's dynamics and mechanics help create it?

Games to Avoid Making

Over the years of teaching game design, I have discovered that certain game genres have stumbling blocks that tend to trip novice game designers. I strongly recommend that you avoid working on any of the following types of games while working through this book:

1. Children's games
2. Roll & move games
3. Playing card games
4. Simulations
5. Statistics games
6. Content-heavy games

This is not to imply that you should never make, for example, a children's game. There are wonderful games in every one of the above categories, and the world can certainly use more of them. However, while you are still mastering the fundamentals of game design, it is probably best to steer clear of attempting to design these sorts of games.

Children's Games

Children's games can be problematic in that they call for game mechanics that are extremely simple. This is not necessarily a terrible thing, but can be a disadvantage for someone who is trying to learn to make imaginative and original game designs. In the same way that creative writing students who wish to learn the craft of writing fiction are well-advised to avoid writing *Dick and Jane* style books, you should avoid designing children's games—at least for the purposes of this book and its exercises.

Another, more problematic issue is the challenge of properly evaluating your work when its intended audience is children. It is very difficult to put oneself in a child's mindset and determine where the game is fun and where it needs work. Is the game too difficult? Is it too easy? Is it at an appropriate level, but boring nevertheless? Without access to numerous playtesters who are of the game's target age, it is not really possible to bring the game design to a finished state.

Even if you do have access to playtesters of the right age, you probably should still refrain from making a children's game as a class assignment (unless, of course, the assignment itself is to make a children's game). When critiquing someone else's game, it is important to try to set aside one's own predilections and evaluate it with an attempt at objectivity. When evaluating someone's fantasy-themed game in which chance plays a significant role, it does not matter whether or not you like fantasy tropes or the element of luck in games. What matters is whether the theme of fantasy and mechanics of luck are working well (on their own terms) in the game. While it is possible for your instructor and classmates to set aside their own preferences when evaluating a game, it is asking a lot of them to also view the game through the eyes of a child.

Roll & Move Games

Novice game designers who have not played many tabletop games have a tendency to create roll & move games along the lines of *LIFE* and *Snakes & Ladders*; games in which players spend most of their time moving pieces as dictated by dice rolls. Creating these sorts of games sidesteps creativity; they use what is essentially a prefabricated game mechanic.

Setting aside concerns of originality, roll & move games are a bad starting place for game design because they offer players little choice in regard to what actions can be taken. Giving players multiple pieces to move (along the lines of *Pachisi* and *Sorry!*) or grafting on other mechanics that offer some form of choice can help to a degree, but almost invariably the resulting game is one of monotonous rolling and moving that is only occasionally punctuated with interesting choices. If you find roll & move mechanics sneaking their way into your designs, visit www. funmines.com/roll-and-move to discover some strategies for extricating them.

Playing Card Games

Novice game designers sometimes gravitate towards creating a game using a standard deck of playing cards. Playing cards possess a readymade set of traits (four suits, numerical sequences of one through ten, face cards) that lend themselves to a variety of mechanics (matching suits, matching numbers, collecting sets, collecting numerical sequences, trumping, etc.).

It can be difficult, however, to design a playing card game that feels very original. Doing so requires a designer to be both thoroughly aware of the conventions of card games *and* able to design mechanics that subvert or step outside of them. It is not impossible (*Switch*, for example, is innovative in how it uses a grid of playing cards as a game board), but it is difficult.

For an experienced designer, creating a truly original playing card game can be an interesting challenge. But a novice designer is better served by pursuing less well-trodden paths. Original designs are more likely to arise when a designer does not build upon an existing framework such as the one offered by standard playing cards.

Bear in mind that simply "re-skinning" a deck of cards (keeping its fundamental characteristics, but changing its graphical surface) does not sidestep this problem.

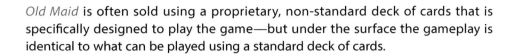

Old Maid is often sold using a proprietary, non-standard deck of cards that is specifically designed to play the game—but under the surface the gameplay is identical to what can be played using a standard deck of cards.

Simulation Games

Choosing a theme can be a great way to start the game design process. A farm-themed game can immediately spur ideas for game mechanics and pieces. Perhaps each round of player turns represents a season. A game economy can be based on players taking out farm loans and selling their harvest. Perhaps the gameplay involves strategic choices regarding farm improvement, what kinds of crops are planted, and what animals are raised.

Theme-guided design can go wrong, however, if the designer becomes beholden to the game's fiction and it becomes the major consideration for all design decisions. Imagine our farm game has a mechanic in which the plants need to receive just the right amount of rain—too little they wither, too much they drown. The playtester feedback suggests that the mechanic is too complicated and that perhaps rain should be simplified so that rain always has a positive effect. If the designer resists this idea because it is not "realistic," then she is really creating a farm simulation, not a farm game.

Vino is a real-life example of an agriculture-themed game whose designer did not allow realism to override his discretion. The game has players acquiring vineyards and making money by selling grapes. However, for some unexplained reason, selling grapes causes the vineyard to disappear. This makes no logical sense and would be entirely out of place in a grape-growing simulation, but it works well in *Vino* and is a core part of the game's dynamics.

Generally speaking, "fun" should take precedence over realism. It is worth noting, however, that there are game designers and players for whom detailed realism *is* the fun. Ultimately, the designer should not lose track of what type of game is being made and for whom.

Statistics Games

Video games are adept at running complicated algorithms and dealing with data. Tabletop games, however, need to be more streamlined, otherwise they risk overwhelming their players with bookkeeping and minutiae. If your game playing experience is primarily in video games, you may find yourself trying to apply comfortably familiar video game mechanics onto the tabletop. If so, be conscious and cautious of the inclination.

A hit-point style combat system has a drawback in addition to its reliance on bookkeeping and number crunching. It can serve as a kind of off-the-shelf design module that is easily plopped into a game's design.

This is not necessarily a problem. A recognizable game system can be easier for players to learn and can allow a designer to increase depth and complexity in other areas of the game. But in the absence of meaningful innovation elsewhere, a standard-issue combat system (or other common game structure) can result in a lackluster, unoriginal game.

For example, when called upon to create a tabletop combat mechanic, the first thing that might come to mind is the ubiquitous RPG system of percentage chances to hit and damage done in hit points. This sort of combat system tends to make heavy use of randomness and data. If each player is controlling multiple characters and each character has hit points that need to be tracked, the game can quickly devolve into a stream of throwing dice and updating numbers. The result is lots of tedious work and little decision making (a combination that is rarely fun). In contrast, consider how simple combat is in *Chess*—no hit points and no die rolls, just moving and capturing. Yet *Chess* offers deep and varied gameplay.

This issue of how data is best incorporated into tabletop games is covered in more depth in Chapter 9, "Choices."

Content-Heavy Games

Trivia games, such as *Trivial Pursuit* and *Cranium*, can be fun to play. However, if your goal is to learn how to design games, it is best to avoid taking one on as a project (at least for now). At issue is that the fun these games offer usually has less to do with the game mechanics themselves (which tend to be relatively simple) and more to do with the quality of their trivia. The typical trivia game comes with hundreds of trivia cards, each of which might hold a half-dozen questions and answers. Making one of these games would mean spending your time researching and writing down trivia instead of designing actual game mechanics.

This applies to any game that is heavy in its use of data (such as *Apples to Apples* and *Taboo*), and not only trivia games. Card games such as *Magic: the Gathering* and *Dominion* fall into this category. So do most roleplaying games (both tabletop and computer-based), which tend to be rules-light and content-heavy. In a nutshell, if your idea for a game involves hundreds of unique items, it is probably best to set the idea aside for now and learn your craft by focusing on something more contained.

If this advice shatters your plan to create the game of your dreams, there is an alternative. Go ahead and design the game, but keep it manageable. Want to make a trivia game? Do it with ten trivia cards, no more. Want to make a collectible card game? Ten different cards (though you can print multiple copies of each, if you wish). Designing a roleplaying videogame? Make it playable to completion in 5 minutes. Making a tabletop roleplaying game? Keep the entire "rulebook" to one double-sided page (using a readable font size).

These constraints are incredibly challenging, but they will keep you focused on design and not content-creation. And if you can pull it off, the result could be a small masterpiece—and perhaps serve as a prototype for a full-fledged version to be created down the road.

Shoot-Out

A game for two players by Reiner Knizia

It is high noon in Silver City, Texas. The sun burns down relentlessly. A little drink in the saloon, an argument . . . and the shoot-out is on!

Your opponent faces you on the other side of the street. Deadly silence. Step by step, you edge closer towards your foe. Your hand wavers above your gun belt. Face to face, eye to eye. A drop of sweat trickles down your neck. Suddenly your opponent's hand twitches towards his Colt—there is a flash of light—then a sharp crack! But who fired first?

Required Materials (see pages 63–64)

- Playing board and two pawns
- Six cards with values from 2 to 7
- Twenty-four revolver bullet counters and twelve rifle bullet counters
- One 20-sided die with numbers from 1 to 20

Setup

Place the board between the two players, who should sit directly opposite each other. Each player takes one pawn. Shuffle the cards and place them as a face-down deck beside the board.

Both players receive twelve revolver counters (representing the bullets in two fully loaded Colt revolvers) and six rifle counters (representing the bullets in a fully loaded Winchester rifle). The bullet counters are placed openly in front of the players.

The Game

The game proceeds over several duels. At the beginning of each duel, the players set their pawns on space number 17 on their side of the board, and the top card is turned up from the deck. The player to start the first duel is chosen at random. Later duels will be started by the player who lost the previous duel.

Players move alternately. On her turn, a player has two choices: either to move, or to shoot.

Moving: The player advances her pawn by one space towards the center of the board. Then play moves to her opponent.

Shooting: The player can fire either a Colt or the Winchester, as long as she has bullets remaining. When firing a Colt, she discards a revolver bullet counter and throws the 20-sided die. If the result of the throw is smaller than the space number of her own pawn, it is a miss. In this case, the player's turn is over and play moves to her opponent.

If, however, the throw is greater than or equal to the space number her pawn is on, it is a hit. In this case, the opponent's pawn is moved back by three spaces (but not beyond space 20), and the opponent loses his turn. Therefore, as long as she is successful, the shooting player can continue to shoot, or she can decide to advance her pawn by one space and finish her turn.

When firing the Winchester, the player discards a rifle bullet counter instead of a revolver bullet counter. In this case, the throw of the die is increased by 3, which improves the chances of a hit (a Winchester is more accurate than a Colt).

Example: Player 1 fires the Winchester and discards a rifle bullet counter. Her pawn is located on space number 10. Therefore, she needs to throw a 7 or higher. She rolls a 9—a hit! Player 2's pawn is moved back from space 8 to space 11. Player 1 continues her turn.

The End of a Duel

At the beginning of his turn, a player may decide to retreat and finish the current duel. If he retreats with his opponent's pawn being on space number 6 or higher, the retreating player receives a reload of two revolver bullet counters; otherwise he receives none. The winner of the duel receives the face-up card and places it openly in front of him. The winner does not receive any new bullets.

With no player retreating, a duel ends when one player's pawn reaches the center space of the board. This player wins the duel and receives the face-up card. No player receives any reload bullets.

The player who lost the duel takes the first turn in the next one.

The End of the Shoot-Out

The game continues from duel to duel until one player succeeds in receiving cards with a total value of 14 or more. This player wins the shoot-out and the game is over.

Veteran's Variant l

Add a seventh card with a value of 8, and the first to gain 18 points or more is the winner. The game is longer, but there is a lot more tension as your supply of bullets dwindles.

Tournaments

With more than two players, tournaments can be held. In this scenario, each player plays one game of *Shoot-Out* against another player. The scores are added up, and the player with the highest point total wins the tournament.

Game Materials

In order to play *Shoot-Out*, you will need to create the game's board and components. Doing so will give you practice for prototyping your own games. There is no need to be elaborate—the idea is to create the necessary materials as quickly and easily as possible.

You will need a pawn for each player. Almost anything will do: *Chess* pawns, coins, dice, Lego pieces—whatever is convenient.

The board consists of thirty-two spaces laid out linearly. The spaces are numbered as shown in figure 3.14. Drawing this on a piece of paper (or pieces of paper taped together) is probably the easiest option. Make sure that the spaces are large enough for a pawn to easily fit inside without overlapping into an adjacent space.

The game requires a 20-sided die. If you do not already own one, you can buy one at your local game shop or online. Better yet, fulfill your dice needs for a long

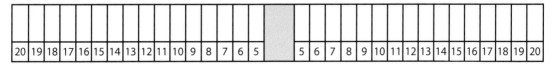

Figure 3.14 *Shoot-Out's* game board.

Reiner Knizia

Dr. Reiner Knizia is one of the world's most successful and prolific game designers. He has had more than 500 games and books published in many countries and languages with sales totaling over 15 million games. He has won numerous game of the year awards from around the world.

Knizia has a Master of Science degree from Syracuse University (USA) and a PhD in Mathematics from Ulm University (Germany). Before dedicating himself to the full-time development of games, he was the Operations Director of a £10 billion mortgage company based in the United Kingdom.

Photo 3.2 Reiner Knizia

Knizia has taught at universities and institutions including the Massachusetts Institute of Technology and the ABECOR Banking Institute.

time to come by purchasing a "Pound-o-Dice" (see "Items for your prototyping kit" at www.funmines.com/resources for details). Alternatively, you can use the dice simulator at www.funmines.com/dice-simulator.

The game requires six cards, numbered 2 through 7. Borrowing cards from a deck of playing cards would be ideal—they are ready made and their slick surface makes them easy to shuffle. Alternatively, any card stock (such as index cards) will work fine. Standard printing paper will work in a pinch, though you will need to make sure that the values you write on them do not show through the paper when they are face down.

The game requires game pieces that represent twenty-four revolver bullets and twelve rifle bullets. Twenty-four pennies and twelve nickels would work well. Alternatively you could use poker chips, M&Ms, or anything else handy. Some game designers like to use dice for tracking this sort of thing. This approach involves each player using a 12-sided die to track the revolver bullets and a 6-sided die for the rifle bullets. Players start the game with their revolver dice set to "12" and their rifle dice to "6." Each time a bullet is used, the appropriate die would be rotated to show the next lower number. Using dice in place of counters conveniently reduces the number of components needed to play, but requires more care in play—accidentally nudging a die can cause a player to lose track of her resources.

Prototyping

When building a prototype, keep in mind that the quicker you put it together (and later, revise it), the more time you will have to playtest it—which is the whole point of building the prototype in the first place.

Cheap, ugly, and fast are virtues during the early stages of prototyping. A designer needs to be clear-sighted about what is not working in the game and ruthless about cutting or modifying it. The more time and money invested in making a prototype, the harder it is to ditch the chunks of it that are not working well. Even if you are capable of merciless revising, keeping the early prototypes fast and ugly can help your playtesters feel more comfortable about suggesting major changes. There is a balance to strike, however, because some testers may be distracted by the roughness of an early prototype. For your earliest, crudest prototypes you may be best off testing with other game developers (who will be forgiving of the clunkiness of games at this stage) and close friends and family (who will be inclined to humor you).

Look for ways to cut corners. Rather than make your own play money, cannibalize a *Monopoly* set. Use coins as game pieces instead of making your own. If the game's components are complicated enough that they cannot be quickly thrown together, ask yourself if a scaled-down version could serve as a proof-of-concept before devoting the time to making a full version.

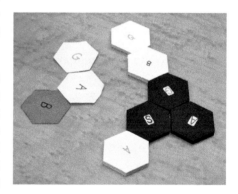

If you were designing *Hive*, your first few prototypes might be simply cut out of paper (figure 3.15). Paper is easy to work with and is a good way to try out the first few iterations of the game's mechanics. However, the flimsiness of the paper pieces can be distracting and frustrating for playtesters. So after a few playtests, you might opt to remake the pieces in foam core. It is a bit more difficult to work with, but the thicker material is much easier to play with.

Figure 3.15 *Hive* prototypes in paper and foam core.

As you playtest your prototype (the topic of the next chapter), you will find problems. Whenever possible, update the game immediately (mid-game) so that you do not waste time playing something you know needs to be changed. The board can be marked up, a card's text can be scratched out and rewritten, the players' pieces can be reduced, and so on. In the case of a foam core prototype of *Hive*, it would be a good idea to have spare blank pieces on hand in case any ideas for new pieces came up during a playtest.

Pandemic's First Prototype

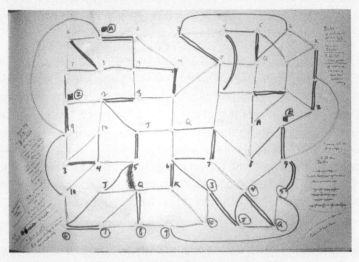

Figure 3.16 Matt Leacock's first prototype of *Pandemic*. Used with permission.

Pandemic's core mechanic involves disease counters being added to cities on the game board. When a fourth counter is added to a city, it causes an "outbreak" and a disease counter is added to every adjacent city. This mechanic can result in a single outbreak erupting into a chain reaction of outbreaks that spread across the adjacent cities and beyond.

The game's designer, Matt Leacock, came up with the idea for it during a walk with his daughter. Returning home, he created a prototype of the board (figure 3.16) in 15 minutes. After playing it by himself a few times, he sought out another playtester:

> My wife humored me by playing this version with some cubes, pawns, and a standard deck of cards. After I "discovered" the rule where players shuffle up discards to place back on to the disease draw pile, I knew I was on to something.
>
> Other rules that survived from the very first prototype included the need for five cards of the same suit to discover a cure and the ability to use a card as a plane ticket to the pictured city.
>
> Rules that didn't make the cut: colored routes (for connecting flights), the ability to buy another pawn with cards, the use of a pair of cards as a wild card, and quarantine cubes.
>
> (Leacock, *Pandemic Version .1* 2008)

Leacock refers to the typically ugly first prototypes as the "spark stage." It is here where the designer explores the first "spark" of an idea. If the game seems worth pursuing, it moves into a "wireframe stage." This means that the game's components are not distractingly

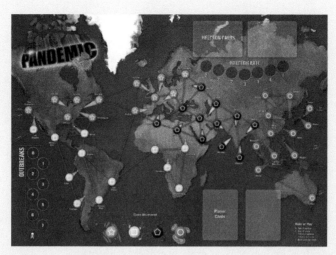

Figure 3.17 *Pandemic*'s board (prior to its 2013 update). Used with permission of Z-Man Games.

ugly, but the time and expense of creating them is kept to a minimum. Most importantly, everything in the wireframe stage should be easy to change. The "final stage" (figure 3.17) is where the game takes on the appearance it will have when published. Often this stage is the responsibility of the publisher, not the designer. Making changes to the final stage is expensive, so it should be avoided until the game is essentially done (Leacock, "Cooperation and Engagement" 2008).

Raph's Prototyping Kit

A prototyping kit is a set of materials and tools that can be used to create new games. The contents of game designer Raph Koster's prototyping kit include:

- Two decks of regular cards
- One deck of *Uno* cards
- One *Go* board
- One *Checkers* board
- A half dozen 6-sided dice
- One full set of polyhedral dice
- A large stack of differently colored index cards
- Craft store items:
    - Twelve pounds of differently colored beads for fish tanks and potted plants
    - Square glass chips

- Blank wooden clock faces to use as game boards
  - Wooden pieces to include cubes, flat squares, dowel rods, pawn pieces, circles, and other shapes
- Wood glue
- Dremel tool

(Koster 2010)

Koster uses his kit for video game paper prototypes, but it would work just as well for tabletop games. In addition to the items on Koster's list, you may want to have on hand:

- Markers, regular & colored pencils, regular & colored pens
- Card stock, blank paper, lined paper, grid paper, and hex graph paper
- Blank adhesive labels, colored sticky dots, masking tape, transparent tape (single & double-sided)
- Scissors, straight edge, box-cutter or craft knife, cutting mat
- Game components cannibalized from boardgames found in junk stores and tag sales

As Koster's list suggests, craft stores (such as Michaels, Jo-Ann Fabrics, etc.), have many bits and pieces that can be used as game components, even if that is not their intended purpose. Before getting too carried away, however, keep in mind that a perfectly workable kit can be had with just paper, pencils, and a set of dice—or even no components at all. That is the spirit of prototyping: making do with what is on hand.

Rapid Prototyping

Practice your prototyping skills by making a playable prototype of an existing game as quickly as possible. The game could be *Backgammon, Risk, Candy Land,* or anything else that strikes your fancy.

Give yourself a time limit of 10 minutes for making the prototype. Then start over and see what you can do in 60 seconds. (You probably will need to make a scaled down version of the game in order to keep within the time limit.) In a group setting, this rapid prototyping exercise can take the form of a race to completion.

For an added challenge, incorporate a rules change so that your prototype is a variant of the original game.

Start With the Core

Core mechanics are a game stripped down to its essence. They are the parts of the game that most characterize it—what could not be eliminated or changed without making the game unrecognizable. Abstract games tend to be streamlined and their core mechanics may not be much smaller than their entire set of mechanics. *Chess*'s core mechanics, for example, include how the pieces move and capture. The mechanics for castling, pawn promotion, and en passant are outside the game's core—even in their absence we can still recognize the game as *Chess*.

Core mechanics are the engine that makes a game run. They provide the primary gameplay experience. Often a game's core mechanics form the actions and events that occur turn after turn. Sometimes a core mechanic is less constant, but its impact looms large and is a major consideration for the players as they make their choices each turn. When developing a new game, focusing on its core mechanics is a good way to start. Even when you have an idea about what the secondary mechanics might be, it is useful to make sure the game's metaphorical engine is running smoothly before adding hubcaps and air fresheners. As Schreiber explains:

> If the basic, core rules don't work, then adding extra rules on top of it will generally not make it work. Get the basics working first, before you start adding complexity.
>
> In fact, if you build extra rules on an unstable foundation, the real underlying problems in your design could be obscured! Something might seem wrong, but if there are a lot of systems and resources and game objects it can be hard to tell if you're experiencing a problem with the core mechanics, or the balance of a particular resource, or the design of the map, or something else.
>
> (Schreiber, *The Early Stages of the Design Process* 2009)

Having a clear vision for the game's core can help anchor your design process. Designer Matt Leacock says being unclear about the game's core can result in aimless iteration. If you do not know what the core of the game is, then you do not know what you are trying to do, and you will not know when you have achieved it and the design is finished. Without a crisp goal, a game in development can meander for years (Leacock, "Cooperation and Engagement" 2008).

In its early stages, it is fine for your core mechanic to be something that can be played with, but does not have any set goals. For example, the first step in creating a farm-themed game might involve creating the rules for how crops are planted, grown, and harvested. This sort of core mechanic would certainly suggest a goal

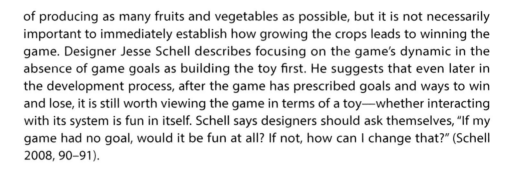

of producing as many fruits and vegetables as possible, but it is not necessarily important to immediately establish how growing the crops leads to winning the game. Designer Jesse Schell describes focusing on the game's dynamic in the absence of game goals as building the toy first. He suggests that even later in the development process, after the game has prescribed goals and ways to win and lose, it is still worth viewing the game in terms of a toy—whether interacting with its system is fun in itself. Schell says designers should ask themselves, "If my game had no goal, would it be fun at all? If not, how can I change that?" (Schell 2008, 90–91).

Shoot-Out's Core

This takes Reiner Knizia's *Shoot-Out* and strips it down to its core mechanics. The actual Knizia game can be found on page 61.

Players:

■ Two players

Required Materials:

■ Playing board (page 63) and 2 pawns
■ One 20-sided die with the numbers 1 to 20

Object of the Game:

■ Reach the center of the board.

Setup:

■ Arrange the board so that the line of spaces runs between the two players.
■ Each player has a pawn which should be placed on the space numbered 17 on their side of the board.

Rules:

1. Players alternate taking turns.
2. On a turn, a player can either shoot or move (but cannot do both).
3. When moving, the player's pawn advances one space towards the center of the board and the turn ends.
4. When shooting, the player rolls the 20-sided die.
   ■ If the result of the roll is smaller than the space number of the player's own pawn, it is a miss and the player's turn is over.

- ■ If the result of the roll is greater than or equal to the space number of the player's own pawn, it is a hit.
5. When a pawn is successfully hit, it moves back three spaces (but not beyond space 20) and its owner loses a turn.
6. After a successful hit, the shooting player can choose to shoot again or to move. As long as the shots are successful, a player can continue taking turns. After a missed shot or a move forward, the player's turn is over.

EXERCISE Coring a Game

Try playing the bare bones version of *Shoot-Out* just described as well as the full version on page 61. How do they compare? Are they recognizably the same game? Are they equally as fun? The "core" version of the game removes the bullet resource management, the scoring, and the structure of having a game made up of multiple duels.

What purpose do each of those secondary mechanics serve in the full version of the game? Are there any gameplay issues in the core game design that are solved by the addition of one of the secondary mechanics?

Following the example of how the core mechanics were pulled out of *Shoot-Out*, try stripping *Zombie in my Pocket* (page 114) down to its core mechanics—the mechanics that are providing the primary gameplay experience. There is no precise answer here, so you have some discretion in deciding what constitutes the game's core mechanics. That said, if a mechanic is not happening almost every turn, then you should question whether it is really part of the core. Also, keep in mind that it is perfectly acceptable for a core mechanic to not include the means for achieving the full game's goal; the core mechanic can be a toy.

Build the Pillars

Once you have a core mechanic playtested to your satisfaction (the topic of the following chapter), the next step is to start adding "pillars" to your game design. Pillars are the secondary mechanics that flesh out the core mechanic's skeleton. Core mechanics tend to be the actions and events that occur almost every turn in a game. A game's pillars constitute the game mechanics that are more conditional and less frequently encountered, but are still crucial in terms of the players' gameplay experience.

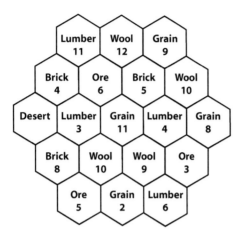

Figure 3.18 A simple (prototype-style) version of a *Settlers of Catan* board.

For example, *Shoot-Out*'s pillars include the bullet resource management mechanic that interacts with its core mechanics of movement and shooting. *Monopoly* might be said to have core mechanics of piece movement and the ability for spaces to be "owned" by players. Its pillars are the mechanics involved in its monetary economy, the ability to upgrade properties (adding houses and hotels), property trading, and the random events of the Chance and Community Chest cards.

The Settlers of Catan is a tabletop game that every designer should know as part of a basic game literacy. Its core mechanics involve players collecting and trading resources. The game's board is made up of hexes, each of which is designated with a number (between 2 and 12) as well as a particular type of resource (ore, grain, wool, lumber, or brick). Players start the game owning two hex corners, from which they expand using the hexagons' sides as paths (figure 3.18). Each turn, two 6-sided dice are rolled and their combined value indicates which hexes are producing resources. Every player who controls a corner on the producing hexes receives a corresponding resource.

Does *The Settlers of Catan*'s resource acquisition mechanic remind you of any game we have examined earlier in the book? In some ways, it is very similar, in its skeletal form, to *The Tower*. In both games, players are linked to a number that provides them a resource whenever it comes up in a dice roll.

While the core mechanics of *The Settlers of Catan* and *The Tower* are very similar, the actual experience of playing the games is wildly different. The difference comes from the pillars that *The Settlers of Catan* adds to its core: area control, purchasing, and upgrading. *The Tower*'s own gameplay does not extend much beyond its core mechanic.

Usually the best a core mechanic can do is provide a somewhat engaging or satisfying activity. True fun usually arrives with the addition of the pillars. Some designers like to add everything at once to the core mechanic, while others prefer to add pillars one by one (Daviau 2011, 45). The former approach requires a designer who can detect where there is fun in an unwieldy mess of gameplay and does not hesitate to pare away the mechanics that do not support it. It is like starting with a big block of stone and then chiseling away to create a statue. The latter approach, in contrast, requires a designer who can look beyond the game in

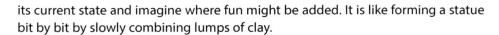

its current state and imagine where fun might be added. It is like forming a statue bit by bit by slowly combining lumps of clay.

Neither approach is inherently better than the other. As a starting place, it is recommended that you take a moderate approach. After designing and testing the game's core mechanic, take a stab at adding the pillars you think are needed to make a full-fledged game, but do not overload it. If there are some mechanics that you think might not be absolutely critical, leave them out for the initial version of the game. As you playtest the game, remove what you think is not working. If the game is seriously lacking in fun, then you may need a systemic change— something along the lines of adding, dramatically changing, or replacing a pillar.

Keep in mind, however, that the heart of the game is its core mechanic. Every secondary mechanic should support and not detract from it. Even if a mechanic is fun or interesting, it is usually best to remove it if it is taking the focus away from the core. In such a situation, make sure you write down the idea in your designer's notebook to use in some future game (perhaps promoted to serve as a core mechanic itself).

Whenever you have a difficult decision regarding whether to include some secondary mechanic, just ask yourself, "Does this make the core stronger or weaker?" and there is your answer.

CHAPTER FOUR

Playtesting Tabletop Games

INTRODUCTION

Making the first prototype of a game is only a small part of the overall design process. Much more time and effort goes into properly playtesting and developing a game than is spent creating its first incarnation. Playtesting can strain your patience and bruise your ego. But it can also be exciting and fulfilling. Playtests are where your game comes alive and (hopefully) evolves to reach its full potential.

The learning objectives for this chapter are:

1 Become aware of the various types of playtests, the purposes they serve, and the processes for conducting them.

2 Explore what is meant by "fun."

3 Understand the importance of playability.

Solo Playtesting

After coming up with a new core mechanic or pillar (or doing a significant revision to an existing one), a designer's typical next step is to test it out. When designing collaboratively, this can be easily accomplished by simply playtesting the game with your design partners. When a designer works alone, however, it is wise to conduct a solo playtest before bringing in additional playtesters.

A solo playtest involves setting up the game as if it was being played by multiple people, then making the moves for each "dummy player" in turn. A dummy is an imaginary player whose moves are controlled by another player (the designer in this case). This simulation of playing against other people often unearths unforeseen design problems.

It is certainly possible to skip the solo playtest step and simply find other people with whom to play the game. However, doing so risks wasting the playtesters' time (which is a valuable commodity for a designer). When playtesting an initial prototype for the first time, it is not unusual to discover huge design flaws before even the first turn in the game is completed. Solo playtests serve the same purpose as re-reading the first draft of a term paper and putting it through a spell-checker before asking someone else to read it (i.e., it saves you from looking incompetent).

Solo playtests have three primary goals:

1. Identify game situations that the designer did not anticipate.
2. Confirm that the game's dynamics are working as the designer expects and desires.
3. Improve the design as much as possible prior to presenting it to another playtester.

It is surprisingly easy to overlook obvious holes in a game's design. The author cannot count the number of times one of his students brought in a game to playtest only to discover that some fundamental aspect of the game's design (such as defining the number of resources each player starts with) had been overlooked. A solo playtest serves as a sanity check to insure there are no glaring holes in a game's rules. If you have not participated in many game playtests, it is easy to underestimate the likelihood of an unanticipated game situation derailing the game. For example, consider *Hive*'s "One Hive Rule" (page 49). The ruleset for *Hive*'s first prototype did not anticipate the problem of a move dividing the hive into two. However, the very first time the game was played, it became clear that a rule was needed in order to keep the pieces connected.

Solo playtests are unlikely to catch every single problem in a game's design, but they certainly can help a designer spot the most obvious ones. Beyond uncovering holes in the design, solo playtests are a way to confirm that the game's dynamics are working reasonably well. For example, if you were designing *Hive* you would want to make sure that it is indeed possible to surround an opponent's Queen Bee—that the pieces' movement abilities do not provide so much flexibility that the game never ends. In the case of *Shoot-Out* (page 61), the designer might use a solo playtest to see if the bullet allotment is approximately correct. Are there enough bullets that players do not run out of them too early in the game? Are the number of bullets limited enough that the players feel pressure to conserve them?

As much as possible, you want to exhaust your ability to improve the game on your own before bringing in other people to playtest it. Even if you have captive playtesters (such as family members or roommates) who are available and willing to play your game whenever you want, you should be wary of having them play the game too early in its development. Playtesters are a valuable commodity and you should not waste them on testing anything that you can test on your own.

As the saying goes, you can only make one first impression, and in regard to games, the feedback you get from the first time someone plays the game is often the most valuable. After playing a game a few times, players begin falling into patterns of thinking and play that can blind them to other possibilities. A first-time player who has not yet figured out what is possible (or is supposed to be possible) is the tester most likely to find a radically different strategy or a hole in the rules. This also points to why playtesters are important and why solo playtests are only a small part of the playtesting effort. The more you play a given set of mechanics, the less you are able to see the flaws.

Conducting a Solo Playtest

A solo playtest can feel awkward. Assuming the game is intended to involve more than one player, a solo playtest requires taking on the roles of all the opposing players. To do this, you simply set up the game as if it were to be played normally, then take each player's turn one at a time. As you step into each player's shoes, you want to be invested in that player winning the game. Additionally, you want to vary the play style and strategies employed by each of the virtual players. For example, if you were playing a solo game of *Chess*, you might decide that one player is going to

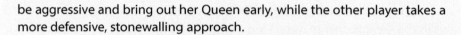

be aggressive and bring out her Queen early, while the other player takes a more defensive, stonewalling approach.

Solo playtests can require a fair amount of mental juggling if the game being tested allows players to interrupt each other's turns or move simultaneously. A game that allows players to take actions during other player's turns (such as *Magic: the Gathering*'s "instant" spells and *Kill Doctor Lucky*'s "failure" cards), requires being mindful of not only the current player's actions, but also the counteractions that opposing players might want to take.

Battleship (aka *Sea Battle*) has a core mechanic in which players place their own ships in secret locations and guess where their opponent has hidden his ships. In such situations, a solo playtest requires the designer to "forget" about the information that a given player would not know. Likewise, mechanics that have a large degree of player interaction (such as making alliances and trading resources) require a true act of imagination on the part of the solo playtester to represent the interests of all the parties involved.

Here are some things to keep in mind when conducting a solo playtest:

- Put together a list of the concerns and uncertainties you have about the design. Try to steer your solo playtests towards exploring and resolving those issues.
- Use a solo playtest to stress-test the game. If the game involves player choices (and hopefully it does), see what happens when a player becomes single-minded about making a particular choice. For example, if you were solo playtesting *Shoot-Out* you might experiment with seeing what happens when one player always chooses to shoot or always chooses to move.
- If the game supports a varying number of players (for example, two to four players), be sure to do solo playtests for each of the possible numbers of participants.
- Vary your playing style as much as possible. Try playing aggressively, conservatively, and in a middle-of-the-road manner. Try out various combinations of these styles (for example, see what happens if all the players are playing defensively).
- Consider basing some of the decision making on chance. For example, you could use a coin flip or die roll to decide whether a *Shoot-Out* player opts to shoot or move.

EXERCISE Making Your Own Game

Up until now, the book's hands-on design exercises have involved tinkering with someone else's design. This exercise gives you the freedom (and obligation) to create your own game from the ground up. You will spend about 40 minutes total coming up with an idea, prototyping it, conducting solo playtests, and revising the prototype. You should spend the time focusing on the core mechanics. An exercise later in the chapter will have you expand upon this core.

1. Spend about 10 minutes coming up with a core mechanic for a two-player game. Try to be creative—avoid simply copying the core mechanic of another game. You can borrow elements from other games, however, if you can find a way to make them your own.
2. Next, spend 10 minutes thinking about the game dynamics that are likely to arise from your mechanic. Do the choices that players are incentivized to make lead to the sort of gameplay you want? If not, is there a rule addition or adjustment to the core mechanic that can be made that would solve the problem?
3. The previous step involved thinking about the mechanic and anticipating how it might play. Now you want to get ready to actually play it. Spend about 10 minutes prototyping the mechanic. This means creating the materials necessary to play it. Do not get caught up in trying to make the physical components aesthetically appealing, just make them functional.
4. Now that you have physically made your game's core mechanic, spend at least 10 minutes solo playtesting it. As you run into problems, revise the mechanic to fix them. It is fine to have some part of your mechanic (say, an action card) scrawled over with annotations and scratched out text.

For step 2, if your predictions regarding game dynamics prove completely inaccurate, do not despair. If nothing else, realizing your limitations in this regard will help you appreciate the value of playtesting. An ability to anticipate dynamics can be improved both through practice and by expanding your exposure to mechanics through learning and playing more tabletop games.

You are free to devote extra time on step 4 (conducting solo playtests and revising the core mechanic). Avoid stretching out the earlier steps, however. It is easy to get bogged down trying to come up with the perfect idea or creating great looking game pieces.

Given the exercise's time constraints, you will not be able to create something epic. Your core mechanic should be small in scale, certainly nothing more broad or complicated than the core of *Shoot-Out*, *Marrakech*, or *Zombie in my Pocket* (page 114).

Anticipating a Game's Dynamics

An important skill for game designers is the ability to anticipate the dynamics of a game—the sorts of choices players are incentivized to make. The better a designer is able to do this, the more effective she will be at ideation and the stronger her initial design will be.

One way to build this ability is to practice predicting how a game will work based on its rules alone. After reading the rules to a game, but before you have played it for the first time, try to imagine how playing the game will feel. What sort of player strategies do you think will be most effective? In what ways do you think the game will be fun and what aspects of it do you think will be less engaging? Compare your initial having-read-the-rules-only impression of the game with the actual experience you have playing it.

When designing collaboratively, keep in mind that simply playing the game with your co-designers and seeing how it plays is better than getting bogged down in theoretical discussions about how a design change might affect the game. Also, be aware that a talent at foreseeing a game's dynamics is not a substitute for playtesting. To draw an analogy, a chef may have a skill for imagining how several unusual flavors might taste when combined, but only an incompetent chef would skip taste testing the result before serving it to customers. Likewise, having a sense of what dynamics arise out of a set of mechanics is useful for coming up with initial designs, but only a naïve game designer would believe that it can take the place of playtesting.

Playtesting with Others

At some point, probably sooner rather than later, you will want to move from solo playtesting to playtesting your prototype with other people. As you do so, your playtest objectives usually shift to become one or more of the following:

1. Performing a "sanity test" on the game's design
2. Gauging how fun the game is to play
3. Balancing the game
4. Testing the game's playability

The order of these goals roughly corresponds to how a game's development usually proceeds. The first stage of creating a game focuses on simply getting it blocked out. Sanity testing the game system is really a continuation of what was being done during the solo playtests. The game is likely to still have kinks that need shaking out, and playing against another person often exposes obvious (in retrospect) problems that did not surface during solo playtests. The goal is to have a game system that runs smoothly and does not lead to any gameplay dead ends.

Once the design is deemed "sane," the effort shifts towards making the game fun. This is where things get hard. It can be disheartening to have your idea for a game finally coalesce into a system of mechanics that functions well, only to realize that while the game "works," it is not fun. In such a situation (which is the norm), revisit your core mechanic to assure yourself that it is reasonably engaging on its own—that it is a "toy." If it is, then you need to work on your game's pillars. Doing so may require dramatic changes in order to create a setting in which the core's brilliance can shine. If the core mechanic is weak, then spending time re-arranging the pillars is probably pointless and the best course of action may be to start over and try to come up with a new and better core.

Once the fun is established, the game needs to be balanced to insure that it is fair to all the players and supports a variety of effective player strategies. Balancing a game (the topic of Chapter 12) typically involves tweaking and testing its quantifiable aspects. For example, John Yianni was balancing *Hive* when he conducted the many playtests that helped determine that 11 pieces is the ideal number for each player to have.

Finally, when the game is nearly done, making sure that it is easy to learn and play becomes the most crucial task. The sections on "Playability" later in this chapter and "Writing Rules" in the next will both discuss this further.

Game development is an iterative process. Each iteration is a development cycle of designing (or revising) game mechanics, implementing the design, and playtesting the implementation. What is learned in the playtests informs the next round of revision, implementation, and testing. Developing even the most simple game requires a daunting number of iterations.

With any luck, the general trend of the game's development will be one of advancing through the stages described above: blocking out the game, making the game fun, balancing the game, and making the game as playable as possible. However, there will inevitably be revisions and backtracking that require a shift (hopefully brief) to the earlier testing goals. For example, if playtesting reveals that giving the players additional resources will help with playability (objective #4), then the change should be tested to make sure it does not break the game (objective #1), does not have a negative impact on the fun (objective #2), and does not hurt the game's balance (objective #3).

> "Your game's not as good as you think it is. At least not until you've had people who don't hold it—or you—near and dear to their hearts, play it and agree with you."
>
> Teeuwynn Woodruff (2011)

Fun

What are you trying to do when you create a game? The top priority for designers is usually to provide a fun experience for the players. But what does that mean? What makes a game fun?

It is tempting to treat "fun" as being an objective (and perhaps measurable) trait. We often declare that a game is fun (or not fun) in the same sweeping way that we might declare a game piece is blue (or not blue) in color. But you will be a much more effective designer if you approach fun as a subjective experience rather than an absolute characteristic.

"Fun" does not describe a single kind of experience. Sunbathing, riding a roller coaster, going to the mall, and working out are all very different activities, yet each of them would be described as fun by some people and unpleasant by others. Similarly, games offer all kinds of experiences that might be enjoyed by some and disliked by others. For example, it is not unusual for a hard core gamer to dislike games in which chance plays a major role, yet for many game players the ability to push their luck is thrilling.

On its own, the question of "How can I make my game more fun?" has no answer. It is too broad a query. Two kids playing *Candy Land* might be having a blast, possibly more fun per second than is being had by their parents playing *Chess*. But you are unlikely to ask "How can I make my game more like *Candy Land*?" And swapping games so that the *Chess* players are playing *Candy Land* is unlikely to increase the amount of fun they are having. Fun is a property of the fit between player and game, not a property of the game itself.

Before you can ask how to make your game more fun, you need to establish the kind of fun you are trying to provide and know what type of player enjoys that kind of fun. Or to approach it from the other end, if you are designing a game for a particular audience, how can your game be shaped to increase the fun for them?

If you are someone who is learning the craft of game design, it is a good idea to create games that are meant for the kinds of people who you can most easily access for playtesting. If that is your family, then you may want to create family games. If you are taking a game design course, then your target player might be the type of person who would enroll in a game course.

EXERCISE A Fun Exercise

Designer Marc LeBlanc is known for his list of eight kinds of fun (LeBlanc n.d.):

1.   Sensation (game as sense-pleasure)
2.   Fantasy (game as make-believe)
3.   Narrative (game as unfolding story)
4.   Challenge (game as obstacle course)
5.   Fellowship (game as social framework)
6.   Discovery (game as uncharted territory)
7.   Expression (game as soap box)
8.   Submission (game as mindless pastime)

The kinds of fun do not end with LeBlanc's eight. For example, game as ruining other people's enjoyment ("griefing") is not on his list (Schreiber, *Kinds of Fun, Kinds of Players* 2009). Can you think of any other kinds of game fun?

What are your favorite games? What kinds of fun are they providing you?

Of the games you know, which appeals to the broadest array of players? In what ways does it satisfy its various types of players.

What games do your friends find fun, but you do not? What is the kind of fun that they are having?

Working with Playtesters

The tenor of playtesting will change as your game progresses through the development process. In the early stages (while you are still sanity testing the game and seeking out its fun), you want to iterate as rapidly as possible. You should encourage your playtesters to give feedback while they are playing and you should not hesitate to make changes to the rules mid-game. If something is not working or you want to experiment with a change, do not wait for the next game to try it—go ahead and institute the change immediately. The quicker you can make your iterations, the more iterations you will have, and the better your final game will be. It is very possible to pack several iterations into a single playtest.

Changing the rules of a game does break many people's conception of game etiquette, so you will want to prepare your playtesters for the process. You want playtesters striving to win, yet not so caught up in the game that they become aggrieved if the game's rules suddenly shift.

As the playtesters give you feedback, treat it as the gift it is. Anyone who plays your half-baked game is doing you an immense favor. Being dismissive of someone's feedback (even if it is a seemingly innocuous statement of, "Oh yeah, I know about that problem"), means you are less likely to receive a following piece of feedback that *is* useful. Also, keep in mind that feedback that may not seem relevant at first glance may end up being useful once you have had a chance to mull it over and absorb it.

As the game design settles down and you start bringing in new playtesters, you should pay special attention to their first time playing the game. You only get one first encounter per playtester, so it is an opportunity not to be wasted. Video game companies have a special term for playtesters who are specifically used for their first impression: Kleenex testers. "Kleenex" because they are "used once and then thrown away." Having a steady stream of "throwaway" testers is not practical for most independent designers, but you do want to be aware that a tester's first encounter with a game is a unique playtest opportunity. In the later stages of development, a playtester's first time with the game is your ideal chance to test the game's written rules.

You are not required to act on every piece of information gathered during playtesting. In fact, doing so is impossible because inevitably the feedback you glean from one playtester will be contradicted by another. Contradictions aside, your game does not need to be fun for everyone who plays it. Even jaw-droppingly great games are not to everyone's taste. That said, your first inclination *should* be to embrace the criticism and only later, after thoroughly thinking it through, weed out what is not useful.

Sometimes playtesters will present you with great ideas for improving the game, and when they do, you want to be able to recognize and embrace it. In some cases you may learn that you are entirely wrong about what your game is about—that what people find most engaging is some aspect of the game that is secondary to the main gameplay (Extra Credits 2011). When that is the case, ask yourself whether you may have stumbled upon a gem and should revise your game to center on the part of it that is capturing people's attention.

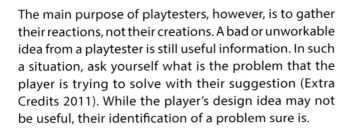

The main purpose of playtesters, however, is to gather their reactions, not their creations. A bad or unworkable idea from a playtester is still useful information. In such a situation, ask yourself what is the problem that the player is trying to solve with their suggestion (Extra Credits 2011). While the player's design idea may not be useful, their identification of a problem sure is.

In addition to being open to any impromptu lessons learned during the playtest, you should have specific questions in mind that you are hoping to answer. Does the scoring system seem fair? Can players who fall behind catch up? Does the turn order seem to advantage a particular player? And so on. Depending on the situation, you may or may not want to share your specific playtest goals with the testers.

Playtesters for early prototypes are usually whoever is most convenient. As a game begins to take shape, however, it is a good idea to seek out a variety of testers. Friends and family can be handy, but their feedback is not necessarily the most objective. Fellow game designers, hard core game players, people in your target audience, and random strangers will all bring different perspectives to your game and each can give you valuable insights that you might not otherwise have.

On Getting Criticism

by Raph Koster

Raph Koster is a video game designer whose online persistent world games have been particularly influential. He was the lead designer on the seminal Ultima Online game, as well as creative director for Star Wars Galaxies. Koster is the author of A Theory of Fun for Game Design, one of the classic books on game design.

Lately I have been working on multiple new games. And whenever you are working on games, of course, you get people to try them, and a lot of them don't like what they see.

I've gotten a lot of criticism over the years, and I haven't always taken it the right way. These days, criticism comes from all directions, and work is often shared before it's really done. It can be hard to know what to listen to and when to stick to your guns.

Ultima Online is a Hall of Fame game. It averaged 6/10 in reviews. *Star Wars Galaxies* got a famously mixed reception, and closed down a while back; I still get fan mail.

So here's my takeaway from all those years of being told that my work sucks.

Everyone Who Dislikes Your Work is Right

This is the hardest pill to swallow. I've never gotten a piece of feedback that was wrong. You see, you can't deny a player their unique experience. Whatever they felt, was true. For them. And *something* in your work triggered it.

It is useless, and worse, actually self-defeating, to attempt to deny the critique. Sure, there are sometimes reviews that seem spiteful, unfair, and the rest. But the vast majority of the time, people are giving their honest reaction.

And the bottom line is, you put the game out there in order to get reactions. If it were not for reactions, you could have just kept the game in your drawer and gotten everything you needed out of it.

The criticism that is useful is that which helps you do it better

People make games for different reasons. Some do it just because it is fun. Some do it as a form of personal expression. Some have a message to get across, and some are out to make money to put food on the table.

Whatever your goal is, doing it better is held in common. That sense of craftsmanship is the common ground that unites us all. Do what you do better, serve the work better, and you get to do it again.

That means there are two aspects of your work that you want to hear about the most. What you did right, and what you did wrong.

Nothing's perfect

All our babies seem perfect until that first player touches them. We have to learn they are not. Nothing is. People who point out flaws are just pointing out reality. If you can't see the flaws in your own work, you probably need to get some distance. You can't do your best work if you cannot get that distance, because you will learn to gloss over problems. It is amazing how they will vanish into a blind spot.

In my case, I often have to let stuff sit for a long time. A year, or more. The fastest way to short-circuit this process is to stand behind someone who tries to play my game, and shut up and say nothing. It's awesome: suddenly everything in it sucks! Then I furiously take notes.

The fact is that to do creative work is to know that most of what you do is shit. And we feel that way because we know we can do better. Honestly, if you aren't pushing the boundaries of what you can do, you're probably not working hard enough. And working at the edge means a lot of screw-ups.

You often have to choose between your ideals and your message

One of the commonest pieces of feedback I get is that I am choosing some philosophical ideal over the player's experience. It might be getting wedded to an aesthetic or visual I love that is just confusing the issue. It might be sticking with PvP (see note at the end of this essay) for too long in order to serve an ideal of virtual citizenship, not paying attention to how many players are being chased out of the game.

The irony here, of course, is that if I can't make the player's experience positive enough, my ideal is failing to reach them anyway. And what good is it then?

It doesn't mean I have to give up on the philosophical ideal. But it does mean that there are many many ways to compromise, and not all of them leave you compromised. In fact, being uncompromising may be the *least* successful way to achieve your artistic goal.

You have to dig to get the gold

Most feedback you get isn't going to be from fellow practitioners. Even when it is, they are not going to know as much about the specific ways in which you did things, the tools you used, the practices you follow, to be able to pinpoint exactly what's wrong without a pretty deep dive.

This means that usually, when someone tells you that something is wrong or broken, it's going to be wrong. But wrong in the sense that it will be imprecise. You need to find out what the problem is underlying the problem. In other words, the symptoms described will almost always be right, and the diagnosis will often be wrong.

Don't discard the feedback because of this. Look at it as a door you need to push on. Dig deeper and find out what the *real* issue is.

Good feedback is detailed

Sometimes you get a piece of feedback that is highly specific. It offers alternate word choices. It tells you the basics like you're an idiot. It offers suggestions that are likely

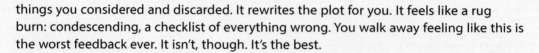

things you considered and discarded. It rewrites the plot for you. It feels like a rug burn: condescending, a checklist of everything wrong. You walk away feeling like this is the worst feedback ever. It isn't, though. It's the best.

Look past what may feel like condescension. This sort of detail is impossible for someone who has not *engaged fully with your work*. The sign of a critic who does not care is brevity, not detail. It's dismissal.

Now, all the other caveats about whether or not this feedback is right still apply. It can be detailed and not right. But never dismiss serious thought.

People who tell you you're awesome are useless. No, *dangerous*

They are worse than useless because you *want* to believe them. They will defend you against critiques that are valid. They will seduce you into believing you are done learning, or into thinking that your work is better than it actually is. Especially watch out for the ones who tell you that nobody understands your genius.

Honestly, this is going to sound horrible, but self-doubt is one of your most powerful tools for craftsmanship. None of the designers you admire feel self-confident about their work in that way. None of them think that they are awesome. They all suffer from impostor complexes the size of the Titanic.

I am not saying that you need to lack confidence in yourself. (Heck, you'll never put anything out if that's the case! You need to have the arrogance to assume anyone will care in the first place.) I am saying that nobody is ever done learning, and people who tell you you have arrived will give you a sense of complacency. You should never be complacent about your art.

Someone asked for feedback will always find something wrong

This is super simple. When someone is asked to critique something, they will feel like they have failed if they don't find something wrong. So everyone will always find something, even if there's nothing major to fix.

That doesn't mean that the thing they mention is wrong. If the only feedback you get from multiple people is the same minor thing, you should feel pretty good!

Good work may not have an audience

This is a sad truth. There is no correlation between quality and popularity. You may make something that is sophisticated, subtle, expressive, brilliant, and lose out to what is shallow

and facile and brash. Oh well. And that really is the right attitude to have about it, too: oh well. Getting bitter about it is pointless.

That said, don't underestimate the skill required in being simple, polished, and accessible. Dense and rich is *easy*. Simple is *hard*. You denigrate "pop" at your peril.

Any feedback that comes with suggestions for improvement is awesome

That's because it means the person offering the criticism actually thought about your goals. So either you get avenues to explore that assist you in your artistic goal, *or* you get told that your goal is invisible to an audience! Both are highly valuable information.

If you agree with the criticism, say "thank you." If you disagree, say "fair enough," and "thank you"

Complaining about a critique, or about a bad review, is utterly pointless. You can't deny the subjective experience of the reviewer. You also have to be thankful that they paid enough attention to actually say anything at all. The fact is that *indifference* is the enemy, not engagement, even if that engagement doesn't get the results you want.

You're going to face way more indifference in your career than anything else. There are a lot of people out there working really hard, and they all want the audience attention that you do. Always be grateful for the attention. Someone takes the time to let you know what they thought? That's already one in a thousand. *They cared*.

You are not your work

Above all, don't forget this. Oh, be personally invested, of course. Your art will be poorer if you are not. But every little ship we launch is just our imperfect crafting of the moment. And we move on. We create again, and again. Each can only ever express a fragment, a tiny fraction of ourselves. And if you are trying to always improve in your craft and your art, then every old fragment, everything out there in the world already, that's *old news*. You are on the next thing. Your next work, that's who you are. Not the work that exists, but the work that does not yet.

So if someone savages it, who cares? That was *yesterday*. It's not who you are now.

Hold on to that, because a lot of people can't separate the work from the artist. Including a lot of artists.

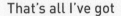

x

That's all I've got

And really, this advice is as much for myself as it is for anyone else. Because we all need reminding.

In his essay, Koster references "PvP," an acronym for "player versus player." The term describes video games in which players are in competition with one another, as opposed to the conflict being against computer-controlled antagonists exclusively.

EXERCISE Expanding Your Core

In the "Making Your Own Game" exercise (page 79), you created a core mechanic and solo playtested it. This exercise asks you to develop that core mechanic into a full-fledged (but short) game. It should take no more than 10 minutes to play it start to finish—the quicker the game, the better.

Recruit someone to playtest the core with you. Iterate on the core mechanic until you are satisfied it is solid and promising. When you are ready, begin adding more gameplay. You can add pillars one at a time or pile them on all at once, whichever way you prefer. Whatever method you choose, consider trying the other one for your next game design so that you can compare the techniques and see what actually works best for you.

After adding the pillar(s), return to solo playtesting. When you are confident you understand the impact of the change and that the new game mechanics have not introduced any systemic problems to the game, playtest it again with another person.

Continue with this iterative process until you have a game that is fun to play. Be sure that you return to solo playtesting whenever you add, remove, or significantly change a game pillar (or the core itself).

Playability

Playability refers to how easy it is to learn and play a game. As a game's design begins to settle into its final form, you should make sure that your players are not only having a fun playing experience, but a smooth one as well. As much as possible, you want to eliminate any confusion about how a game is played and make the experience of updating and interpreting the game state as easy as possible.

One way this is done is by adjusting the game's mechanics themselves. Game designer Rob Daviau recommends reconsidering any oddball, special case mechanics, "If you have mechanics in there that come up extremely infrequently, try hard to close the loophole so you don't need the 'patch.' Don't fall in love with a fringe element to your game" (Daviau 2011, 45). He goes on to suggest that designers look for alternative ways to achieve whatever effect is being provided by mechanics that players tend to forget or stumble over. It is not always possible to create a perfectly streamlined game, but it is certainly worth striving for.

Consider the Income Tax space on the *Monopoly* board. The long-standing rule for landing on Income Tax required the player to choose between either paying 10% of her worth or $200. The rulebook adds that the decision must be made prior to calculating the value of the player's properties, cash, and buildings. The decision between paying a percentage or flat rate adds little to the game and the worth calculations slow the game down unnecessarily. In 2008, the Income Tax rule was simplified to always be a flat $200.

A great deal of a game's playability comes from the design of its physical components. As a designer you should ask yourself whether there is anything that burdens the players that could be made less onerous by adding or changing some game component.

For example, *Zombie in my Pocket* (page 114) requires players to track their attack and health scores, the items they pick up, and the passage of game world time. While a player can track all this with pen and paper, a better solution is to add a card to the game (figure 4.1, page 92) that helps the player manage the information (including "sanity" for a variant, see www.funmines.com/zimp). In addition to making the bookkeeping easier to manage, the card also makes the game easier to learn because it presents the game's variables so clearly.

Ticket to Ride provides another example of designing playability. In the game, players create railroad lines between cities (see figure 8.6 on page 157). The particular cities that players try to connect are determined by drawing "destination cards." To help players find the cities on the game board, each card includes a mini version of the game board's map with the relevant cities highlighted. So if a player is a bit hazy as to where Calgary is situated, the card provides a quick tutorial.

Ticket to Ride's scoring is not entirely straightforward. The number of points a player earns for laying track increases exponentially based on its length. Rather than force players to memorize the details (or constantly look them up in the rules), the scoring details are printed on reference cards as well as on the board itself.

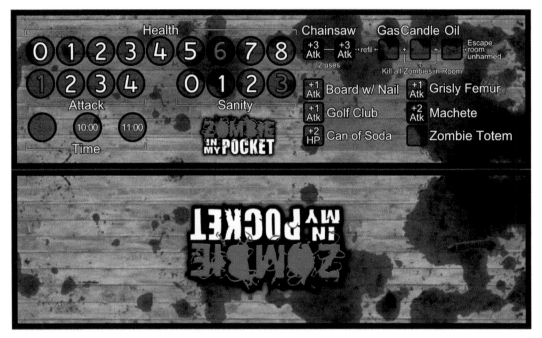

Figure 4.1 *Zombie in my Pocket* player board by Kris Barton.

EXERCISE Reference Cards

When you start playtesting a game, you may find that there are details that the players constantly forget. For example, when you learned to play *Hive*, you may have had trouble remembering how the various pieces moved. If so, a movement reference card might have helped. A reference card is something like a rules cheat-sheet. Typically reference cards do not attempt to capture a game's entire set of rules; instead they summarize a few details about the game that players tend to have trouble remembering.

This exercise asks you to design a reference card for a game you know well, but does not already come with reference cards. Teach the game to someone who does not know it. While teaching the game, try to determine what parts of the game are difficult for a beginner. For example, if you chose to teach the poker game *Five Card Draw*, you may have noticed that the beginner had trouble remembering which poker hand beats what.

Create a reference card that will serve as an aid for playing the game. In our poker reference card example, you might choose to list the rank of the various types of hands (figure 4.2). Try to keep the card's size manageable—perhaps no larger than a 4" × 6" index card. A playing card-sized (2.5" × 3.5") reference card would be natural for a poker game.

Try introducing the game to another person using the assistance of your reference card. Did the card help the person play the game? Are there any improvements you could make to it?

Figure 4.2 Ranking of poker hands.

CHAPTER FIVE

Rules

INTRODUCTION

How the rules of a tabletop game are presented to players is largely an issue of documentation. There are very few situations in which a designer would intentionally choose to obscure how a tabletop game works. Video gameplay, on the other hand, often depends on players starting the game without having a full understanding of its rules/mechanics. Learning the rules to a video game can be an act of discovery and a large part of what makes the game fun. For video games, the way in which rules are presented is very much a design consideration.

The learning objectives for this chapter are:

1 Explore the ways in which rules can be presented to players and understand the meaning of explicit, implicit, discoverable, and hidden rules.

2 Understand why edge cases are important to identify.

3 Gain some insight into the process of writing a rulebook.

Explicit Rules

When people talk about rules, they are usually referring to explicit rules. An explicit rule is one that is expressly stated to the players: it is written in the rulebook, it is discussed before play, or it is formally declared in some other manner. While most tabletop mechanics are presented explicitly, video game mechanics often are not. This is why we tend to refer to tabletop games as having rules and video games as having mechanics. For the purposes of this book, however, the terms "rule" and "mechanic" are largely synonymous and interchangeable.

Because video game players do not necessarily need to know much about a game and its rules in order to start playing it, video game designers can be selective in which rules they choose to make explicit. A video game's explicit rules are typically those which are explained during introductory tutorial levels, through in-game hints and tips, and on help screens (figure 5.1).

> The terms "rule" and "mechanic" are largely synonymous and interchangeable.

Figure 5.1 *The Last of Us* in-game instruction.

Implicit Rules

In addition to explicit rules, every game has an amorphous set of "implicit rules" that constitute the unwritten rules of a game (Salen & Zimmerman 2004, 130). Implicit rules are ones which a designer can reasonably expect a new player to already know—and as such, does not bother to explicitly state them.

Implicit rules have been characterized as the rules of etiquette and good sportsmanship. It is certainly true that rules regarding polite game behaviors are often implicit, but not every implicit rule is about social niceties. Game mechanics that have nothing to do with politeness, such as how to determine who takes the first turn, can become implicit if they are conventional enough that players can be expected to follow them without any explicit guidance.

Implicit Politeness

For example, a common implicit rule is to avoid distracting the other players during their turns. Another implicit rule is to avoid making the game drag on too long, which might lead a player facing a difficult choice to make her decision quicker than she really wishes. These types of normally implicit rules might be made explicit when a designer believes that the players need extra motivation to adhere to them. For example, the World Chess Federation tournament rules state:

> It is forbidden to distract or annoy the opponent in any manner whatsoever. This includes unreasonable claims, unreasonable offers of a draw or the introduction of a source of noise into the playing area.

Because more is at stake in a tournament game than in a friendly one, some players are willing to flout social conventions—so the normally implicit rules about distracting behavior are made explicit. Similarly, the social conventions that normally discourage poor sportsmanship are weakened in online games because players do not face each other in person and very well may never encounter one another again once the game concludes. Because of this, an online, tabletop-style game might require special mechanisms for enforcing rules that would normally be implicit. For example, a turn timer might be added to the game to insure that players complete their actions in a reasonable amount of time.

Implicit Mechanics

Some implicit rules, such as the playing card rule of waiting until the deal is done before picking up your cards, have little impact on the game's outcome. In the absence of being made explicit (and penalties applied to its violation), this sort of implicit rule is not really a mechanic and is an exception to the idea that "rule" and "mechanic" are synonymous.

Not every implicit rule is simply about playing with good form. Game mechanics that are well known and widespread can become unstated and implicit. For example, in the United States the implicit rule is that player turn order proceeds in a clockwise direction, based upon where the players are seated. In other places (such as South America) turn order is implicitly counterclockwise.

Not every implicit mechanic is as mundane as this. The order in which poker hands beat one another is (from worst to best): high card, one pair, two pair, three of a kind, straight, flush, full house, four of a kind, and straight flush (see figure 4.2, page 93). By definition, every game of Poker uses this ranking (Morehead & Mott-Smith 2001, 242) and Poker players can be expected to know it. Because of this, when the rules of a specific Poker game are being presented, the very important detail of determining who wins can be left unstated and implicit.

Similarly, the roleplaying game convention of using statistics such as Strength, Dexterity, and Constitution is so widespread, that the details regarding the statistics and how they affect the gameplay can be left implicit.

It is important to note that not every unstated rule is implicit. The rules to *The Tower* do not specify how to handle the situation in which there are fewer counters remaining in the tower than there are players whose number have been rolled. However, the handling of the situation does not involve an implicit rule because there is no standard etiquette or convention that can be applied to it. It is a case of an absent explicit rule, not an existing implicit rule.

Trouble can arise when players follow different sets of implicit rules. These situations can lead to a lot of player frustration, anger, and bruised feelings. It might seem that differing ideas regarding implicit rules would not be an issue for a video game since the software mediates the players' actions—arguably whatever a player is able to do is allowable and within the scope of the game. Yet players can still hold strong opinions about whether a game's implicit rules forbid, for example, "spawn camping" (i.e., lurking near the place a just-killed opponent will re-materialize in order to immediately kill him again).

This is not to imply that explicit rules are preferable to inexplicit rules. Few people would be stymied by a rulebook that did not specify how to determine who plays first (or even notice the rule's absence). Including unnecessary details risks bloating the rules and obscuring the more critical information. That said, most novice game designers have a strong tendency to overlook edge cases (see sidebar on page 99) and omit rules that should be explicit.

Designers should be conscious of where an implicit rule might lead to disagreements getting in the way of an otherwise positive player experience. In such situations, it may be worth making the rule explicit or altering the game in such a way that does away with the issue (e.g., giving a short period of invulnerability to a just-spawned player).

Edge Cases

An "edge case" is a circumstance in which one of the factors that influences it has been taken to an extreme. It is another word for what might be called a borderline situation.

The rule for who goes first in *Button Men* (page 184) is dealing with an edge case when it specifies what happens when the players roll their five dice and come up with identical numbers. The edge case of a tied roll is not a common occurrence, but it is certainly possible.

It is important for designers to identify all the edge cases in their games. Edge cases are often the source of "holes" in a game's rules—situations that are not handled by the rules as written. The *Button Men* identical roll rule is an example of this sort of edge case being solved with the addition of a rule.

Sometimes an edge case causes an undesirable dynamic even when it does not result in a hole in the rules. For example, a game in which a limited number of resources are intended to circulate among the players might be brought to a standstill if players begin hoarding. A situation like this might require the addition of a mechanic to encourage the spending of resources. *The Settlers of Catan* accomplishes this with a rule that any player holding more than seven resources loses half of them whenever a seven is rolled on two six-sided dice.

Discoverable and Hidden Rules

While video games can have explicit rules and implicit rules, many of their mechanics are often not readily described as either.

For example, *Full Throttle* (a well-received adventure game from 1995), had a puzzle in which the player's character needs to cross a mine field. In order to do so, the player must perform the following actions:

1. Steal a mechanical bunny from a store.
2. Blow up the bunny in the mine field.
3. Recover the bunny's batteries.
4. Go back to the store and distract the store's clerk by using a radio control car (powered by the bunny's batteries).
5. Steal an entire box of mechanical bunnies.
6. Use the bunnies to (finally) clear a path across the mine field.

While crossing the mine field is an explicit goal, the means of accomplishing it must be deduced by the player. The series of actions that the player must take do not constitute a strategy because they are not just a possible way of accomplishing the goal, they are the *only* way.

The rules for crossing the minefield are not explicit, but they are not implicit either because players are not expected to come to the game knowing how to accomplish the task. They are expected to discover it—and the process of doing so forms the gameplay.

Playing a tabletop game can involve discovering its rules. For example, someone new to *Monopoly* may only learn of the various effects of the Chance and Community Chest cards as he encounters them in play. Even so, this kind of discovery is really an artifact of learning the game rather than a part of the game itself. Tabletop games whose rules are intentionally designed to be discovered are rare. One such game, however, is *Penultima*, a variant of *Chess*. The game is played by having non-playing spectators devise secret rules for how the pieces move and capture. Each time the players attempt to move, the spectators inform them whether the move is legal or not.

Some video game mechanics are meant to remain hidden from players. For example, a designer probably does not want players to gain much insight into how the actions of a computer-controlled character are determined. If players gain too clear an understanding of the underlying algorithm, the illusion of its lifelike behavior is undermined.

EXERCISE Analyzing Rules

Choose a video game you have not already played—*Kingdom Rush* would be a good choice if it is a new game for you. Play the game and compile a list of the rules you encounter during the first five minutes of play. (You may want to record your notes in audio and transcribe later, so that you do not need to pause the game every time you encounter a new rule.) Categorize the rules as to whether they are explicit, implicit, discoverable, or hidden.

Other Classifications

Categorizing rules as being explicit, implicit, discoverable, or hidden provides a way to think about and discuss how players encounter and learn a game's rules. Let us look at two additional ways of classifying rules that may provide useful insights to you as a designer.

In *The Grasshopper*, Bernard Suits identifies three types of rules: constitutive rules, rules of skill, and what might be termed "rules of infraction" (Suits 2005, 37–38).

"Constitutive rules" are the rules about what is permitted and prohibited in a game. For example, the rule about how a *Chess* king can be castled and the rule against doing it while the king is in check are both constitutive rules. If a constitutive rule is broken by agreement with the other players, then the result is a variant of the original game. On the other hand, if a constitutive rule is broken intentionally and without the agreement of all involved, then the rule breaking amounts to cheating.

In contrast, the violation of a "rule of infraction" is part of the gameplay. For example, a *Basketball* player possessing the ball who collides with a stationary defensive player is breaking a rule of infraction. A player who breaks a rule of infraction is still playing the game—and in fact, a strategic violation might well be considered the game well played. In comparison, a player who breaks a constitutive rule is no longer really playing the game. A *Basketball* video game might very well provide its players with the ability to break rules of infraction and commit personal fouls. It would be very unlikely, however, to provide an in-game means for breaking constitutive rules—players would simply not be able to commit technical and flagrant fouls.

Suits's "rules of skill" are rules that players should, but are not obligated to, follow. These rules are similar to strategies, but are so fundamental to how a game ought to be played that there are few (if any) situations in which a player would choose to break them. For example, attempting to score against one's own team in *Soccer* is violating a rule of skill. While *Soccer*'s constitutive rules specify what happens when an "own goal" is scored, its rules of skill dictate that players avoid having it happen. Violating a rule of skill may result in a game being played poorly, but the game is still being played nevertheless. Constitutive rules and rules of infraction are explicit while rules of skill are usually implicit.

In *Rules of Play*, Salen and Zimmerman proposed categorizing rules as being operational, implicit, or constituative. This book's "explicit rule" is synonymous with "operational rule." Likewise, the meanings given to "implicit rule" are nearly identical. The term "constituative" was probably inspired by Suits's constitutive rule, but has a very different meaning (as well as an 'a' that somehow slipped into the latter half of the word). The constituative rules of a game are the abstract game mechanics that underlay it. As a case in point, Salen and Zimmerman describe Marc LeBlanc's *3-to-15* game. Its rules are:

1. Two players alternate turns.
2. A player's turn consists of picking a number between 1 and 9.
3. No number can be picked more than once.
4. If any three of the numbers picked by a player add up to 15, the player wins the game.

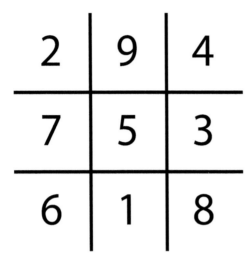

2	9	4
7	5	3
6	1	8

Figure 5.2 Adapted from *Rules of Play* (Salen & Zimmerman 2004, 129).

3-to-15 shares the same constituative rules as *Tic-Tac-Toe* (see figure 5.2), even though their explicit (or operational) rules are entirely different. Try playing a few games of *3-to-15*. Is it the same game as *Tic-Tac-Toe*, or do you think the differing explicit ruleset and presentation of the game state results in it being a different game?

Writing Rules

Writing a good rulebook is a major undertaking. Doing it too early in your game's development risks wasting time on something that can easily become obsolete due to changes to the game. Worse yet, you might hesitate to change the game because of the amount of time and effort that went into documenting it.

Eventually, however, you do need to write down the rules. Novice game designers often make the mistake of treating a game's rulebook as an afterthought. Having the best rulebook possible is absolutely critical for a game's success—after all, there is little point in designing an amazing game if nobody can understand the rules well enough to play it.

Rulebooks are difficult to write. Games are complex, non-linear systems and it is often impossible to describe how to play a game without at some point referencing a mechanic or other facet of the game that has not yet been explained. Even the most complete and well-written rules are apt to be a bumpy ride for the reader—all the more so if the reader is not someone who has played many tabletop games.

While rulebooks are usually compiled in the later stages of development, the early playtests can help inform its eventual format and content. As you explain the game to people, pay attention to what they misunderstand or find confusing. It will be an indication of a section of the rulebook that will require special attention. If something is difficult to explain orally, it will be doubly so when you try to do it in writing.

When you do find yourself writing a rulebook, try to be as comprehensive as possible. Keep in mind that graphics are sometimes the best way to present or clarify a confusing rule. Consider how much more difficult it would have been to understand how to play *Hive* if the pieces' movements were described solely in text.

Test the rulebook by having playtesters try to learn the game by reading it. The early drafts of the rulebook will probably leave your testers confused and you may need to step in and provide additional guidance. If you do, it indicates an area where your rulebook needs improvement.

You may want to delay providing help, however, in order to see how your players misinterpret the rules or fill in its gaps. When they do so, they are following their natural instincts as players and are demonstrating to you how they think the game should be played—valuable information to you as a designer. Similarly, if the players ask you to clarify a rule, before providing an answer you may want to first ask them "What do you think? If I was not here in the room, what would you do?"

Eventually you will need to take the plunge and conduct a "blind playtest." A blind playtest is the point at which your rulebook sinks or swims. Whereas in earlier playtests, you might allow yourself the wiggle room to occasionally step in and provide some guidance, a blind playtest is a strictly hands-off affair. The playtesters must attempt to learn the game from the rulebook alone with absolutely no guidance. This means that the testers must use their best guess whenever they are uncertain about something. While observing the playtest, take copious notes about everything that the players had trouble with or caused a question to be raised.

It can be a painful experience, but you need to resist (and refuse) helping the testers figure out how to play the game. You may find it best to capture the game session in video and not be present at all.

A blind playtest is not about the rulebook alone—it can teach you a lot about your game in general. Perhaps there are aspects of the game that are overly complicated and even though the players understood the rules, they still stumble over them. If players constantly circle back to the rulebook to look up some detail, it is a sign that you need to improve the game's playability. It is easy to overlook this sort of thing when you are able to interact with the people playing the game. You may be entirely unconscious of providing little clarifications to players throughout a game. When that is the case, a blind playtest will almost certainly bring the problem to your attention.

Designer Rob Daviau likes to conduct a type of test that is even more extreme than a blind playtest. Daviau sets the game up for play and then has new testers try to play the game with no direction at all—not even a rulebook. Daviau explains that while testers are unlikely to play the game properly, knowing what assumptions they made can help you learn what is and is not intuitive about the game (Daviau 2011, 47).

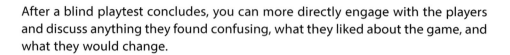

After a blind playtest concludes, you can more directly engage with the players and discuss anything they found confusing, what they liked about the game, and what they would change.

EXERCISE Rulebook Roundup

Before you go to write your first rulebook you should take the time to make a formal, comparative study of how professional game publishers write their rules. This will help you understand the level of detail required to properly explain game mechanics and give you a toolbox of techniques for doing so.

Choose five commercial tabletop games whose rulebooks you would like to analyze. If you do not own the games, you can probably access their rulebooks online at the publisher's website. If you have trouble locating suitable rulebooks, visit www.funmines.com/rulebooks for links.

As you read each rulebook, keep notes regarding how the information is presented. Does the game use any special terminology? How and where does the rulebook present the definitions of its terms (if at all)? Does the rulebook use graphical examples? If so, what sorts of things are best explained using a graphic in addition to text?

A typical game rulebook has the following sections:

1. Thematic backstory
2. List of game components
3. Setup
4. Objective
5. Turn overview
6. Details regarding various game mechanics
7. Ending the game
8. Examples of play

Are any of these sections (or their equivalents) missing from the rulebooks you read? Are there any additional sections—if so, what purpose do they serve? Do any of the rulebooks have particularly innovative or effective ways of presenting their information?

CHAPTER SIX

Stories

INTRODUCTION

Storytelling in games is different from storytelling in books, films, and theater. Games are fundamentally interactive, which creates unique challenges and opportunities when crafting a narrative. In this chapter you will explore some of the ways in which game mechanics can spawn narratives and narratives can support gameplay.

The learning objectives for the chapter are:

1 Understand the role of fiction in games.

2 Recognize how the terms "setting," "game world," "world building," "scenario," "backstory," and "flavor text" apply to game narratives.

3 Be able to use a story-oriented approach to game development.

4 Understand the characteristics of embedded and emergent narratives.

Fiction

A game's fiction is an amalgamation of a world in which it takes place and the roles that players take on. "Representational" mechanics are those whose workings can be explained in terms of the game's fiction (Juul 2007). Mechanics that do not reinforce the fiction are "abstract." When a game's mechanics are primarily abstract, then the game itself is often referred to as being an "abstract game." In contrast, a game that utilizes a significant number of representational mechanics is often referred to as being a "thematic game."

On some level, all game mechanics are abstractions. They take the complexity of reality and simplify it into a codified set of rules. Some games, such as *The Tower*, are abstract to the point of being about little other than their own gameplay. Other games present a fiction and have mechanics that reference it. For example, *Shoot-Out* has a fiction of an Old West gunfight and its representational mechanics include the rules regarding bullet expenditure.

When a largely abstract game does have a fiction (such as the medieval war theme of *Chess* and the insect theme of *Hive*), it is often like icing on a cake—the fiction adds to the experience, but is not a fundamental part of the gameplay. This is not to say that the fictions of abstract games are unimportant or should be treated indifferently by designers. A well-chosen fiction can help players learn the game and reduce the chances of them making avoidable mistakes. Consider how the various pieces move in *Hive*. The Grasshopper's jumping movement is the easiest to remember because it aligns so well with the fiction of the piece. The movement would not be so easy to remember if it were associated with a wasp.

The fact that fiction can help players understand and remember representational mechanics allows thematic games to be more complicated than might be palatable in a more abstract game. For example, the multi-purpose use of gasoline in *Zombie in my Pocket* is easy to remember and makes perfect sense within the fiction of the game: gasoline can be combined with a candle to destroy zombies or combined with a chainsaw to extend the number of times the chainsaw can be used. Without the fiction, however, the rules regarding gasoline would be unwieldy: "Item 1 can be combined with item 2 to destroy enemies; alternatively it can be combined with item 3 to increase the number of times item 3 can be used."

Tabletop game designer James Ernest likes to establish the fiction before beginning his designs. Ernest explains, "This gives me more creative ideas when trying to invent the game mechanics, and it makes for a game whose mechanics seem better to suit the theme" (Ernest 2004, 592). Having a theme in mind can spark ideas about how some aspect of the theme might be translated into a game mechanic and brought into the game. This way of working often provides a richer vein of ideas than simply thinking about game mechanics in the abstract.

That said, some tabletop game designers prefer to design in the abstract and allow their game publisher to determine what theme should be applied to the game. Dale Yu explains, "Although some games are completely built around a theme (that is, the story comes first and then a game is built around the constraints of that story), most games can be viewed in an abstract sense and then any theme can be 'pasted' on to it" (Yu 2011, 78). Even when designers do use a theme, it is not unusual for publishers to change it to something they consider more marketable.

A game's fiction can be a great source of ideas, but the fiction does not have to dictate every design decision. As a designer you need to keep track of your goals for the game's dynamics and aesthetics. There are many situations in which eliminating a detail or abstracting a representation may improve the player experience. Sometimes a necessary mechanical change works against the theme, in which case the fiction needs to be reworked so that the new rules make thematic sense.

Being attentive to the balance between representation and abstraction can lead to a discovery-oriented design process in which the game's fiction and mechanics develop together, each informing the other throughout the development process.

EXERCISE *Shoot-Out*'s Fiction

Shoot-Out presents the fiction of a gunfight in the Old West. Which of its mechanics do you think are most representational of its fiction? Do any of the mechanics suggest an alternative fiction to you? Which, if any, of its mechanics are purely abstract?

Do you think there are ways that the mechanics could be made to fit the fiction better? How would making those changes affect the game's dynamics? Would something have to be sacrificed in order to make the game more representational? What would be gained?

Conversely, in what ways could the game be made more abstract and what would be gained and lost in doing so?

Remake *Shoot-Out* using an entirely different fiction: a foot race, spies going after a secret document, a game of *Basketball*, whatever. Shape the fiction as much as possible to fit the gameplay. Then modify the mechanics (while preserving the core gameplay) to fit the theme better.

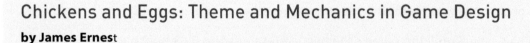

Chickens and Eggs: Theme and Mechanics in Game Design

by James Ernest

I recently read an article about creativity and game design. The gist was "theme or mechanics, which comes first?" It started with a photo of a chicken and an egg, so the predictable conclusion was "it depends." And that's true in a literal sense: sometimes you will start with a theme, sometimes with a mechanic.

But the more important question is not literally "which came into your head first?" but rather, "which matters more?" That means, as you design the game, when the theme and the mechanics don't work well together, which one do you change? In this case, I don't think you can get away with an answer like "it depends."

For me, theme usually comes first, but a lot of board game designers disagree. I've also seen this attitude in both tabletop and computer games: designers start with a core mechanic, develop it, and then "skin" it with a theme. They seem to believe that the game is equivalent to its mechanism, so they treat the theme as an afterthought.

That's so weird to me. It feels like saying that film stock and lenses are more important than the screenplay. It's a technician's perspective on the creation of art.

Defining Theme

Theme is not just story. It's a broad term, encompassing a game's core aesthetic as well as details like story and setting. Games are not great at telling stories; they are more like worlds where players get to tell their own stories. Games are good at delivering emotions, details, and moments of drama. So, even if a game has no story, it can still have a theme.

Here's an example. I recently set out to design a pub game. This was a game that I literally planned to give to one pub. So first, I tried to spell out what "pub game" means.

First thoughts: simple, fast, and portable. It needs to contain "risk," which means a legitimate decision between high- and low-volatility paths. For example, poker contains risk because players can choose to bet (high volatility, uncertain result) or fold (low volatility, certain result), and neither path is the dominant choice. A pub game should also have "craps moments," where everyone shouts together.

So take that list of considerations as a starting point. Is "pub game" a theme, or a mechanic, or just a format? I don't know. You might say that it's a mechanic, but I haven't mentioned any of the rules, just some goals about flow and feel. "Risk" has a very technical-sounding definition, with decisions and volatility, but it's more about the emotions associated with those decisions than any of the specifics. So I'd say, with the considerations above, that "pub game" is a theme.

Another example: I worked on the *Marvel Super Hero Squad CCG* with Devin Low and many other great designers. From the start, we were locked into a form (collectible card game), an audience (kids and Marvel fans), and story elements (Marvel characters). But that didn't define the theme.

We looked for something that distinguished the Marvel universe from the DC universe, and Marvel seemed to be more all about teamwork: The X-Men, The Avengers, The Fantastic Four, and so on. Even the villains come in teams. DC's strongest characters were loners: Batman, Superman, Wonder Woman. From the basic theme of "teamwork," we developed a mechanic that encouraged players to build a team of different characters, striving for a good mix of powers in both attack and defense.

Which Matters More?

Can we prove which matters more, theme or mechanics? Some games with weak themes are popular because of their good mechanics. Some games with weak mechanics are popular because of their strong themes. You can probably think of examples of both.

So why do game designers keep behaving as though theme isn't important? I think it comes down to their personalities. As players, they tend to fall mainly in the "mechanics first" group. They are technicians, not artists. They say things like, "No one cares that *Dominion*'s theme is stupid." But actually, many people do care. And also, *Dominion*'s theme isn't all that bad. More on that in a moment.

Is there any way to test this question? I've published a lot of games, and based on sales and reviews, I can tell you that theme matters to my audience. Here's the clearest example.

I published two games within a span of three years: *Kill Doctor Lucky* and *Save Doctor Lucky*. A few years later, Paizo Publishing repeated this, releasing deluxe versions of the same two games. In both cases, the game with the superior theme sold significantly better than the game with superior mechanics.

In both the original and the deluxe versions, these two games have the same retail price, nearly identical packaging, nearly identical themes, and nearly identical rules. In *Kill Doctor Lucky* (the better story), the goal is to kill Doctor Lucky, who is of course very lucky and hard to kill. In *Save Doctor Lucky* (the better mechanic), the object is to save him from a sinking ship. *Kill Doctor Lucky* is far and away the better seller, and if you ask the players, it is also the game they would rather play.

This phenomenon isn't isolated to the Doctor Lucky games. In my catalog of 150+ games, those with strong themes outsell games with strong mechanics almost without exception. Of course, games with neither aspect do terribly. Games with both do the best.

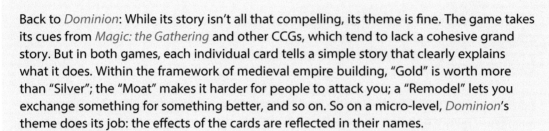

Back to *Dominion*: While its story isn't all that compelling, its theme is fine. The game takes its cues from *Magic: the Gathering* and other CCGs, which tend to lack a cohesive grand story. But in both games, each individual card tells a simple story that clearly explains what it does. Within the framework of medieval empire building, "Gold" is worth more than "Silver"; the "Moat" makes it harder for people to attack you; a "Remodel" lets you exchange something for something better, and so on. So on a micro-level, *Dominion*'s theme does its job: the effects of the cards are reflected in their names.

Crafting Your Theme

To create a theme worth keeping, you have to do some work. Don't expect to pick a winner in an afternoon. Spend effort on it, be smart about it, test it on friends, and don't let unnecessary constraints weigh it down.

Something in the middle of the chicken and egg article really got to me. Here's a paraphrase: "When you are designing a game from a theme, you should pick a theme that you like, and then look for other games with similar themes to find inspiration for mechanics."

That's not designing. It's picking from a menu. If there is already a category of games that have your theme, what value are you adding? Also, one of the benefits of starting with a theme is that it gives you ideas for your own mechanics. Going to the game library for inspiration on any aspect of a new game should be a last resort, not a first step.

Here's an example. Suppose you like "train games." You play a lot of train games. So you decide "I want to make a train game about Eastern Europe." That's starting with a theme, because trains, right? So you draw a map of Eastern Europe, pick some cities, draw some lines, and you're ready to play.

Here's the problem. Games in the "train game" genre are barely about trains. They're resource-management connect-the-dots puzzle games that happen to take place on maps. So if you want to make a game about trains, but it works like all the other train games, you haven't done much game design.

In reality, railroading has many interesting aspects besides competing to connect dots on a map. What if your favorite part about trains is riding them, or repairing them, or robbing them? The only part of your new game that scratches that itch will be a picture on the box.

What do you really like about trains? What story can you tell besides "racing to build rail lines"? How about "closing down an antiquated industry"? Now your story is about the last people in an outmoded industry turning out the lights. There's an emotional theme there, as well as a real-world system that your original mechanics can emulate. Maybe your theme boils down to "Regret." It's about saying goodbye to the age of steam. There, that's three minutes of thinking and it's already a lot more interesting than "trains." And it has nothing to do with connecting dots.

Bending Your Theme

So back to the chicken and egg question. If your theme and mechanics don't play well together, which needs to change? Personally I can't stand sacrificing a theme to fit a mechanic. You're going to change and develop both, of course, but to me, scrapping the theme basically means I'm scrapping the game.

Let's say that in developing my pub game, I wind up with a mechanic that I like, using five dice. It is mostly a race game, with very little risk: just several people trying to get points as fast as they can. Players do a lot of critical thinking, but there is not much talking and never any shouting. There is some tension, but no moments of release. And it's a bit more complex than I intended.

I have two choices here. I can say, "This game isn't delivering on the element of 'risk.' There is no tension and I need to remedy this by changing the mechanics." Or I can say, "This game is fun and challenging but for unexpected reasons; I should consider creating a new theme and a new reason for people to want to play it."

I tried to phrase those choices without bias, but it's hard. Game mechanics are comparatively easy. Good stories are not. Marketing plans, likewise, are not. Should I continue to call this a "pub game" even though it doesn't fit my design goals?

Yet I have been in this situation many times: a finished or half-finished game is looking for a theme. The result is usually a disappointing and hard-fought compromise. Large groups work through long brainstorm and design sessions, months of debate and change, and have nothing to show for it.

Diceland, one of my mechanics-first designs, is a good example. *Diceland* has a strong core mechanic, an uninteresting backstory, and no real theme aside from "look, the dice are fighting!" This game was never a best-selling product, and not for lack of trying. It was more than seven years in development, a mechanic looking for a theme.

In my experience, the more details I add to the mechanics, the harder it is to invent a back story that makes sense. Conversely, when a story has lots of details, it's hard to stop coming up with new ways that the mechanics might work. These are not equivalent processes, not two paths leading to the same goal. They are different approaches that produce different results.

So anyway, that's my opinion. Since this essay isn't exactly aimed at people who agree with me, I'd encourage everybody else to try theme-based design. You might just make the leap from thinking it's terrible to thinking it's obvious. Either way, you'll probably find a better answer to the question of which comes first.

Zombie in My Pocket

Game by Jeremiah Lee, Graphic Art by Kwanchai Moriya. Used with permission.

Players:

Solitaire

Game Length:

5–20 minutes

Components:

Cut out the following from the pages that follow these rules:

- Nine Development cards
- Eight Indoor tiles
- Eight Outdoor tiles

You may also wish to use the player board that can be found on page 92.

Setup:

Take out the **Patio** and **Foyer** tiles; set aside. Place the **Foyer** tile on the table.

Separate the Indoor and Outdoor tiles into two facedown stacks. Shuffle both stacks.

Shuffle the Development ("Dev") cards, and discard the top two facedown (so that you do not see which cards they were).

Record your starting Attack and Health scores (1 and 6, respectively). These numbers will change over the course of the game. There is no upper limit on either. You may wish to use the player board on page 92 to keep track of these numbers.

Note the starting in-game time of 9pm.

Goal:

You must search the house to find the **Evil Temple** and its hidden totem. The totem must be taken outside and buried in the **Graveyard** before the clock strikes midnight.

Indoor Turn Sequence:

1. Choose an exit door. If the door leads to an already placed tile, then you will be revisiting that existing room and proceed to step 3. If there is no tile on the other side of the door, then you will need to place a new room tile per step 2.

2. If it is a new room, draw a room tile and place an Indoor room tile so that it is in the empty space that is adjacent to the exit door. One door on the new tile must line up with your exit door.
3. Draw a Dev card, even if you're revisiting a room. If there are no cards left, see **Time Passes**. Look at the text beside the clock corresponding to the game time.
   a. Item – You *may* draw the next Dev card and find the item shown in the top right corner of the *new* Dev card. If you choose not to draw a card, you do not get an item.
   b. Zombies – See **Combat** below.
   c. Event – Add or subtract health as noted (if any).
4. Follow the instructions (if any) on the room tile, *after* the Dev card has been resolved.

Special Rooms:

The **Kitchen**, **Storage**, **Garden**, **Evil Temple**, and the **Graveyard** are special rooms.

The zombie totem is hidden in the **Evil Temple**, and must be buried in the **Graveyard**. When occupying either room, draw and resolve a Dev card as you normally would, then draw and resolve another Dev card. The second card describes what happens when searching for or burying the zombie totem. If you are still alive and in the room after resolving the card, you have found or buried the totem.

In the **Storage** room, resolve a Dev card as you normally would, then you *may* draw the next Dev card and find the item shown in the top right corner of the *new* Dev card. If you choose not to draw a card, you do not get an item.

In the **Kitchen** or **Garden**, if you end your turn in the room (i.e. you don't run away from zombies), you add one to your Health.

Moving Outdoors:

The only way to exit the house is through the **Dining Room**'s exterior door (indicated with an arrow). When you exit, place the **Patio** tile next to the **Dining Room** tile, then draw and resolve a Dev card as usual.

Outdoor Turn Sequence:

Turns progress outside as they did inside, however, there are no doors outside. New outdoor spaces must connect with open spaces (just like doors inside). You may not pass through a hedge.

Time Passes:

The game starts at 9pm, and time moves forward each time you deplete the Dev card deck. An hour will pass when you need to draw a Dev card after emptying the draw deck. Note the new hour, and use this time when resolving new Dev cards. Reshuffle the discarded Dev

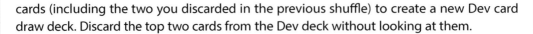

cards (including the two you discarded in the previous shuffle) to create a new Dev card draw deck. Discard the top two cards from the Dev deck without looking at them.

If an Item card was the last card drawn; draw a card from the new Dev card deck to determine which item was found.

Cowering:

You may, at any time after the turn sequence has completed in a room, curl up into a corner and hide. You regain 3 Health points, but you lose time. Discard the top Dev card, do not resolve the card.

Combat:

When you enter combat with a zombie, subtract your current Attack score from the number of zombies you face to find the number of Health points you lose in defeating the zombies. You may never lose more than four Health points in one combat, and you may never gain Health points in a battle, even if your Attack is higher than the number of zombies you face.

 # Zombies – Attack Score = Damage

Example 1: You have an Attack of 1, you come across "3 Zombies": 3 − 1 = 2. You lose 2 Health points in the battle.

Example 2: You have an Attack of 1, but you also have a chainsaw, which adds 3 to your Attack. You come across "2 Zombies": 2 − 4 = −2. You lose no Health points in the battle (but do not gain any either).

Example 3: You have an Attack of 1. You come across "6 Zombies": 6 − 1 = 5. You lose 4 Health points in the battle, because 4 is the most Health you may lose in one battle.

Running Away:

When you draw a Dev card with zombies, you may choose to avoid combat by running through an exit that leads to a room you've already explored (including the room you just came from). The zombies swipe at you as you leave, taking away 1 Health point.

You do not draw a Dev card for the room you're running into. You may Cower in this room.

You take your text turn normally. Draw a new Dev card for the room you next enter, even if it is the room you just ran out of.

Items:

When a Dev card shows "Item" under the time, you may choose to draw the next Dev card in order to gain the item shown in the top right corner of the *new* Dev card. Record the new item you are carrying and discard the Dev card.

You may only hold two items at one time. If you want to pick up a new item, and you're already carrying two, you must drop one of your current items. A zombie carries off the dropped item when you leave the room (i.e. if you come back to the room, you do not find the dropped item). As long as you do not leave the room, you may put down an item to pick up another, and are able to pick up a dropped item again, as long as you never hold more than two items at one time.

You may only use one weapon (and one Attack bonus) at a time, though you may carry two.

The zombie totem does not count against your two-item limit.

Oil: Throw at zombies as you run away to avoid taking damage from running away. Alternatively, instead of running away, oil can be combined with the Candle to destroy a group of zombies without giving them a chance to deal damage. May only be used once.

Gasoline: Can be combined with the Candle to destroy a group of zombies without giving them a chance to deal damage. Alternatively, gasoline can be combined with Chainsaw to give two more Chainsaw uses. May only be used once.

Board with Nails: A simple, yet effective weapon; add 1 to your Attack score when using this weapon.

Cola: Drink this delicious Cola to add 2 Health points.

Grisly Femur: Hey, it might have been your uncle's leg, but now you can use it to bash zombies. Add 1 to your Attack score when using this weapon.

Golf Club: It's hard to whack a ball with one of these, but it's easy to whack a zombie. Add 1 to your Attack score when using this weapon.

Candle: Can be combined with either Oil or Gasoline to destroy a group of zombies without giving them a chance to deal any damage. The Candle can be used more than once.

Chainsaw: Sweeeeet! Add 3 to your Attack score when using this weapon. The Chainsaw only has enough fuel to be used in two battles. Can be combined with Gasoline to give you two more uses. There is no limit to the amount of Gasoline that can be held in the Chainsaw at one time. You may carry an empty chainsaw, and use it again if you find gasoline.

Machete: A fine slashing weapon for cutting through zombies. Add 2 to your Attack score when using this weapon.

Zombie Doors:

Sometimes after you place a room tile and attach it, there won't be any exits available (e.g., the **Bathroom** directly after the **Foyer**). It is also possible that all exits have been explored without finding a necessary room. When this happens, three zombies open a doorway in the wall of your choice in the room you're currently in, after all other events in the room have been resolved. You must fight them normally. Use this door for your next turn's tile placement.

You may not cower before a **Zombie Door** attack.

Ending the Game:

The game can end in several ways. You could be eaten by zombies (die in combat), an event could cause you to lose your last Health point, time could run out (all Dev cards are played in the 11pm hour without burying the zombie totem), or you could win the game (see below).

Winning the Game:

After you've buried the zombie totem in the **Graveyard**, the zombies collapse and you've won the game. In game terms, after you resolve the second Development card in the **Graveyard**, as long as you're still alive, you've won.

Scared of Zombies?

Optional rules to make the game easier (for the kids, you know):

1. Do not draw a Dev card when moving into a room you've already explored.
2. Zombie doors are created by two zombies.
3. You may carry any number of items.

© 2007–2008 Jeremiah Lee

Jeremiah Lee

Jeremiah Lee is a game designer and game marketer who is known for designing *Zombie in my Pocket*, which has spawned dozens of " . . . *in my Pocket*" games (see www.funmines.com/zimp for links). Lee is part of Indie Boards & Cards, running the game publisher's convention booths and events. He started gaming with a *Dungeons & Dragons* box set at the age of 10. He went on to learn *Diplomacy* in college, which became the only game he played for many years. Lee is the full-time father of four unschooled children.

Photo 6.1 Jeremiah Lee

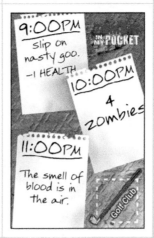

Print and Play

Zombie in my Pocket (or *ZimP* as its fans like to call it), is a "print-and-play" success story. Print-and-play games are a recent phenomenon. They are tabletop games, usually free, that can be downloaded, printed out, and played. At the time of this writing, there are 3,647 print-and-play games available on BoardGameGeek (see www.funmines.com/pnp) with more being added every day.

Some designers worry that giving a game away for free will eliminate its commercial potential. While that is not an unreasonable concern, a free print-and-play distribution can gain exposure for the game and its designer and build an audience for a commercial version of the game. *Coin Age* and *Tiny Epic Kingdoms* are both small, free print-and-play games that went on to be sold very successfully through Kickstarter campaigns, raising $65,195 and $286,972 respectively. Similarly, the print-and-play success of *Zombie in my Pocket* led to its designer, Jeremiah Lee, creating a multiplayer version of the game that was published commercially by the Cambridge Games Factory.

Game Worlds

When a game space is representational, it creates a "setting." A game's setting is the fiction that describes where the game's action is taking place. *Shoot-Out*'s setting is a street in Silver City, Texas; *Zombie in my Pocket* takes place in a suburban home; *Tic-Tac-Toe* does not have a setting because its game space is abstract.

Some games have a fiction that expands beyond the area of active play to suggest a "game world" in which the game's setting exists. Despite its name, a game world is not necessarily planet-sized. *Shoot-Out*'s game world, for example, is a romanticized version of the Old West as depicted in novels and films. The game's mechanics involve no cattle drives, stagecoach holdups, or sheriffs—but all of those elements may be part of the designer's and players' conception of the game world.

Marrakech's setting is the rug market in Marrakech, Morocco. Its game world is less certain—it is hard to say whether the game's actions are taking place in the present day or 200 years ago. *Hive*'s setting is a hive of insects—not a bee hive, but one that integrates a variety of insect types. There is little suggestion of what world might lie beyond the setting of the game.

The more representational and story-oriented a game is, the more a designer should have a detailed understanding of the world in which it takes place. This usually involves research on the designer's part. For a Napoleonic-era naval game, a designer might want to acquaint herself with the nautical terms of the era, the various types of ships and their component parts, the histories of famous sea battles, and so on. Knowing how the subject has been fictionalized and presented in films, books, and other games is just as important as researching the raw facts. Towards that end, the designer might watch *Damn the Defiant!*, read the Aubrey/ Maturin series of novels, and play *Sails of Glory*.

When a game takes place in an imaginary setting, the designer must do the work of constructing a set of "facts" that have an authenticity and coherence despite their fantastical nature. The invention involved in "world building" does not necessarily relieve the designer of needing to do research, however. There are many ways in which the details of the real world can inform an imaginary one. Author George R.R. Martin borrows extensively from human history when constructing the societies, peoples, and events in his *A Song of Ice and Fire* (aka *Game of Thrones*) series of books.

Research and world building serves your game by providing information that can inspire game mechanics and the fictions that envelop them. Even the research that does not directly appear in the game may end up shaping what *is* in the game and help contribute to its thematic richness. Research and world building also provide you the opportunity to reflect on the clichés of the genre you are working in and discover ways in which you might transcend them. Keep in mind, however, that the danger of all this research and world building is that you might become so invested in your source material that you end up swamping your game in the details. How much research and world building should you do? More than appears in your game!

Scenarios and Backstories

A game's "scenario" describes what players are trying to do—it is the part of the fiction that frames the actions of the game's characters. The scenario is where the game's fiction ties in with its mechanics and the players' goals. Because of this, the scenario is an area of the game's fiction that typically receives the majority of a designer's attention. Yet it is often a game's setting and world that is most central to a player's decision to buy and play a game. What a potential customer/player is likely to find enticing about *Zombie in my Pocket* is its zombie theme, not the scenario of finding and burying a totem.

The game's "backstory" is the events that led up to the scenario as well as the aspects of the game world that are made known to players. In tabletop games it is typically revealed through artwork and the game's "flavor text"—writing that exists to enrich the game's narrative atmosphere. While backstory and flavor text usually exist simply to entertain the reader and to evoke the game world, they serve a practical, mechanics-oriented purpose as well. For example, the flavor text and card names of some cards in *Magic: the Gathering* were chosen specifically to let the player know how to use the card, or to help the player to conceptualize effects that might otherwise seem odd. If you want to nudge the players towards certain strategies in the game, well-placed backstory can be a great way to do it.

EXERCISE Story-Oriented Design

For this exercise you will design a game using a story-oriented process. It begins with you figuring out the kinds of stories you want your game to tell, and then has you work towards designing mechanics that can provide those sorts of narrative experiences. The goal is to create a satisfying game that can be played in about 15 minutes. In order to accomplish that, you will need to be careful about how many narrative elements you incorporate, otherwise you risk burying the game in detail.

1. Your first step is to determine the subject matter. Is there a subject that interests you that is not already a common game theme? Perhaps your topic could be inspired by the books and movies you love? You might try compiling a list of possible topics and see what happens when you mash two of them together.

2. After you determine the topic for the game, the next step is to define the game's scenario. What are the players attempting to do in terms of the game's fiction? If your game's topic falls within a common game genre, this is where you can differentiate it. Research your subject matter (and world build, if applicable), keeping your eye out for ways that you could frame the subject that you have not encountered in games before. For example, suppose you would like to do a game about World War II. The standard issue war game is about battles being fought and won using artillery, infantry, and armor units. What other war stories can be told? If nothing comes to mind, think about the war movies you have seen—what are they about besides the battles themselves? This line of thinking might suggest scenarios such as: tracking down looted art, receiving a "Dear John" letter, hunting for foreign agents, having fun while on leave, or simply getting out of the war alive. There are many more war stories to tell besides capturing a hill and winning a battle.

3. As you consider scenarios, think of the typical events that arise in that kind of storyline and how they might crystallize into compelling game pillars and mechanics. Where might the mechanics reflect your topic in detail and where might they become more abstract? Perhaps your war game could be unusually detailed in how its mechanics

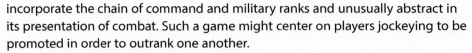

incorporate the chain of command and military ranks and unusually abstract in its presentation of combat. Such a game might center on players jockeying to be promoted in order to outrank one another.

4. Your next step is to prototype the core mechanic. Rather than simply choosing one idea to proceed with, try prototyping at least a couple of the ideas you think are most interesting.

5. Finally, if any of the prototypes proves promising, proceed to expand upon it and develop it into a full game. Otherwise, revisit the earlier steps and come up with some new ideas for core mechanics.

Narratives

Game narratives are often divided into two types: "embedded narratives" and "emergent narratives." An embedded narrative is a story written by a game developer that is presented to the players in a scripted, largely non-interactive form. This type of game narrative inherits the storytelling techniques of more traditional storytelling media. An embedded narrative has the game developer serving as the story's author and the players as the story's readers.

Embedded narratives are created at "design-time" and emergent narratives are created during "play-time."

Emergent narratives are the stories that are created through the act of playing a game. The narrative that emerges from a game of *Shoot-Out* might tell of a gunslinger who has run out of bullets, yet is victorious because (against all odds) he is able to survive a sprint to the center of town through a hail of bullets. This is not a narrative that was written by a designer, instead it grew out of the player's interactions with the game's mechanics.

Embedded Narratives

Embedded game narratives are stories that were written by a developer. These narratives sacrifice a portion of the players' autonomy in return for providing the game developers more control over the storylines within their game. There are three common structures for embedded narratives: linear, plot tree, and web.

"Linear narratives" are the most tightly controlled. In fact, linear narrative games are sometimes referred to as being "on-the-rails," a reference to how a roller coaster ride can offer thrills and excitement, but no ability to deviate from its designated path.

The implicit goal (and reward) of a linear narrative game is experiencing the story from start to end. This is the case for the critically acclaimed *The Last of Us* (a screenshot of which graces the cover of this book), which has garnered particular praise (and awards) for its narrative. The game begins with an introductory scene that shows the beginning of the end for human society due to a zombie apocalypse in the form of a fungal plague. The story then jumps years into the future and we step into the shoes of Joel (who we met in the introductory scene). Joel is a man who does what is necessary—it is clear that he has had to do unpleasant things in order to survive. Joel reluctantly agrees to become the protector of a 14-year old girl, Ellie, and help her travel across the country. Joel and Ellie encounter a series of hardships and challenges (such as running into a band of cannibals) and eventually the story concludes.

This description of the game's story is not just one person's experience playing the game, it is the narrative that is encountered by anyone and everyone who plays the game. The reluctance with which Joel agrees to help Ellie is fixed. The player can neither choose to eagerly offer assistance nor outright refuse it. The storyline is unabashedly predetermined. The players' freedom (and responsibility) lies in overcoming the various obstacles the game puts in the way of advancing that storyline.

If *The Last of Us* allowed the player to occasionally make narrative decisions regarding how the story proceeds, then its structure would expand from a linear form into a branching "plot tree." Figure 6.1 is a simple narrative tree that outlines some ways in which a "boy meets girl" plot might develop. At each step in the story, the reader has two choices as to how the narrative advances.

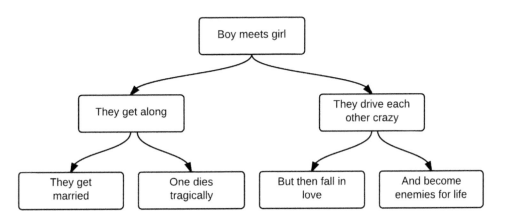

Figure 6.1 An interactive "boy meets girl" story.

While manageable on a small scale, creating a substantial plot tree narrative can become prohibitively time-consuming. The content path followed by a player requires a disproportionately larger, unseen amount to be created. In order to provide the reader with three plot points in the "boy meets girl" story, the tree had to contain seven. To add a fourth plot point, eight more would have to be written. A fifth plot point would require an additional sixteen. And so on.

The untaken plot paths do not necessarily remain unseen. If the various narrative threads are compelling enough, players may want to explore all the possible ways that the game's story can unfold. Most often, however, these games are an exercise in playing through many unsatisfying narrative paths in order to uncover the one or two that actually provide an engaging story. We want to uncover the *Romeo and Juliet* story that centers on love, deceit, and death; not the storyline in which they make sensible life choices.

For these reasons, the plot trees that do appear in games tend to be constrained in scope. For example, the *Mass Effect* series uses plot trees in conjunction with their cut scenes (see sidebar on page 126) so that players can select responses and guide the conversation to a limited degree.

Linear and branching structures are often hybridized to create a storyline that allows the player to choose some of the narrative's paths, but those paths ultimately lead to the same destination as the paths not taken. For example, figure 6.2 shows how a "boy meets girl" story can go in two different directions in step 2, both of which converge on the same plot point in step 3. The narrative splits again in step 4 and then rejoins in step 5 for the story's conclusion.

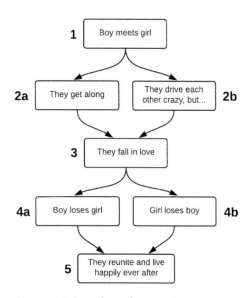

Figure 6.2 Story branching and converging.

Similarly, a plot tree can be structured so that a given plot point can be used in more than one narrative thread (figure 6.3). With enough interconnections, the narrative takes on a "web structure" (figure 6.4) that allows the player to wander back and forth among the plot points. Web structures offer more freedom to the players without requiring the developers to create huge repositories of alternative narrative path content. Because of this, web structures are much more common than plot trees in games.

Web structures typically associate sections of the embedded narrative with the physical locations in the game. The narrative is encountered as the player moves from place to place (and re-encountered if the player retraces her steps). This

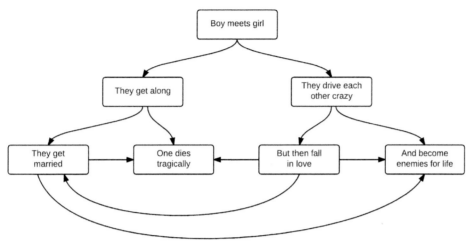

Figure 6.3 A more complex "boy meets girl" plot tree.

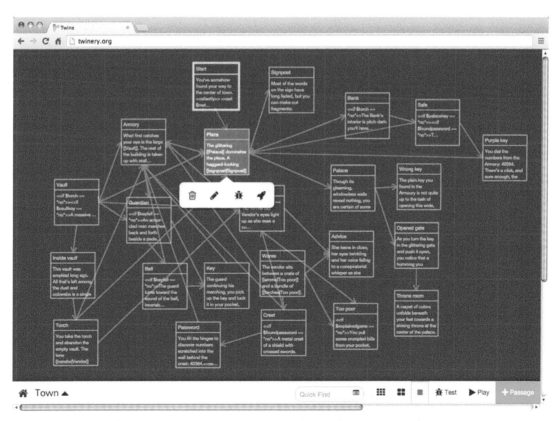

Figure 6.4 Anna Anthropy's *Town* as it appears in Twine (a visual programming language).

125

can lead to a narrative that seems more of an environmental experience than a literary one. Anna Anthropy's *Town* (which was inspired by Tim Sweeney's *ZZT*) is a web structured game in a nutshell—it is a quick play; try it out at www.funmines.com/town.

In practice, games often utilize combinations of linear, plot tree, and web structures. The *Grand Theft Auto* games, for example, have a linear structure for their main narrative; an "open world" in the form of a web structure that allows players to explore when they are not following the main plot; and plot tree structures (typically in the form of the player having the choice to kill or not) that frequently appear at the conclusion of the web structure's side stories.

Cut Scenes

A cut scene is an interlude during which a video game cuts away from the action in order to present some cinematic material, typically expository dialogue or a particularly stunning visual. During a cut scene, the player's ability to impact the game state is reduced (often by having the controls disabled) and the player becomes a more passive recipient of the story.

The cut scenes in earlier generations of games could be particularly jarring. They typically used pre-rendered animations of dramatically better visual quality than the graphics of the game itself. Modern video games tend to better integrate their cut scenes by having them take place in the game's graphic engine.

EXERCISE

Spend at least 20 minutes playing each of the following games: *Kingdom Rush*, *Tactical Assassin 3*, and *Westerado*.

What kinds of embedded narratives does each game utilize and how? In what ways do the embedded narratives add to the experience of playing the games? Do they detract in any way?

Emergent Narratives

Emergent narratives are created through the act of playing a game. In storytelling games, this can involve players taking on the role of a storyteller who directly creates what could be called a "composed narrative." Aside from tabletop roleplaying games and some online persistent world games, this form of narrative is rarely seen in games (the tabletop card games *Once Upon a Time* and *Nanofictionary* being notable exceptions).

The more common form of emergent narrative is one which arises from the series of game state changes that occur during a game (what could be called a "transpiring narrative"). These transpiring narratives have no author, rather they are a history of what happened during the game. For example, James Moore's description of his ongoing game of *Sid Meier's Civilization II* (see sidebar below) is a transpiring narrative.

Composed narratives are audience-centric; the events they describe should tell a good story. Transpiring narratives are participant-centric. It does not matter whether the narrative's action is interesting in the retelling so long as it was compelling to experience when it actually occurred. If you ever tried to describe an amazing game you played and saw your listener's eyes glaze over, then you have experienced the difference between a good transpiring narrative and a good composed one. There are many things in the real world that are amazing for the person who experiences it first-hand, but are incredibly tedious to hear retold.

A satisfying emergent narrative requires the game designer to create settings, scenarios, and conflict. The narrative itself, however, is not directly created by the designer, instead it grows out of the game's mechanics. So a designer who has ideas about what sorts of emergent narratives the game should support, needs to work towards designing mechanics that support them.

Even so, this does not necessarily entail a fiction dictating a specific mechanic. A game in which the players are cast into the role of celebrity chefs might include narratives of coming up with exciting new dishes, keeping diners happy, building an empire of restaurants, earning Michelin stars. Each of these narrative elements could be realized using any number of mechanics—finding the right one is the art of game design.

Eternal Civilization

by James Moore

I've been playing the same game of *Civilization II* for 10 years. Though long outdated, I grew fascinated with this particular game because by the time *Civ III* was released, I was already well into the distant future. I thought that it might be interesting to see just how far into the future I could go and see what the ramifications would be. Naturally I play other games and have a

life, but I often return to this game and carry on when I'm not doing anything else. The results are as follows:

- The world is a hellish nightmare of suffering and devastation.
- There are three remaining super nations in the year AD 3991, each competing for the scant resources left on the planet after dozens of nuclear wars have rendered vast swaths of the world uninhabitable wastelands.

The ice caps have melted over 20 times (somehow) due primarily to the many nuclear wars. As a result, every inch of land in the world that isn't a mountain is inundated swamp land, useless to farming. Most of which is irradiated anyway.

As a result, big cities are a thing of the distant past. Roughly 90% of the world's population (at its peak 2,000 years ago) has died either from nuclear annihilation or famine caused by the global warming that has left absolutely zero arable land to farm. Engineers (late game worker units) are always busy continuously building roads so that new armies can reach the front lines. Roads that are destroyed on the enemies' very next turn. So there isn't any time to clear swamps or clean up the nuclear fallout.

Only three super massive nations are left. The Celts (me), The Vikings, and the Americans. Between the three of us, we have conquered all the other nations that have ever existed and assimilated them into our respective empires.

You've heard of the 100 year war? Try the 1,700 year war. The three remaining nations have been locked in an eternal death struggle for almost 2,000 years. Peace seems to be impossible. Every time a cease fire is signed, the Vikings will surprise attack the Americans or myself the very next turn, often with nuclear weapons. Even when the U.N. forces a peace treaty. So I can only assume that peace will come only when they're wiped out. It is this that perpetuates the war ad infinitum.

Because of SDI technology, ICBMs are usually only used against armies outside of cities. Instead, cities are constantly attacked by spies who plant nuclear devices which then detonate (something I greatly miss in later *Civ* games). Usually the downside to doing this is that every nation in the world declares war on you. But since we are already at war, it is no longer a deterrent for anyone. Myself included.

The other two governments are theocracies, my country is a communist state. I wanted to stay a democracy, but the Senate would always overrule me when I wanted to preempt the Vikings in declaring war. This would delay my attack and render my turn (and often my plans) useless. And of course the Vikings would then break the cease fire like clockwork the very next turn. Something I also miss in later *Civ* games is a little internal politics. Anyway, I was forced to do away with democracy roughly a thousand years ago because it was endangering my empire. But of course the people hate me now and every few years since then, there are massive guerrilla (late game barbarians) uprisings in the heart of my empire that I have to deal with, which saps resources from the war effort.

The military stalemate is airtight. The post-late game in *Civ II* is perfectly balanced because all remaining nations already have all the technologies so there is no advantage. And there are so many units at once on the map that you could lose 20 tank units and not have your lines dented because you have a constant stream moving to the front. This also means that cities are not only tiny towns full of starving people, but that you can never improve the city. "So you want a granary so you can eat? Sorry; I have to build another tank instead. Maybe next time."

My goal for the next few years is to try and end the war and thus use the engineers to clear swamps and fallout so that farming may resume. I want to rebuild the world. But I'm not sure how.

EXERCISE Expansions

Successful tabletop games often spawn "expansions"—aftermarket mechanics and components that can be added to the original "base" game to create new gameplay possibilities. For example, *On the Brink* is a *Pandemic* expansion that adds mechanics for virus mutations and bio-terrorism. Expansions are not a new phenomenon (though they are becoming increasingly common); *Stock Exchange* is a *Monopoly* expansion that was published in 1936.

Sometimes game enthusiasts step in and create home-brewed, non-commercial expansions for their favorite games. One such expansion (designed by Sherid Adams) takes the form of a miniature "inner board" that can be placed on top of a standard *Monopoly* board (figure 6.5). The expansion introduces Atlantic City's

Figure 6.5 Courtesy of Sherid Adams.

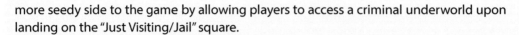

more seedy side to the game by allowing players to access a criminal underworld upon landing on the "Just Visiting/Jail" square.

This exercise asks you to take inspiration from Adams's expansion and create one of your own for an existing commercial tabletop game. Think about the kinds of narratives that the base game supports. What sorts of stories would you like to add? The "story-oriented design" exercise (page 121) presented a process for creating mechanics in support of a narrative. Use a similar process to develop the expansion. Keep in mind that your goal is to extend the gameplay in a meaningful way while maintaining the game's core mechanic.

Narratives on the Tabletop

Even the most linear game has some emergent narratives, and the most emergent game has some of its narrative embedded. *The Last of Us* narrative is primarily embedded, yet many of the story's details emerge out of choices made by the player. For example, when the advancement of the game's linear narrative requires the player to kill someone, it does not dictate how exactly that death must occur. *Chess* is almost entirely an emergent game, but it does have an embedded narrative in the form of its beginning (two opposing and equal forces facing one another upon a battlefield) and its three possible endings (white wins, black wins, or the game ends in a draw).

It is rare for tabletop games to have their core gameplay revolve around an embedded narrative. Why is this so? It may be that embedded narratives fit more naturally in games whose internal workings can be handled by a computer and hidden from the players' view. It could be that an embedded narrative's limited replayability conflicts with what people expect from a tabletop game. Retail tabletop games and video games are comparable in price, but most tabletop games can be played in under two hours whereas video games typically take about 30 hours to complete. So in order to get a similar entertainment hour per dollar value, a player would need to be able to play a tabletop game at least fifteen times before setting it aside for good.

EXERCISE Something in My Pocket

Zombie in my Pocket has inspired a whole series of "in my pocket" games that build upon its mechanics, such as *Fairy Tale in my Pocket* and *Dungeonquest in my Pocket*. Visit www.funmines.com/zimp for links to these and other "in my pocket" games.

This assignment asks you to apply your narrative creativity to come up with a compelling original theme, scenario, and (most importantly) embedded narrative that utilize *Zombie in my Pocket*'s game mechanics.

As a single player game centering on the actions of a protagonist (albeit one that is not represented by a game piece), *Zombie in my Pocket* is particularly well suited for supporting an embedded narrative. You may want to have your embedded narrative use a web structure—the game's core mechanic of laying down randomized tiles easily supports that kind of structure. Alternatively, if you would like an extra challenge, you might try figuring out a way to marry a linear or plot tree narrative structure to the game.

This exercise provides you the opportunity to create an original narrative. However, if you prefer you can borrow a storyline from someone else's writing and adapt it to work within the format of a game. Either way, keep in mind that it is perfectly fine for the game to be a one-shot play experience—the narrative does not need to support replayability.

Modify the rules to *Zombie in my Pocket* however you think best. Do make sure, though, that the resulting game is still recognizably part of the *ZimP* family.

Suspension of Disbelief

Battleship is a 2012 film "based" on the eponymous tabletop game. In order to have a scene that replicates the game mechanics, the plot has the heroes' radar disabled, forcing them to rely on a grid of tsunami detection buoys in order to fire on the enemy (an enemy in the form of invading aliens from Planet-G, of course). Many film reviewers commented (with an appalled admiration) on the pretzel-like narrative twists required to justify the scene's action.

Yet the game itself requires no justification for its own narrative thread. Why would anyone fight a sea battle by firing at random spots in the ocean? If it is not possible to determine whether an enemy ship is in a particular location, how is it possible to determine whether a shot fired at that location hit a ship? For a film, these questions beg to be answered (albeit with buoys); for the game they are generally not even asked.

Perhaps this lack of narrative rigor suggests that when viewed in terms of their backstory, some games are flawed and weak. Yet in the same way that the artificiality of theatrical plays allows for narratives that would be jarring in the cinema, tabletop games' ability to be disconnected from their own narrative logic is a kind of strength. *Battleship* (aka *Sea Battle*) does not require tsunami buoys to work. *Shoot-Out* does not need to explain why the gunfighters' ability to hit one another is based upon their distance to the middle of the board, rather than to each other (or why the two fighters can be hit by so many bullets, yet go on to fight several consecutive duels).

Consider *Marrakech* in terms of its player roles and narrative. The game casts its players as rug merchants competing to be named the best salesperson. Yet the gameplay has nothing to do with selling rugs—rather it is about placing the rugs on the board so that money is received when Assam (the market owner) steps on them. A player's turn involves moving the Assam game piece and paying a penalty if the movement ends on another player's rug (though no penalty is paid for traversing rugs). Assam serves as a transitory avatar that the players take turns possessing. None of this really makes sense, yet it all works within the context of a game.

Taking this sort of tabletop game's narrative on its own terms does not involve a willing suspension of disbelief because the plot holes are not something that most players attempt to resolve. Rather, a game's backstory possesses dream logic that slips around the players' consciousness and sidesteps any methodical thought.

EXERCISE Personal Narrative

Create a game whose inspiration comes from something you have personally experienced. It does not need to be directly autobiographical—the game can include fictional elements and the main character does not need to be you.

If you are unsure how to begin, think about the stories you tell about yourself. What issues do you grapple with? Do not feel obligated to have the game's narrative involve high drama or profound lessons. Someone who is chronically late for appointments might choose to create a game that explores the struggle to be on time and the costs of failing to do so.

You are free to tackle this project using either embedded or emergent narratives. For an added challenge, try creating a second game that explores the same story using the other type of narrative.

Further Reading

If you would like to learn more about game narratives and writing for games, the following books may be of interest:

- *Character Development and Storytelling for Games* by Lee Sheldon
- *Game Writing: Narrative Skills for Videogames* edited by Chris Bateman
- *Kobold's Guide to Worldbuilding* edited by Janna Silverstein
- *Professional Techniques for Video Game Writing* by Wendy Despain
- *The Ultimate Guide to Video Game Writing and Design* by Flint Dille & John Zuur Platten
- *Writing for Video Game Genres: From FPS to RPG* edited by Wendy Despain
- *Writing for Video Games* by Steve Ince

CHAPTER SEVEN

Game Over

INTRODUCTION

When playing a game, the goal is to win, but it is the goal that is important, not the winning.

(Reiner Knizia in Woods 2012, 189)

The quote above says that an enjoyable game requires players who strive to win, but do not view winning as the sole reason to play. An opponent who plays by the rules, but does not pursue the prescribed goals ruins the game. This kind of aimless play can undermine a game's dynamics to the point that they entirely disappear. Just as bad, however, is a player who is entirely fixated on winning. Someone who cannot find satisfaction in a well-played (but lost) game robs his opponents of their own enjoyment.

This chapter focuses on how to design a game's conclusion and the ways in which a game's dynamics can affect the players' experience of it.

The learning objectives for this chapter are:

1   Understand the terms: victory condition, loss condition, and end condition.

2   Understand how stability and feedback loops can affect a game's dynamics.

Winning and Losing

Not every game can be won or lost. For some video games, defeat is momentary—a character's death results in a minor setback rather than the loss of the game. For this kind of game, the player will always be able to finish and win as long as he does not run out of patience. In other video games (such as *Pac-Man* and *Canabalt*) there is no way to win the game (though a high score might be considered a victory). Some games simply do not have an end point at all—games of *World of Warcraft*, *SimCity*, *Farmville*, and tabletop RPGs can all continue indefinitely.

Games that *can* be won have "victory conditions," games that can conclude have "end conditions," and games that can be lost have "loss conditions." Let us take a closer look at each of these kinds of conditions.

Victory Conditions

A victory condition defines how a game is won. Common victory conditions include having the most points/assets when the game concludes (*Marrakech*), being the first to reach a particular destination (*Tabletop Billiards*), eliminating the other players' assets (*Button Men,* page 184), depleting one's own assets (*Hut,* page 137), or simply accomplishing some action (surrounding the opponent's Queen Bee in *Hive*).

Games are sometimes described in terms of their victory conditions, yet the victory condition is not really what a game is about. Achieving victory is the goal of the game, but the final act of winning can be a very minor part of the game's actual experience.

When the mechanics of a particular game are described, it is often possible to guess the nature of the victory condition. There is usually a clear connection between what you *can* do and what you are *trying* to do. The reverse is often not the case: a description of a game's victory condition gives little insight into a game's mechanics. Games with strikingly different mechanics can have nearly identical victory conditions. For example, *Shoot-Out*, *Cribbage*, and *The Settlers of Catan* are completely different in their gameplay, yet they all have a victory condition based upon being the first player to reach a specified score.

End Conditions

The criterion for concluding a game is its end condition. Victory conditions often, but not always, do double duty by also serving as the game's end condition. In *Tabletop Billiards*, moving all three of your pieces into the opponent's home spaces is both the game's victory condition and its end condition. *Marrakech*, however, has different criteria for its end and victory conditions. The game ends when all the rugs have been played; the winner is the player who has the most visible rug halves and Dirhams combined.

A *Pente* game ends when a player manages to either place five stones in a row or make five captures of her opponent's stones. Both of these end conditions double as victory conditions, so *Pente* has multiple victory conditions as well as multiple end conditions.

Loss Conditions

The Tower has a "last person standing" mechanic in which the last player holding counters loses the game. If two people are playing the game, the person who does not lose the game might consider herself the winner. But if more than two are playing, it really becomes a game that can be lost, but not won.

Just as games can have multiple end conditions and multiple victory conditions, they can have multiple loss conditions. *Zombie in my Pocket* is lost when the player either runs out of hit points or runs out of time.

Hut

Reiner Knizia describes this game in his classic book, *Dice Games Properly Explained* (Knizia 2010, 39).

Players:
- Two or more players

Required Materials:
- One six-sided die
- Six cards (numbered 1 through 6) for each player

Object of the Game:
- Be the first player to turn over all six cards.

Setup:
- Each player arranges the six cards in front of them in numerical order with the numbers face up.

Rules:
1. Players take turns rolling the die.

---

2. After rolling the die, the player takes one of the following actions:
    - If the player's card whose number corresponds to the roll is face up, then it is turned over.
    - If the card is already face down, then the player on the left turns her or his card of that value face down.
    - If the player to the left's card is already face down, the player to the right turns her or his card face down.
    - If both the player on the left and the right already have their cards face down, the current player must turn his card face up.
3. Play continues until one player has turned over all six cards and wins the game.

Misère

The Tower has a loss condition of being the only player holding counters after all the other players have returned theirs. When you played the game, did it occur to you that this could just as easily be a victory condition? That the game could be played using the rule that the last player holding counters *wins* the game? Inverting a game's victory and loss conditions in this way creates a "misère" variant.

The Tower is a game in which players just go along for the ride—they roll dice and move counters, but at no time can they make a decision that affects the game state. Because of this, *The Tower*'s misère gameplay does not feel all that different from the standard game.

A misère variant of a game that offers more player choice—one in which players can actively strive to win—often provides a very different, mind-bending play experience. *Misère Chess* (also known as *Antichess*, *Losing Chess*, and *Suicide Chess*) has the victory condition of losing all of one's pieces or being stalemated (having no legal moves). To make the game work, some of *Chess*'s other standard rules must be modified:

1. Capturing is compulsory (players can choose the piece to capture if more than one is possible).
2. The king has no special significance and cannot castle. Losing the king does not win the game.
3. Pawns can be promoted to be a king, if desired.

Some games are more easily converted into misère form than others. *Marrakech* could easily be made into a misère variant—the only rule change required is specifying that the winner is the first player to run out of Dirham coins (or has the fewest coins if no one runs out of coins before the last rug is played).

When developing a game you may want to try playing it in misère form. A misère game can support gameplay that is not simply an inversion of the original game. For example, *Marrakech* usually ends with the last rug being placed. It is much less common for someone to win the game by bankrupting all the other players. This creates a dynamic in which players tend to focus more on avoiding the loss of Dirham than attempting to influence who gains them (at least in games with more than two players). However, playing *Marrakech* as a *misère* game greatly increases the chance that the game will conclude before the last rug is played. As a result, players are much more conscious of the potential of someone winning mid-game by going bankrupt. Strategic players may choose to forgo a potentially larger Dirham loss in favor of making a payment to a player who is very low on coins and close to winning.

Momentum

Think about the last tabletop game you played. Did one of the players gain an early lead? At what point did it become inevitable who would win?

A game's "momentum" describes how the game mechanics tip to favor or disfavor players who are pulling ahead. A given game may have some mechanics that tilt one way and some the other, but generally speaking most games tend to advantage the player in the lead rather than the players who trail.

Consider the game of *Checkers*. If a player falls behind in how many checkers she has on the board, it can become harder and harder for her to turn the tide of the game. With fewer checkers, she has fewer choices regarding what piece to move and her defensive capabilities become weaker. Falling behind increases the likelihood of falling behind further still. A dynamic such as this, which increases the tendency of the player in the lead to build upon that lead, is called a "positive feedback loop."

Strictly speaking, the term "feedback loop" should indicate a snowballing effect—that the effect is proportional to the lead. In practice, however, game designers also apply the term to mechanics that have a fixed effect—that do not increase in proportion with the leader's advantage. It is also worth noting that "positive" in this context does not indicate that the effect is necessarily beneficial to the player it targets. Rather, it simply indicates that the mechanic provides an advantage to the player in the lead.

Games whose core mechanic involve capturing (such as the example of *Checkers*) often have positive feedback loops, as do games with resource gathering mechanics. For example, a player who is doing well in *Monopoly* accumulates the resource of money; that money can be spent on upgrading his properties with house and hotel resources; those houses and hotels increase the amount of money the player collects from opponents who land on his properties, and so on. Doing well in *Monopoly* creates a positive feedback loop.

Shoot-Out is another example of a game that possesses a positive feedback loop. Moving a pawn closer to the center of the board simultaneously brings the player closer to victory and makes it easier to shoot and force the opponent's pawn farther away from the center. Additionally, a successful shot graces the shooter with another turn.

Shoot-Out also has a mechanic that aids a player who is falling behind. A player who is losing a *Shoot-Out* duel can choose to "retreat" (concede the duel's points) and gain back two revolver bullets. A mechanic such as this, which provides a boost to a player who is falling behind (or a penalty to a player pulling ahead), is called a "catchup feature" or "negative feedback loop." A more dramatic example can be seen in the "rubberbanding" mechanic used in many race car video games to insure that a player does not fall too far behind the race's leader. Rubberbanding is a mechanic that slows down the car in front or speeds up the cars falling behind (Rogers 2010, 362–363)—the term is meant to evoke the idea that the cars' positions pull towards one another. Where a positive feedback loop provides the player in the lead with an advantage, negative feedback loops dampen the leader's momentum or aids the players who trail.

Hut has a core mechanic that contains a negative feedback loop. The closer a player is to the goal of turning all six cards face down, the more likely it is that the player's die roll will either aid one of her neighboring opponents (by allowing them to turn one of their cards facedown) or pull the player farther from victory by forcing her to turn a card face up. A typical game of *Hut* involves the players finding themselves quickly advancing towards victory, only to have their progress stagnate just short of winning.

Positive feedback loops create games of increasing momentum. The tide of victory in these games is like a rock at the top a hill. Once it moves in the direction of one player, it picks up speed. The farther it rolls, the more difficult it is to change the outcome of the game.

Negative feedback loops and catchup features inhibit the leading player or benefit the players who are falling behind. These types of mechanics slow down and reverse a player's momentum. Victory in these games is like trying to push a rock out of a valley. It is harder to keep the rock rolling up the hill towards victory than it is for opponents to reverse its direction and have it roll back to the bottom.

These rock analogies beg the question, "What about a flat plain?" And indeed, many games do not provide players in the lead with any advantages or disadvantages, such as *Sea Battle* when played by its basic (non-variant) rules.

Neptune's Pride II Case Study

Neptune's Pride II: Triton is an online game in which players compete to capture planets. The combat system is designed to favor defenders, but over the course of the game the degree to which the defender is favored erodes. This provides a momentum that starts out slowly, but picks up speed towards the end of the game. Early in the game, leads can be easily overcome and turned around, but as the game advances towards its conclusion, leads become more powerful and can provide the opportunity to push through the other players' defenses. Let us look at how that is done.

The game's combat mechanic involves fleets of ships attacking one another. While the results of combat are presented to the players instantaneously, behind the scenes it actually takes place in the form of rounds. During a round, each player destroys a number of the opponent's ships equal to the player's "weapon technology level." Defenders have the advantage of attacking first and at a +1 weapon technology level.

Imagine a combat between two players early in the game. The players both have the starting weapon technology level of 1 (which allows one ship to be destroyed per turn), but the defender's bonus allows him to fight at a weapon technology level of 2 (which allows two ships to be destroyed per turn). The attacker has fifteen ships and the defender has eight. Here is how the combat plays out:

1. Attacker loses 2 ships, has 13 remaining.
2. Defender loses 1 ship, has 7 remaining.
3. Attacker loses 2 ships, has 11 remaining.
4. Defender loses 1 ship, has 6 remaining.
5. Attacker loses 2 ships, has 9 remaining.
6. Defender loses 1 ship, has 5 remaining.
7. Attacker loses 2 ships, has 7 remaining.
8. Defender loses 1 ship, has 4 remaining.
9. Attacker loses 2 ships, has 5 remaining.
10. Defender loses 1 ship, has 3 remaining.
11. Attacker loses 2 ships, has 3 remaining.
12. Defender loses 1 ship, has 2 remaining.
13. Attacker loses 2 ships, has 1 remaining.

14. Defender loses 1 ship, has 1 remaining.
15. Attacker loses 2 ships, has 0 remaining and has lost the battle.

At this early stage in the game, the defender's bonus is formidable and gives the defender twice the attacker's fire power. As the players increase their weapon technology level, however, the defender bonus becomes less and less significant. If the players both have a weapon technology level of 4, the bonus's impact is reduced to giving the defender 1.25 times the attacker's firepower. In that situation, here is how the above combat scenario would play out:

1. Attacker loses 5 ships, has 10 remaining.
2. Defender loses 4 ships, has 4 remaining.
3. Attacker loses 5 ships, has 5 remaining.
4. Defender loses 4 ships, has 0 remaining and loses the battle.

The combat algorithm does not change, but the data it uses does. Because of that, the game's combat dynamic changes as the game develops.

EXERCISE Feedback

Try playing a variant of *Shoot-Out* that reverses its positive feedback loop. Instead of determining a successful hit by rolling a number greater than or equal to the shooter's position, have it based on the target's position. The result is that the closer a player's pawn is to the center of the board, the easier it is to successfully shoot.

The main game of *Sea Battle* does not have any feedback mechanics, but the "Salvo" variant (in which the number of shots a player can take is equal to the number of unsunk ships she possesses) creates a positive feedback loop. As you did with *Shoot-Out*, try playing *Sea Battle* with a negative feedback variation. Instead of having the number of shots be equal to the player's number of ships, play "Anti-Salvo" in which the number of shots is equal to the opponent's number of ships.

How did the negative feedback loops affect the gameplay of *Shoot-Out* and *Sea Battle*? Try varying a few more games by adding positive and negative feedback mechanisms.

Ending the Game

A game's stability refers to how quickly and significantly its game state can change. A game with a stable positive feedback loop tends to have a front runner who slowly builds upon her lead. An unstable positive feedback loop would typically result in a lead rapidly snowballing into a sudden win. A stable negative feedback loop provides gameplay in which players alternate in moving slightly ahead, whereas an unstable negative feedback loop promotes wild swings of fortune with the players taking, and then losing, large leads.

A key challenge in game design is to use these kinds of dynamics to create a game that concludes in a satisfying way. If the winners tend to be determined too early and with too much stability, the game can seem to drag on before it reaches its foregone conclusion. If the winners are determined too late with too little stability, the game will feel random and all but the final few rounds of action will seem irrelevant in determining who won.

When a game's dynamics lean toward one of these extremes, it is important that you recognize it and address the problem. One approach is to modify and moderate the dynamic itself. However, this often requires an adjustment to the core mechanic. An alternative is to look for ways to maintain the dynamic while mitigating its shortcomings. Towards that end, you could try doing one (or more) of the following:

- Adjust the game's starting or end point;
- Obscure the players' relative standings;
- Eliminate players as they fall behind; or
- Increase the players' sense of agency.

Adjust Starting or End Points

If the game's conclusion tends to feel as if a random winner was determined in the last few turns, try adjusting the initial setup so that players begin the game in stronger, more developed positions. The idea is to move the pivotal action that has been happening at the very end of the game so that it occurs earlier in the game. Having the play begin in a more advanced position also provides room to expand the endgame, making it a larger part of the game. This change also insures that players go into this (now earlier) phase of the game on a more equal footing.

Conversely, if the game's winner tends to become obvious too early in the game, you can try adjusting the end condition (or adding an additional one) to be closer to the point at which a player's advantage becomes unassailable. In this way, the game concludes at the point when it is usually clear who will win. For example, a game with a victory condition of being the first to reach 100 points might work better if the goal was reduced to 80. Or perhaps the victory condition of 100 points should be left in place and a second victory condition added so that the game is won when a player earns 100 points *or* has a 20 point lead. That second victory condition would handle the occasions in which a player takes an early, unsurmountable lead.

Obscure the Players' Relative Standings

A player who is uncertain of how close his opponents are to victory is less likely to feel that his continued play is hopeless (even when it is). *Ticket to Ride* takes this approach by keeping a significant portion of each player's accumulated victory points concealed from her opponents. The game's core mechanic involves players gaining points by claiming sections of track. The points gained in this manner are known to everyone playing and are openly scored on a victory point track. The players' main objective, however, is to complete train routes between distant cities. The particular cities a player is trying to connect is determined by drawing "Destination Ticket" cards and is kept secret from the player's opponents. At the end of the game, the Destination Tickets are revealed and points are rewarded for each one completed and deducted for each one that was not. Over the course of the game, the players' score markers may have been neck and neck on the victory point track, but once the Destination Ticket points are added in, it can become clear that one player has secretly dominated the entire game and has won by a substantial margin. This mechanic—having some victory points public and some hidden—allows a game to seem close during the course of its play, but still have a decisive victory whose outcome was determined by choices made early in the game. Part of what makes this mechanic work is that while the extent of the hidden points is not entirely clear, players can deduce the points their opponents are accumulating to a certain degree by observing their choices and actions they take.

Another approach is to allow multiple paths to victory in a game. If players are pursuing distinctly different goals, then their overall progress can be difficult to compare. Is the player who has accumulated 127 of 150 gold pieces he needs to win closer to victory than someone who has captured eight of the ten towns she needs for the victory condition she is pursuing?

Artificially squeezing scores together is another way to obscure that a blowout is in progress. A game whose victory condition is being the first to reach ten points might make the last two points more difficult to acquire than the previous eight. If so, the difference between having eight points and ten is greater than the difference between having six points and eight. So a player losing the game by two victory points may feel that the game was closer than it actually was (Howell 2011). However, this designer tactic works only if the players do not see through the illusion. Pulling it off requires a good understanding of human psychology in addition to game design expertise.

Eliminate Players as They Fall Behind

In some games, such as *Monopoly* and *Risk*, players are eliminated from the game as they fall behind. Player elimination mechanics have fallen out of favor and are fairly uncommon in contemporary tabletop games. This comes from a view that player elimination solves the problem of having to play a hopeless game by creating the problem of not getting to play at all.

Marrakech, however, does include an elimination mechanic. Even so, being eliminated in *Marrakech* is uncommon and not part of the core mechanic—and as mentioned earlier, the elimination mechanic itself was eliminated by its German publisher.

Richard Garfield, who designed *Magic: the Gathering*, argues that player elimination has been unfairly stigmatized. He says that the possibility of being eliminated raises a game's stakes and makes it more interesting—and moreover, that playing a game with no chance of winning is usually less fun than not playing at all (Garfield 2011; Elias, Garfield, and Gutschera 2012).

When implementing a player elimination mechanic, consider minimizing how long the game continues after players start being eliminated. Rikki Tahta's *Coup*, for example, only takes 10 to 15 minutes to play in its entirety, so a player who is knocked out of the game does not need to wait long for the next one to begin.

Increase the Sense of Player Agency

Finally, increasing the players' sense of being able to affect the game's outcome can make end game dynamics more appealing. Falling behind and fighting against a positive feedback loop can be exciting instead of disheartening *if* the player feels that optimal performance could turn the tables. A player who feels in control of his fate may find that as his chances to win diminish, instead of losing interest his excitement increases.

Stability in *Risk*

A game's stability may shift as the play progresses. *Risk*'s core gameplay is a relatively stable positive feedback loop. Players use resources in the form of army pieces to attack and gain territory. The more territory a player controls, the more armies she gains every turn. The game has another mechanic which involves collecting and turning in cards for extra "bonus" armies. In the beginning of the game, the number of bonus armies awarded is modest and tends to have only a marginal impact on the game. However, with each set of cards turned in, the number of bonus armies awarded increases. Eventually the bonus armies dwarf the number of armies received for territorial control. A typical end game of *Risk* involves players taking turns cashing in cards and spending their bonus armies to sweep across the globe in huge swaths of territorial captures.

Risk's bonus cards serve as a catch up feature. While bonus armies can certainly help a player to consolidate and extend a lead, in practice their level of destabilization is so great that it allows players to nullify the lead that an opponent had slowly built up over the course of the game.

EXERCISE Stability

Create six simple core game mechanics. The goal is to have each mechanic demonstrate a different combination of feedback loop and stability as follows:

1. Stable positive feedback loop
2. Unstable positive feedback loop
3. Stable negative feedback loop
4. Unstable negative feedback loop
5. A stable core mechanic without any feedback loops
6. An unstable core mechanic without any feedback loops

Do not worry too much about whether or not the core mechanics have much potential to be fun. The main point of the exercise is to simply wrap your head around creating these sorts of dynamics.

Here is an example of a simple core mechanic for a dice game that features a stable negative feedback loop:

Goal: Be the first to reach 100

Equipment: One 6-sided die for each player

Players roll simultaneously and score as follows:

1. If the player's total score is the same or greater than the opponent's, the player adds the value of her own roll to her score.
2. If the player's total score is lower than the opponent's, the player adds the value of *both* rolled dice (the player's and the opponent's) to her score.

CHAPTER EIGHT

Movement

INTRODUCTION

The movement of game pieces is so fundamental to tabletop games that "your move" is synonymous with "your turn," even for games whose play does not involve moving pieces (such as *Go*, *Sprouts*, and *Pente*). This chapter examines how movement and space can be used in games.

The learning objectives for this chapter are:

1 Understand the characteristics of discrete and continuous space.

2 Become familiar with the typical ways of presenting game space and having pieces move through it.

Continuity

Many tabletop games take place across a series of "discrete spaces." A game space is discrete when all the locations within its boundary are treated as being the same position (Schell 2008, 130). A *Chess* board's 8 × 8 grid provides sixty-four discrete spaces, the 10 × 10 grid in *Sea Battle* (*Battleship*) provides 100 discrete positions, and *Shoot-Out* takes place on a row of thirty-two discrete positions.

The square that a *Chess* piece occupies is relevant; but because the space is discrete the precise position *within* that square is not. As far as the game's rules are concerned, situating a pawn near the edge of its square is no different from placing it in the center.

When a game's mechanics do take into account an element's precise location, it is utilizing "continuous space." For example, the space in *Jetpack Joyride* is continuous. The precise location of Barry (the player's character) matters—even a slight alteration of his position can make the difference between slipping past an obstacle and crashing into it. The use of continuous space is common in video games and sports, but is rare in tabletop games. Tabletop continuous space primarily shows up in "dexterity" games (such as *Jenga* and *Pick Up Sticks*) and miniatures war games. In miniatures games, the precise locations of the pieces is relevant to the game's mechanics—movement and attack ranges are typically specified in millimeters and measured using rulers.

A game does not need to have its space uniformly continuous or discrete. In fact, a game may treat the same section of space as continuous in some of its mechanics and discrete in others. For example, when a *Tennis* ball is served, the server must stand behind the fault line and the ball must travel into the diagonally opposite service box without touching the net. The fault line, the net, and the service box are treated as discrete spaces for the purpose of determining whether the serve was legal or not. The precise location of where the ball lands does not matter so long as it is within the box, the server was behind the line, and the ball did not brush the net. Simultaneously, the game's space is continuous for the player receiving the ball—her racket cannot simply be swung anywhere within the service box, it must connect with the ball in order to return it.

Continuous *Shoot-Out*

Let us take a closer look at how discrete and continuous spaces work by converting *Shoot-Out* to use continuous space. The game has thirty-two discrete spaces in a line. For our continuous space version, we will simply translate each discrete space into 1 cm of continuous space. This gives us a play area that is 32 cm long.

Street width is not part of the original game (the mechanics do not recognize any side-to-side movement), but we will incorporate it into the continuous space variant. Since the fiction of the game is that it takes place on a street, the width should be narrow in comparison to its length. We will use a width of 8 cm.

Using continuous space allows the pawns' movement to be more flexible. Rather than having a movement of exactly one space per turn, players can be given the ability to move the pawn any distance up to a maximum per turn—we will use 1 cm per turn in this case. When a pawn is successfully shot, we will have it pushed back 3 cm (instead of three spaces) in a direct line away from the opposing pawn (but not off the board).

It is worth noting that, as it stands, there is little reason for a player to choose anything other than to move a pawn as fast as possible towards the center of town. A later iteration of the design might expand the game to give players incentives to move at various rates of speed and in various directions. To give players a reason to move slower, for example, the rules might allow a player to move and shoot simultaneously, with the shot's accuracy decreasing as the movement distance increases. Game objects might be scattered around the board to motivate players to move towards and away from them: barrels that offer cover, ammo that can be picked up, perhaps even dynamite that can be picked up and thrown (and run away from).

Converting the game's shooting mechanics to work in continuous space is a bit more complicated than the movement conversion. The original game's discrete spaces are numbered from "20" at the far ends to "5" in the middle two spaces (see figure 3.14, page 63). In order to successfully shoot, a player must roll a number on a 20-sided die that is equal to or higher than the number of the space occupied by her pawn. This means that if the pawn is at the furthest possible point from the center (square 20), there is a 5% chance (1 in 20) of making a successful shot with a revolver. At the closest point (square 5), there is an 80% chance (16 in 20) of making a successful shot with a revolver.

Our goal is to have the continuous space version of the game supporting similar shooting probabilities with an 80% probability at the center of town; a 5% probability at the furthest point from the center; and a continuous range of probabilities for all the points in-between. The playing field's corners are the furthest points from the center, so as a starting place we need to determine that distance. We could do this by drawing out the board and using a ruler to measure it, or we could use high school geometry and calculate it using the Pythagorean theorem ($a^2 + b^2 = c^2$). For the purposes of the theorem, the distance from the corner to the center forms a hypotenuse—which is the "c" in the formula. Taking the square root of the sum $4.5^2 + 16^2$ tells us that the distance in question is 16.492 cm.

Rounding off that distance and converting it to millimeters gives us 165 mm as the playing field's longest distance. That number becomes the cornerstone of the algorithm that determines the percentage chance to hit when using a revolver:

Percentage = ((165 − [distance to center in mm]) * 0.45) + 5

How was this algorithm determined? The starting point was finding an algorithm that calculates the desired results of 80% and 5% when the distance extremes (0 mm and 165 mm) are plugged into it. At 165 mm the first half of the algorithm zeroes out and the "+ 5" at its end establishes the 5% chance to hit. In pursuit of having an 80% for 0 mm, we subtract 5 from 80 and divide it by 165, which results in $0.\overline{45}$. This value (rounded off) provides the algorithm's multiplier. In short, we worked backwards by starting with our desired outcomes and then sought an algorithm that provides them. This process of concocting an algorithm like this may seem baroquely complicated, but with experience it becomes more straightforward and natural.

Using the algorithm, we can determine that a pawn has a 43.25% chance to hit at 80 mm and a 5% chance to hit at 165 mm distance. The probability at 0 mm is 79.25%—not precisely the same as the 80% chance to hit from the discrete "5" space, but close enough for our purposes.

When playing the game, a player's process for attempting to shoot involves the following steps: 1) measure the distance to the center of town to the nearest millimeter; 2) calculate the probability to hit; 3) round off the probability to be an integer; 4) roll two 10-sided "percentile dice" (see sidebar on facing page) to determine whether the shot was successful.

So that's a continuous space game!

Or is it?

Arguably, this continuous space *Shoot-Out* is still a discrete space game because the smallest unit of measure is a millimeter—any fractions of one are rounded off. Essentially, we have changed the game from using a line of thirty-two discrete spaces to using a grid of 320 × 80 discrete spaces. Still, we could call this *effectively continuous*—that the 25,600 discrete 1 mm square spaces making up the board provide the same experience that would be had if the space was truly continuous.

Continuous space on computers is very similar. What seems continuous to the player is actually discrete—but the units are small enough that the result is effectively continuous. Imposing a discrete structure on game space, allows you to create mechanics that evaluate and affect these seemingly continuous occurrences.

In chapter 13 ("Turns, Ticks, & Time") we will take a similar look at continuous time and how it works in the context of turn-based and real-time games.

Playing Dice with the Game Universe

Many games involve an element of chance. Tabletop games often incorporate chance through the use of shuffled cards and dice rolls. Video games simulate chance by using "pseudorandom number generators," which work along the lines of obtaining an arbitrary number by asking a friend to pick a number between 1 and 1,000.

Depending on the types of tabletop games you have played in past, you may be most familiar with cube-shaped dice. However, there are many more options available. In addition to the ubiquitous 6-sided die, game designers often make use of 4-, 8-, 10-, 12-, and 20-sided dice. When dealing with this multitude of dice options, a given type of die can be abbreviated as the number of dice followed by "D" followed by the number of sides on each of the dice (as in "*Monopoly* requires 2D6").

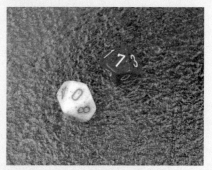

Figure 8.1 10-sided dice.

A 10-sided die (or D10) usually is numbered 0 through 9 with the 0 representing a roll of 10. The reason for this is that it enables using two 10-sided dice (or 2D10) to roll a number between 1 and 100. This is done by having one die represent the 10's place and the other die represent the 1's place (the two dice need to be different colors so that the 10's place roll can be distinguished from the 1's place roll). For example, if the red die in figure 8.1 is rolling the 10's place, the pictured roll would be 70. If the white die is the 10's place, then the roll is 7. If both dice had rolled a 0, then the result would be 100.

For a tabletop game, a set of dice may be part of the final, boxed product. But the usefulness of dice is not limited to physical games—they are also often used in creating paper prototypes of video games. A paper prototype may use dice to simulate the output of a pseudorandom number generator in order to develop and playtest a game mechanic that will eventually be translated into computer code.

Adjacency

Dividing a game space into discrete units creates a network of positions. A given array of game spaces might be presented in any number of visual forms, but it is the game mechanics regarding movement that really dictate the physical relationship between one space and another. Let us take a look at some of the ways that game spaces are presented.

Grids

Grids are the most common layout for discrete game spaces. You have already encountered a number of games in the book that utilize grids: *Marrakech*, *Tabletop Billiards*, and *Zombie in my Pocket*.

How do *Marrakech* and *Tabletop Billiards* differ in their treatment of adjacency? *Tabletop Billiards* allows both orthogonal (non-diagonal) and diagonal movement, so adjacency in that game includes the neighboring squares at the corners as well as the sides. In contrast, *Marrakech*'s rules do not allow rugs to be placed diagonally or Assam to move diagonally. In effect, *Marrakech*'s game mechanics do not treat squares touching on a corner as being adjacent. It would take Assam a minimum of two turns to land on a square that is immediately diagonal from his current position.

Orthogonally oriented grid games are fairly common. In addition to *Marrakech*, this book includes the rules to three other games with this sort of board adjacency: *Zombie in my Pocket*, *Three Musketeers*, and *Cathedral*. Grid-based games that have both orthogonal and diagonal adjacency are also common and include *Reversi* (*Othello*), *Chess*, and *Tic-Tac-Toe*. Diagonal-only adjacency is uncommon and is most notably used in *Checkers*.

Nodes and Irregular Areas

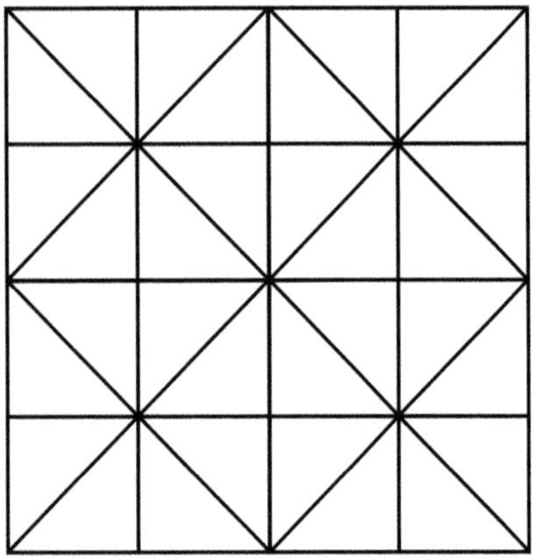

Alquerque is *Checkers*'s Middle Eastern forefather. The game's board is an array of geometric crisscrossing lines (figure 8.2). The line intersections themselves, rather than the spaces in between them, are where *Alquerque*'s game pieces are positioned. Line intersections used in this way are called "nodes" or points—the games themselves can be characterized as using "nodal mechanics." The lines, called "paths," indicate which nodes are directly connected.

In contrast to nodes and nodal games, games which make use of space that is surrounded by lines (such as *Marrakech*, *Shoot-Out*, *Chess*, etc.) could be said to use "area mechanics." A game that uses a grid can

Figure 8.2 *Alquerque* board.

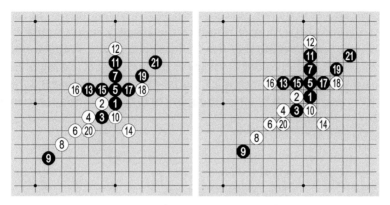

Figure 8.3 *Pente* as played on nodes (left) and on areas (right).

be transposed from area mechanics to nodal mechanics (and vice versa) without affecting the gameplay whatsoever. For example, *Chess* could be played on the nodes of a 7 × 7 grid. In fact, the Chinese and Korean siblings of chess (*Xiangqi* and *Janggi*, respectively) do exactly that (albeit on a more spread out 9 × 10 grid). Likewise, *Pente* is traditionally played on orthogonally connected nodes (figure 8.3, left), but could easily be played on area spaces instead (figure 8.3, right). In fact, since *Pente* has diagonal adjacency, using areas would probably better reflect the game's mechanics.

Alquerque's board has a uniform geometry, but nodal structures can be more irregular. The real power of nodes is the ability of a designer to easily manipulate how they connect to one another. For example, nodes that are spatially close to one another can be made distant in terms of their connection. In *Pandemic*, there

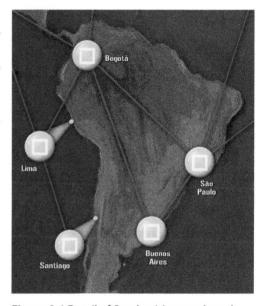

Figure 8.4 Detail of *Pandemic*'s game board (the full board can be seen on page 67). Used with permission of Z-Man Games.

are two intervening nodes between Santiago and Buenos Aires even though the nodes are quite close to one another on the board (see figure 8.4). Likewise, nodes that are spatially distant can be made adjacent via a direct connection. *Pandemic*'s rulebook explains:

> Cities are adjacent if they are connected by a red line. Red lines that go off the edge of the board "wrap around" to the opposite board edge and continue to the indicated city. (For example, Sydney and Los Angeles are considered to be adjacent.)

Irregular area spaces in games typically represent map boundaries, as can be seen in the city districts on a *Mapple* board or the country/regions on a *Risk* board (figure 8.5). It is worth noting that the distinction between irregular nodes (such as *Pandemic* uses) and irregular areas (such as *Risk* uses) is merely presentation. A *Risk* board can use area-mechanics, nodal-mechanics (figure 8.5, right), or a mixture of the two (figure 8.5, left) without impacting the game's actual mechanics in any way.

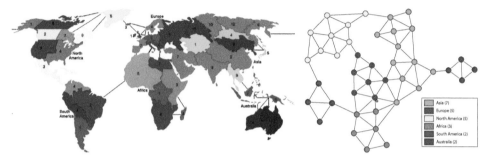

Figure 8.5 *Risk* boards by Orthuberra (left) and Fanblade (right), Creative Commons Attribution-Share Alike 3.0 Unported license.

Hexes

Games that use square grids tend to support an adjacency of up to either four or eight neighbors. Using hexagonal spaces creates an adjacency of up to six neighbors (see figure 8.7). If the hexagon's sides are used as nodal paths (as is the case in *The Settlers of Catan*, see figure 3.18 on page 72), each node can support up to three paths.

Hexagonal game boards and pieces (such as the ones used in *Hive*) are generally a modern convention (and are particularly prevalent in war-themed games). The traditional game *Agon*, however, is an interesting antecedent dating back at least to the 1870s (Bell 1979, 61–64).

There are any number of ways to combine and expand upon these ways of laying out game spaces. *The Settlers of Catan* not only uses its hexagons as nodal paths, but as areas as well. The nodal paths that connect *Ticket to Ride*'s cities are divided into a series of discrete rectangles (figure 8.6). This means that *Ticket to Ride*'s lines take a varying amount of resources to use—they are "weighted paths." When designing your own games, keep in mind that there may be more than one way to present the game's spaces.

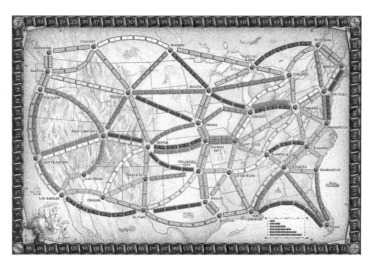

Figure 8.6 *Ticket to Ride*, used with permission of Days of Wonder.

Contiguity

Contiguity (not to be confused with continuity) describes a group of items that share a trait and are not separated from one another. For example, in figure 8.7 the land hexes on the right are contiguous as are the water hexes on the left. The water hex that is surrounded by land is not contiguous with the other water hexes.

The movement of the ship in figure 8.7 would typically be limited to water spaces contiguous with its current location. A railroad hex might provide the ability for units to immediately move to any contiguous railroad hex.

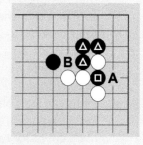

Figure 8.7

Contiguity is fundamental to the game mechanics of *Go*. In the game, pieces that are adjacent orthogonally (but not diagonally) are considered contiguous. In figure 8.8, the black stones (*Go*'s game pieces are known as stones) marked with triangles are contiguous with one another, but not with the other black stones. Their contiguity is important because any stone that does not have an empty space (called a "liberty") next to it or one of the other stones in its contiguous group is captured by the opponent and removed from the board. The black stone marked with a square would be captured

Figure 8.8

by a white stone being placed at point A. Playing at point B would not capture the black stone to the right of the point. That individual stone would not have any adjacent liberties, but would be safe because of the four remaining liberties adjacent to its contiguous group.

Sprouts

Sprouts is a nodal game invented by the mathematicians John Horton Conway and Michael S. Paterson. What makes it unusual is that the gameplay involves the players creating the nodes and paths instead of playing within an existing set of nodes and paths.

Players:

- Two players

Required Materials:

- Pen & paper

Object of the Game:

- To leave the opponent with no legal moves.

Setup:

- The game begins with players sketching a few nodes on a sheet of paper. The exact number does not matter, but for your first few games you probably want to keep it to four or fewer.

Rules:

- Players take turns drawing a path from one node to another. Paths do not need to be straight, but they cannot cross one another.
- New paths can only be added to nodes that have fewer than three paths already connected to them.
- After drawing a new path, players should draw a new node on it. Because they are drawn on a path, these new nodes start with two paths already connected to them.
- Paths can start and end on the same node. Paths beginning and ending on the same node count for two of the node's paths. This means that these types of paths can only be drawn on a node that has one or no paths currently connected to it.

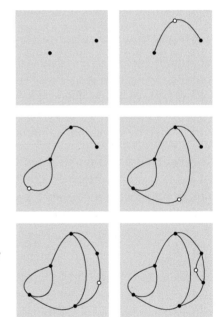

Figure 8.9 example *Sprouts* game.

Variant:

- *Sprouts* can easily be played as a misère game (see page 138) in which players are striving to have no legal moves for themselves.

Movement

As suggested earlier, a game's space is truly defined by the game's rules of movement. Typical movement mechanics include having each turn: a single piece to move (*Shoot-Out*); the selection of one piece from a set to move (*Chess*); an ability to select more than one piece to move (*Backgammon*); and the ability to move every piece (*Diplomacy*).

Pandemic, which allows players to move one piece per turn, provides four methods of movements. The first is a straightforward movement from one city node to a connecting one. The second is called a "Shuttle Flight," which allows a pawn to move from a city with a Research Station to any other city with a Research Station. The third and fourth ways of moving involve using one of the game's cards to do a "Direct Flight" or a "Chartered Flight." A Direct Flight allows a pawn to move to a city pictured on a card. If the player happens to have a card whose city corresponds to a pawn's current location, the card can be spent on a Chartered Flight which allows the pawn to move to any city node on the board.

The instantaneous movement provided by *Pandemic*'s Shuttle, Direct, and Chartered flights could be described as "teleportation"—a movement from one game space to another without visiting the spaces in-between. Teleportation is movement that does not take distance into consideration and is not affected by game spaces between the departure and destination spaces.

Despite its science fiction flavor, teleportation game mechanics has been around for a long time and is seen in such time-honored games as *Backgammon*, *Pachisi*, and *Nine Men's Morris*. Teleportation in *Backgammon* and *Pachisi* involves landing on an opponent's piece and sending it off the board, from where it must re-enter the game in a starting position. *Nine Men's Morris* bestows teleportation powers on a player who is about to lose the game. When a *Nine Men's Morris* player has only three remaining pieces, the pieces are no longer bound to moving from node to node (what is usually referred to as "point-to-point movement"). Instead, the pieces can teleport to any vacant spot on the board.

"Jumping" is another kind of game movement. As with teleportation, jumping allows a piece to move directly to a non-adjacent space without the intervening spaces having any gameplay affect. Jumping differs, however, in that the distance moved has a cost or limit. Jumping is how players move their own pieces in *Backgammon* (the game's teleportation only happens when landing on an opponent's piece). The places to which a *Backgammon* piece can be moved are dictated by dice rolls, but the game spaces between the starting and landing positions (called "points" in *Backgammon*) have no effect. Movement in *Monopoly* similarly ignores the property spaces through which the game pieces travel.

"Sequential" movement indicates that the game spaces between a piece's departure and destination have some impact in terms of game mechanics or state. For example, *Chess* pieces (aside from knights) cannot pass through other pieces. *Marrakech*'s fiction (Assam, the owner of a market, walking across rugs laid out by vendors) suggests sequential movement. However, in terms of game mechanics, Assam is jumping from spot to spot—the intervening spaces he passes through have no impact on the game.

The knights in *Chess* have a jumping movement—but the knight equivalent in *Xiangqi* and *Janggi* ("ma" or horse) moves sequentially. A horse's move is done in two steps: first an orthogonal move to an adjacent node followed by a diagonal move that is 45 degrees to either side of the direction of the orthogonal move (figure 8.10). If the orthogonal space is not vacant, then the move cannot be made.

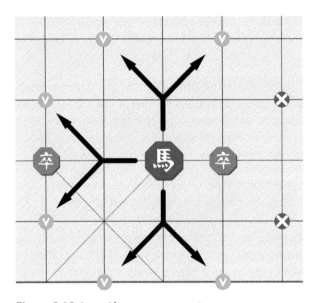

Figure 8.10 *Janggi* horse movement.

EXERCISE Movement

Choose an existing tabletop game (perhaps one in this book or from www.funmines.com/games) and analyze how its pieces move. Is their movement sequential, teleporting, jumping, fixed in place, or something altogether different? Make a variant of the game by changing the forms of movement used by the pieces. Your goal is to make an interesting new variant, so you want the game mechanic implications to be reasonably significant. Adjust the game's rules accordingly.

Diagonals

The geometry of a game space can impact the speed at which game pieces move. Diagonal movement on grids, in particular, can distort a game piece's rate of travel. The diagonal distance between the centers of squares on a grid is √2 (approximately 1.41) times longer than the orthogonal distance between the centers of squares on a grid. This means that a game piece that moves one square diagonally is moving 1.41 times as fast as a game piece that moves one square orthogonally.

In abstract games (such as *Chess*) the difference in diagonal and orthogonal speed may not be an issue, but it can be undesirable for more simulation-oriented games. Consider the map in figure 8.11. The distances from London to Moscow and to Cairo are equal in terms of squares—five orthogonal squares to Moscow and five diagonal squares to Cairo.

The actual distance from London to Moscow is 1550 miles (2500 km) versus 2175 miles (3500 km) to Cairo. If you were designing a game about World War II, it may be desirable to have the game mechanics treat London as being farther from Cairo than it is from Moscow.

One solution commonly employed by wargames is to use hexes instead of a square grid because the distances from the center of one hex to the center of each of its adjacent hexes is the same. In figure 8.12, London is five hexes from Moscow and seven hexes from Cairo. Five hexes is 71.4% of the distance of seven hexes, very close to the 71.2% in real-world geography.

The drawback of hexes is that unless one is creating a game about beehives or chicken wire, their shape does not correspond to anything we generally encounter. Rectilinear grids may not be particularly suited for representing geographical and political boundaries, but do tend to work well for representing rooms, buildings, and cities. Figure 8.13 illustrates four methods for handling diagonal movement within a square grid (Fisher 2011).

One possibility is to simply disallow diagonal movement (as shown in the bottom left quadrant in figure 8.13) and require two orthogonal moves to reach the adjacent diagonal square. The disadvantage is that this approach results in diagonal movement being slower than orthogonal movement (represented by the gray shading). It takes twice as many moves to reach a diagonal as it takes to reach an equivalent orthogonal—whereas spatially it is only 1.41 times as far.

As we saw in the London/Moscow/Cairo example, having diagonal movement cost the same as orthogonal movement allows quicker movement on the

Figure 8.11 Measuring distance in squares.

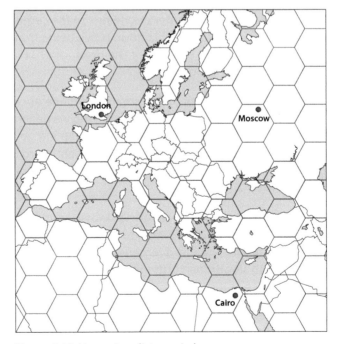

Figure 8.12 Measuring distance in hexes.

diagonal. The shading in figure 8.13 shows that this method (bottom right quadrant) results in four diagonal moves covering the same distance as six orthogonal moves.

The method employed by Wizards of the Coast's *d20 System* is to have diagonal movement alternate between costing one and two movement points (Wizards of the Coast 2003). This means that a game piece that moves one orthogonal square a turn could make its first diagonal move whenever the player wanted. After making a diagonal move, however, the piece's owner would have to wait two turns to save up the two movement points to make a second diagonal move. The third time the piece was moved diagonally, the movement cost would return to one (so a third diagonal move could be made immediately following the second one). And so on. The upper right quadrant in figure 8.13 illustrates this kind of movement.

Similar to the *d20 System*'s alternating cost method, but less complicated, is to simply not allow a piece to make two consecutive diagonal moves. This method has the advantage of not requiring a piece with a base movement of one space per turn to sit still for a turn in order to move diagonally. The piece can move every turn, it just cannot make a diagonal move two turns in a row. However, this method is slightly less accurate than the alternating cost method in terms of the distance covered. The alternating cost method treats the distances between diagonal spaces as being 1.5 times farther apart than orthogonal spaces (which is fairly close to their real distance of 1.41 orthogonal square lengths). In contrast, the non-consecutive diagonal method treats diagonal moves as being 1.2 times the orthogonal length, allowing for five diagonal moves to cover the same distance as six orthogonal moves (see the upper left quadrant in figure 8.13).

No consecutive diagonal movement

Diagonal movement cost alternates between 1 & 2

No diagonal movement

Diagonal movement costs 1

Figure 8.13 Each quadrant of this image (based on images by Robert Fisher) uses a different rule for diagonal movement. The colored squares indicate the number of steps to reach that position when using the quadrant's rule. The circle's radius corresponds to the distance covered in six orthogonal steps.

CASE STUDY *Kill Doctor Lucky*

James Ernest's *Kill Doctor Lucky* is something of a prequel to *Clue*. In the game, players vie to be the one to do away with the doctor. The game is set in Dr. Lucky's mansion, which is represented by irregular areas (figure 8.14). Each room, hallway, and staircase is a discrete space. The players are each represented by a game piece representing their character, over which they have exclusive control. The players also have a limited degree of control over a shared game piece that represents Dr. Lucky.

The gameplay involves players making many attempts on Dr. Lucky's life. In order to make a murder attempt, a player's game piece must be in the same room as Dr. Lucky's game piece and out of sight of any other player piece. The line of sight rules are:

> If a player can stand in one room and look straight (perpendicularly) through any number of doorways into your room, he can see you. So, for example,

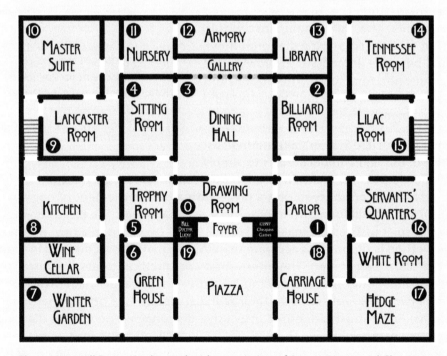

Figure 8.14 *Kill Doctor Lucky* used with permission of James Ernest and Cheapass Games.

someone standing in the Kitchen can see (and be seen by) people in the Master Suite, the west stairs, the two adjoining hallways, the Trophy Room, the Wine Cellar, and the Winter Garden.

(Ernest 2011)

For the purposes of murder attempts, the line of sight rule defines a kind of adjacency, although not one related to movement.

Players can move their game piece one "step" each turn. A step means moving from one room/hallway/staircase to another through a doorway. In addition to this one step move, players can use a Move Card or a Room Card for additional movement.

Move Cards provide up to three extra steps, which the player can use on her own piece or to move Dr. Lucky's piece. This movement could be either sequential or jumping since there is nothing in the game mechanics that would require it to be one or the other. Room Cards allow players to teleport their own playing piece or Dr. Lucky's to the room indicated on the card.

Dr. Lucky makes a jumping move after every player's turn. This jumping is Dr. Lucky's primary way of moving, though (as noted) players can move him using cards. When Dr. Lucky makes his standard jumping movement, he jumps to the room that is numbered one higher than his current room (19 moves back to 0). For example, if Dr. Lucky is in the Kitchen (room 8) at the end of a player's turn, he would jump to the Lancaster Room (room 9). For the player's pieces, the Kitchen is three steps away from the Lancaster Room, but for Dr. Lucky's jumping move the two rooms are adjacent. Conversely, the Green House (room 6) and the Piazza (room 19) are adjacent to the player's pieces, but are thirteen jump moves apart for Dr. Lucky.

CHAPTER NINE

Choices

INTRODUCTION

It is a basic paradox of games that while the rules themselves are generally definite, unambiguous, and easy to use, the enjoyment of a game depends on these easy-to-use rules presenting challenges that cannot be easily overcome.

(Juul 2005, 5)

The learning objectives for this chapter are:

1 Understand the differences between actions and events.

2 Learn to identify when a game offers boring choices.

3 Understand how conflicting goals can create interesting choices.

Actions and Events

Actions are game mechanics that involve some form of player choice. Examples of actions include deciding where to place a rug in *Marrakech*, what nodes to connect in *Sprouts*, and whether to shoot in *Shoot-Out*. Actions are defined by the game's mechanics and impact the game state. Not every choice a player makes over the course of a game is an action. The way a player organizes the cards in his hand is a choice, but not one that typically involves a game mechanic or impacts the game state. Similarly, two players may choose to ally themselves against the game's frontrunner, but that choice is not an action unless the game has formal rules regarding player alliances.

The flip side of actions are events. Events are game mechanics that are triggered by the game's rules and do not incorporate player choice. Examples of events include paying for landing on a rug in *Marrakech*, adding a node on a just-drawn line in *Sprouts*, and ending a turn after a missed shot in *Shoot-Out*.

"Event" is a term that is often applied to secondary game mechanics that are conditional—that happen in response to a particular game state or other mechanic. This book's use of the term is broader and includes core (not just secondary) game mechanics if they do not involve player choice. The player dice rolls in *The Tower* and *Monopoly* are events that are part of their games' core mechanic.

Insofar as a distinction is useful, we could describe events happening on a regular cycle (such as every turn) as "fixed events" and events that are triggered less uniformly as "conditional events." Rolling dice in *Monopoly* is a fixed event; getting an extra turn by rolling doubles is a conditional event.

Because tabletop games require player intervention to update the board's representation of the game state, it can sometimes be unclear whether a particular mechanic is a player-driven action or a system-driven event. The aforementioned dice rolling events in *The Tower* and *Monopoly* might seem better categorized as actions because they are activated by a player's hand. However, the player does not have any choice about whether to roll the dice or not; nor does the player have any real way of influencing the roll's outcome; nor does the player have any influence over how the roll affects the game state. This lack of player agency (control over one's fate) is why the dice rolls in *The Tower* and *Monopoly* are events, not actions.

Another situation in which a player has no choice can be seen in Move 6 of the *Tabletop Billiards* example game on page 31. The only legal move is the one shown (and the game's rules require the player to take it). The player has no choice in the matter whatsoever. Given the definitions that have been put forth, it may seem natural to categorize this *Tabletop Billiards* move as an event. However, this risks obscuring the fact that the game's movement was designed primarily to be a mechanic that involves player decision. So it is useful to maintain the distinction between a mechanic for which a player never has a choice (such as a *Shoot-Out* pawn moving back three spaces when shot) versus a situation in which a mechanic typically supports player choice, but the choices have been winnowed down to one due to the particular game state. For example, if it is white's turn in figure 9.1, the player has only one legal move: the king must move to square h2. When a player has only one "choice" in this way, it could be called a "forced action."

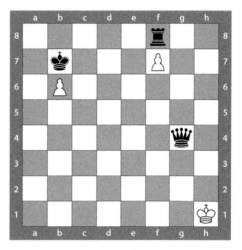

Figure 9.1 *Chess* pieces by Colin M.L. Burnett, CC-BY-SA-3.0.

Games often have actions that players are required to take, but have some choice in regard to how it is done. For example, if it were black's turn in figure 9.1, the player does not have a choice about whether to move a piece (she *must*), but she does have a choice about which piece to use for the required action. This sort of situation in which a player must perform the action, but some choice in regard to how it is done, could be called a "required action."

The *Marrakech* action of placing a rug is a required action. The action of rotating Assam is something that a player can freely choose to do or not. An action that is entirely optional could be called a "voluntary action."

Table 9.1

Actions: mechanics that involve player choice
Voluntary action: completely optional
Required action: must be performed
Forced action: a required action with only one possible "choice"
Events: mechanics that do not involve player choice
Fixed event: occurs on a regular cycle
Conditional event: occurs intermittently in response to particular game states or actions

EXERCISE Action!

Start by taking a look at the list below of forty kinds of actions (Järvinen 2008, 385–394). For each of them, see if you can think of an instance where you have encountered it in a game. For example, the act of playing a rug in *Marrakech* involves "placement." For the actions you cannot tie to a particular game, can you imagine a design that might incorporate it? Can you think of any actions in addition to the ones listed?

Select a game that you would like to modify (perhaps one of the traditional games at www.funmines.com/tag/traditional-game). Play the game several times and compile a list of the actions and events it contains. Classify each *action* as being voluntary or required and by type (either from the list below or your additions to it). Classify each *event* as being fixed or conditional.

After analyzing the game's actions and events, choose one or more of the events to convert into an action. You accomplish this by changing the event's mechanic so that it incorporates some form of player choice. Try playing the game a few times to test out your change. How did it affect the game's dynamics? Does it improve the game or detract from it?

Accelerating/Decelerating	Information-Seeking
Aiming & Shooting	Jumping
Allocating	Maneuvering
Arranging	Motion
Attacking/Defending	Moving
Bidding	Operating
Browsing	Performing
Building	Placing
Buying/Selling	Point-to-Point Movement
Catching	Powering
Choosing	Sequencing
Composing	Sprinting/Slowing
Conquering	Storytelling
Contracting	Submitting
Controlling	Substituting
Conversing	Taking
Discarding	Trading
Enclosing	Transforming
Expressing	Upgrading/Downgrading
Herding	Voting

Boring Decisions

Game designer Sid Meier famously stated that, "A game is a series of interesting choices" (Rollings & Morris, 2003, 38). According to Meier, the characteristics of an interesting choice are:

1. No single option should be best;
2. The options should not be equally good; and
3. The player must be able to make an informed choice.

(Rouse 2005, 27–28)

Another way of putting this is that decisions are uninteresting if they are obvious, meaningless, or blind (Brathwaite & Schreiber 2008).

Obvious Decisions

Any decision is obvious when one of the player's options is clearly superior to the others. For example, the choice between being paid $5 or $20 is an obvious one (or at least it is for most people).

Imagine if it were black's turn (instead of white's turn) in the *Chess* game shown in figure 9.1. Black has thirty-nine possible moves. However, one of those moves (the rook to h8) puts the white king into checkmate and wins the game for black. Given that, even though the choice is not literally forced, there is obviously only one move for black to make.

When you played *Marrakech*, at several points in the game you probably had the choice to either rotate Assam towards a direction where he could land on an opponent's rug, or a direction where there were no rugs at all within his movement range. The choice to face him away from the rugs is obvious.

"Obvious" should not be interpreted as meaning immediately apparent. What it means is when the implications of the choices are fully understood, there is a clear best choice (Extra Credits 2010). Because players have varying levels of skill and insight, an obvious decision for one player may not be so for another. The decisions in *Tic-Tac-Toe* are obvious for adults, but interesting and not obvious for small children. The reason *Tic-Tac-Toe* becomes boring as its players grow up, is that they become able to foresee the lines of play that extend from each possible move. Keep this in mind whenever you are designing a game with choices that can be quantified and calculated. For a player who is able to do the calculation, the decision may not be any more interesting than making a move in *Tic-Tac-Toe*.

Meaningless Decisions

A meaningless decision is one that does not offer a real difference. The choice between being paid two $10 bills or one $20 bill is meaningless. In game terms, a meaningless decision is one that does not have any impact on the game state and, therefore, cannot affect how the game plays out.

At the start of a game of *Tabletop Billiards* (page 29), there seems to be six possible opening moves (see figure 9.2).

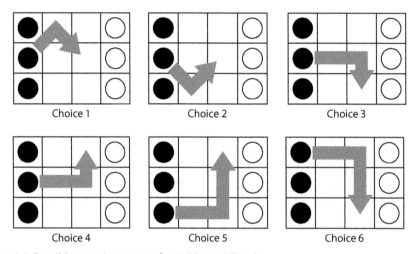

Figure 9.2 Possible opening moves for *Tabletop Billiards*.

However, the six moves do not result in six truly unique game states. Choice one and choice two have the same outcome. The positions resulting from choice three and choice four are mirror images of one another, as are the positions stemming from choices five and six. These mirrored positions are identical in the same way that the choice to mark one corner in as the first move in a *Tic-Tac-Toe* game is really the same as marking any other corner. So while there seems to be six possible choices for the first move in *Tabletop Billiards*, those choices actually boil down to three unique possibilities. The difference between choices one and two is meaningless, as are the mirrored outcomes of choices three and four and choices five and six.

Some decisions are meaningless in terms of their effect on the game state, yet are still important in terms of the game's fiction and/or the player experience (Schreiber, *Decision-Making and Flow Theory* 2009). *Mass Effect* gives players the choice of having Shepard, the player's character, be male or female. The gameplay impact of the choice is minimal, yet it is something that generates a lot of passion in the game's players ("FemShep is best Shep"). Similarly, the choice of what player piece to use in a game of *Monopoly* is meaningless for purposes of winning, yet everyone has their favorite piece (to the point that a fight over the tokens could break out before the game even begins).

Blind Decisions

A blind decision is one in which the player is unable to apply any strategic reasoning. Unlike a meaningless decision, a blind decision affects the game state (or at least has the potential to do so). One way of determining who plays which color in a game of *Chess* is for one of the players to hide a pawn of each color in either hand. The other player chooses a fist; the piece that it concealed becomes that player's side. The choice of left fist or right fist is a blind decision; there is no strategic reason to prefer one hand over the other. However, the decision is not meaningless because the option selected will determine which player has the advantage of moving first.

Dominant Strategies

A dominant strategy is a player choice or set of choices that provide a marked advantage over players who are not employing the same strategy. Essentially, it is an obvious choice that has taken over the game.

Suppose a coin flip is not entirely fair—that there is a slightly better chance for one side to come up than the other. If a coin has a 51% probability of landing heads side up, which side would you choose when flipping it? The logical choice would be heads since there is a greater chance of that being the winning side. A player who continually chooses heads will come out ahead over the course of many flips. This is a dominant strategy because the effectiveness it offers leads to it dictating the player's actions—there are no real choices to be made.

Players who discover a dominant strategy for a game may enjoy it for a while—especially if it sets them on a winning streak. However, the enjoyment can quickly stale from the dominant strategy robbing the game of interesting choices.

Zamboni Doodle is a Google Doodle game in which the player is tasked with smoothing out the ice on a skating rink. The Zamboni's fuel is limited and the player's challenge is to smooth the ice using as efficient a path as possible (so as to not run out of fuel before completing the task). If the Zamboni is driven too quickly, control can be lost as it slides during turns. The problem with driving too slow is . . . well, there is no problem. The fuel depletes based on the distance moved, not the amount of time it is driven. This means that there is no disadvantage to driving slowly and carefully. The dominant strategy in the game is to move at a snail's pace. Doing so is not fun, but it gets the best results.

It is not practical (or even necessarily desirable) to try to make every player decision in a game an interesting one. Interesting choices are stressful, and players may welcome some relief from them in the same way that a horror film has suspense that ebbs and flows in order to allow the audience recovery time. Obvious choices can occasionally also be satisfying in their own right—especially if the obviously good choice was made possible from earlier less obvious choices.

Even if you wished to, it would be very difficult to have every player choice be interesting. Games are dynamic systems—the pressures they place on players shift, which in turn can cause a given choice to shift in how much interest it might generate. At the start of a *Shoot-Out* duel, the decision to move rather than shoot is usually an obvious one. At some point during the game (at exactly what point varies based on the game state), the choice between shooting or moving becomes less obvious and more interesting. Why this is the case is explored in the next section of this chapter, "Interesting Choices."

Interesting Choices

Games usually present players with a number of goals. The primary goal is (usually) winning the game, and along the path to achieving that goal are incremental milestones in the form of sub-goals. A *Chess* player might have a goal of capturing her opponent's queen. Someone playing *Shoot-Out* might have a goal of having his gunslinger/pawn reach a certain spot before attempting to shoot. In *Monopoly*, players are almost certainly striving to collect all the properties in a particular color-group in order to fulfill a goal of building houses and hotels.

These goals provide the game with structure and give the players something immediate to do when the end of the game still seems remote. Ideally, a player feels that she is actively working towards one or more goals every turn of the game. Sid Meier is a master at finding ways to layer goals. His games usually involve players simultaneously pursuing big, long-term goals and one or two more immediate, less major goals. The result is that players continually want to play a few more minutes to finish the next minor goal, which is then conveniently replaced with a new goal that is just a few minutes off. It is all to easy to have one's entire evening disappear in this manner.

The places where a player's goals do not align can be particularly fertile ground for generating interesting choices (Extra Credits 2010). A *Hive* player wants to surround his opponent's Queen Bee while keeping his own Queen Bee protected—the choice of what to do becomes interesting when these goals conflict and the player has to choose one over the other.

As long as a computer roleplaying game character can freely pick up and carry every item she comes across, the decision to pick items up is not interesting. It becomes interesting, sometimes wrenchingly so, when the character's pack becomes full and the player has to start choosing things to throw away.

Driving slowly in *Zamboni Doodle* is boring because it does not conflict with another goal. It could be made interesting if a conflicting goal was designed into the game—perhaps one that puts time pressure on the player. For example, perhaps the game is lost if the rink is not cleared fast enough. Or perhaps moving slowly uses the gas less efficiently. Or perhaps if the player takes too long, skaters come out and cut more lines into the ice.

When you are looking to add interest to your designs, try taking a similar approach. Think about situations you could introduce that would force the player to prioritize and choose one goal to favor over another. These kinds of choices can be interesting not only as intellectual challenges, but also emotionally because they can tap into the powerful human fear of regret—that the consequences of not giving priority to the unpursued goal will prove to be worse than expected.

In *Challenges for Game Designers*, Brenda Brathwaite and Ian Schreiber categorize these sorts of "prioritizing" decisions into three types: trade-offs, dilemmas, and risk versus rewards (Brathwaite and Schreiber 2009, 85–87). To these, a fourth might be added: sacrifices.

Trade-Off

A trade-off involves a player not being able to take every action he desires. Instead, the player must choose which actions (and goals) to favor. The option to retreat in *Shoot-Out* involves a trade-off. When a player retreats, he is choosing to favor gaining two revolver bullets over continuing to contest the duel. The benefit of one action (possibly winning the duel) must be weighed against the benefit of the other (gaining two bullets).

Dilemma

A dilemma, like a trade-off, requires the player to prioritize an action to favor over the others. However, where a trade-off involves choosing between actions that the player wants to do, a dilemma forces the player to select between actions that are disadvantageous. *Shoot-Out*'s choice between spending a rifle bullet or a revolver bullet is a dilemma—a player would prefer to spend nothing when shooting, but that is not an option.

Risk Versus Rewards

Risk versus rewards are choices in which the more a player risks, the more she stands to gain. The risk can come from varying levels of likelihood and/or from varying levels of the potential negative consequence.

For example, playing red on a roulette table has a 47.37% chance of success and will pay out $1 for every dollar bet. Betting on a single number has a 2.63% chance of success and pays out $35 for every dollar bet. Winning a bet on a single number provides a greater reward because it involves a greater risk of losing. Similarly, betting $5 on red provides a greater reward than betting $1 because the player is risking more money on the bet.

Shoot-Out's choice between shooting and moving is a risk versus reward choice. Shooting pushes back the opponent three spaces and gives the player an additional turn, but only if the die is rolled high enough. Moving advances the player only one space and ends the turn, but its outcome is certain and does not require a successful die roll. Shooting provides a greater reward, but at a greater risk. *Shoot-Out* is designed so that this choice's level of risk (and the importance of the reward) fluctuates throughout the duel, which helps keep the game interesting.

Sacrifice

A sacrifice comes when an option contains both positive and negative consequences. For example, a fantasy game might contain a powerful sword that makes the wielder more vulnerable to magical attacks. Choosing to use that sword involves a sacrifice—making oneself weaker against wizards. In *Shoot-Out*, using a rifle bullet sacrifices a scarce resource in return for adding three to the die roll's result.

But Aren't These All the Same Thing?

It may have struck you that any one of the above *Shoot-Out* examples could have been used to illustrate a different decision type. In fact, the use of a rifle bullet was described as both a sacrifice and as part of a dilemma. Rifle bullets could also be used in an example of a trade-off: the choice between having a better chance to hit (rifle bullets) or using a more abundant resource (revolver bullets). Or they could be an example of risk versus reward—the risk of wasting a valuable rifle bullet versus the reward of a successful shot.

What decision type a choice entails is a matter of perspective. While a given decision may more naturally be categorized as one type or another, ultimately it is the player's frame of mind that determines what kind of decision she is making as she weighs the options. If the player is running low on bullets, she may be more conscious of the sacrifice in using one. If the opponent is getting close to the center of town, the player may be most conscious of the risk and reward of shooting this turn as opposed to simply moving her pawn.

These categories of choices are useful because they help you think about and be intentional in terms of the experience you are trying to provide players through the choices you pose. A vampire-themed game that is supposed to be dark and brooding might be best served by dilemma and sacrifice oriented choices. A children's game might call for trade-offs and risk versus reward choices. If you find that your design choices are all framed in a similar manner, you may want to try varying their choice types. If your core mechanic seems tedious, perhaps it is too static in terms of the types of decisions it offers the players. See if you can revise the mechanic in such as way that the choices tend to shift from one decision type to another, based on the state of the game.

Marrakech for Two

The rules for playing a two-person game of *Marrakech* demonstrate how introducing conflicting goals can make a choice more interesting. In a two-person game, each player uses two colors of rugs instead of only one. The two colors are mixed together, put into a stack, and played in order.

When landing on an opponent's rug, the colors are treated as separate. A player only has to pay a number of Dirham equal to the number of contiguous squares of the color landed upon, not the contiguous squares of both of the opponent's rug colors.

When playing with a single color of rug, the choice of where to lay it has the conflicting goals of wanting to improve one's own rug layout and wanting to weaken the opponents' rug layouts. Playing with two colors of rugs adds an additional conflicting goal—the desire to increase the scoring capability of the color being played while wanting to avoid diminishing the scoring capability of the player's other color.

Ultimate *Tic-Tac-Toe*

This game revitalizes *Tic-Tac-Toe* by adding interesting choices. In this case, each player's move determines the places where the opponent can move next. Players have to weigh the benefit of making a desired move against the moves it enables the opponent to make.

Players:

■ Two players

Required Materials:

■ Pen & paper

Object of the Game:

- To achieve a three-in-a-row in three small *Tic-Tac-Toe* boards, which themselves form a three-in-a-row in the large *Tic-Tac-Toe* board. If neither player accomplishes this, the winner is the player who has achieved the most small three-in-a-rows overall.

Setup:

- Draw a large *Tic-Tac-Toe* board. Draw a small *Tic-Tac-Toe* board in each of the large board's nine cells (see figure 9.3a).

Rules:

- The first player marks an "X" in one of the small board's spaces (see figure 9.3a).
- The position of that "X" within its small board dictates in which of the nine small boards the second player's next move must occur. In the example game below, the first "X" was placed in the left of the small board's center row. This means that the second player must place an "O" in one of the unfilled spaces in the small board that occupies the left of the large board's center row (figure 9.3b).

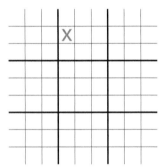

Figure 9.3a Move 1.

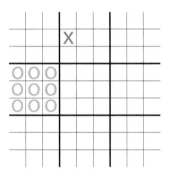

Figure 9.3b Possible positions for Move 2.

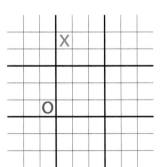

Figure 9.3c Move 2.

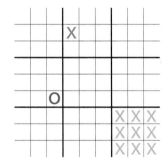

Figure 9.3d Possible positions for move 3

- The players continue taking turns claiming unfilled spaces in the small board that corresponds to the opponent's previous move. For example, in figure 9.3c the second player chose to claim the small board's bottom-right space. Therefore, the first player must make his next move in one of the nine spaces that make up the small board that is located in the large board's bottom-right (figure 9.3d).
- A player who achieves three-in-a-row on a small board "owns" it. *Note: both players own a board if they both have three-in-a-row on it.*
- A player sent to a small board whose spaces are already all filled, can claim any open spot on any small board.
- The first player who owns three small boards in a row, wins the game. If neither player achieves this, then the winner is the player who has achieved the most small three-in-a-rows.

Variations:

- If a player is sent to a small board that is owned (i.e., a three-in-a-row already exists on it), but not entirely filled, the player can take an additional turn in the small board that is associated with the space she claims in the owned board.
- For a quicker game, the winner can be whoever is the first player to get three-in-a-row on a small board.
- Instead of having the victory determined by three-in-a-row, the winner is the player who has the longest consecutive line of Xs or Os across the entire large board.

EXERCISE Adding Choice

Ultimate Tic-Tac-Toe improves *Tic-Tac-Toe* by adding meaningful choice to it. Pick a game that lacks choice (such as *Hut, The Tower, Candy Land, Snakes & Ladders*, etc.). Add to or alter its mechanics in order to create goals that conflict and lead to interesting choices for the players.

EXERCISE Reviewing Your *ZimP*

Chapter 6 included an exercise in which you applied your own theme to the mechanics of *Zombie in my Pocket*. Replay your "in my pocket" game several times. While you play the game, track every choice you make and the type of choice it is. What goals are you pursuing in the game and how do they conflict? Based on what you have learned in this chapter, can you think of any ways that you might improve the number of interesting choices in the game?

CHAPTER TEN

Chance

INTRODUCTION

Games are engines of uncertainty. It is one of the traits that makes a game a game. Even games whose outcomes seem inevitable contain some spark of uncertainty. It is not *entirely* impossible that a *Chess* novice beats a Grandmaster or that *Tic-Tac-Toe* does not end in a draw. It is true that a game of *Tetris* cannot end in anything but a loss, but the final score is unknown in advance of playing.

Game designer Greg Costikyan has pointed out that it is human nature to dread uncertainty. An uncertain good thing (the possibility of promotion) can be nearly as stressful as an uncertain bad thing (the possibility of being laid off). In the same way that we enjoy experiencing the thrill of fear in tamed and nonthreatening constructs (horror films and roller coaster rides), games give us the opportunity to dive into uncertainty without putting anything real at risk (Costikyan 2013, 1–2).

This chapter explores how certainty and uncertainty can be incorporated into games and the kinds of roles they serve.

The learning objectives for this chapter are:

1 Understand the meanings of determinism, nondeterminism, certainty, and risk.

2 Understand the differences between perfect and imperfect information.

3 Be able to determine probabilities for common game situations.

Determinism and Risk

The way a *Chess* or *Ultimate Tic-Tac-Toe* game progresses is wholly determined by the players; there are no dice rolls, shuffled cards, spinners, or any other agents of randomness involved. Such games are known as "deterministic" games. A deterministic game's uncertainty comes from not knowing what choices the other players will make—but the effect of a given choice is entirely certain. If a deterministic game is played with the same set of choices that were made in a previous game, the outcome will be entirely identical. This is why we can recreate a *Chess* game from 400 years ago by simply replaying its recorded moves.

A nondeterministic game is one that incorporates some form of randomness. *Shoot-Out*'s use of dice rolls and *Zombie in my Pocket*'s use of shuffled decks make both games nondeterministic. Because the tiles are shuffled, a game of *Zombie in my Pocket* cannot be replayed by simply making the same choices. The position, rotation, and placement of the tiles may be the same, but the tiles themselves will be different. The only way to replay the game is to remove the nondeterministic element, stacking the deck so that it matches the previous game. In other words, making it a deterministic game.

Nondeterminism in games often takes the form of a player attempting an action whose outcome is decided using some random factor (such as a dice roll). For example, the action of moving Assam in *Marrakech* involves a player choosing a direction and then rolling a die to determine the distance traveled. That action would not be as interesting if the distance was fixed and not determined randomly. Nor would it be as interesting if the distance was determined prior to the player choosing his direction. What makes the choice interesting are the situations in which the player is taking a chance and the die roll will decide whether or not the player will lose Dirham.

Marrakech uses a custom die. It has one side marked "1," two sides marked "2," two sides marked "3," and one side marked "4." When deciding how to rotate Assam, savvy players take into account that he is most likely to move two or three spaces. When a player knows an action's possible outcomes and their likelihoods (as is the case for Assam's movement), then the player choice involves what game theorists call "risk" (Klibanoff 1996). In contrast, if the action's possible outcomes or their probabilities are not known, then the player is dealing with what game theorists term "uncertainty" (Rasmusen 2007, 49–50).

It is worth noting that a mechanic that is designed to incorporate risk does not mean that every player will approach the decision in such a manner. A player who does not understand (or has not thought through) the probable outcomes of a decision is experiencing uncertainty rather than risk. The difference between uncertainty and risk may seem slight, but the experience can be markedly different for a player. Have you ever felt a bit lost when playing an unfamiliar game because you do not understand the implications of the choices you are making? That is uncertainty. As you gain a better understanding of the game's system and scope, your choices become better informed and you feel more comfortable making them. That is risk.

Most tabletop game mechanics are designed to incorporate risk rather than uncertainty. This is because tabletop game players need to fully understand the game's actions, their possible outcomes, and how those outcomes are determined. Video games, with their ability to hide their inner workings, are much more able to incorporate uncertainty into their gameplay, which is why they can provide a sense of discovery not readily available in tabletop games.

Another way that nondeterminism can be incorporated into games is by having a random event precede a player's choice rather than follow it. For example, a player might be presented with a randomly determined set of choices, of which the player is free to choose any of the options and knows the certain outcome for each. For example, *Zombie in My Pocket*'s tile placing mechanic could be converted to using this kind of preceding nondeterminism by having the decision of where the tile is placed occur after it is drawn, instead of before it.

Pachisi, *Yut Nori*, and *Backgammon* all involve players first generating a random number for movement and then deciding how to allocate the movement points to their pieces. The player has to utilize a randomly determined resource, but the outcome of the choice itself is not subject to randomness. Game theorists would describe such a decision as having "certainty" because the player knows the precise outcome for each possible choice (Rasmusen 2007, 49–50). Certainty in a nondeterministic game can de-emphasize the role of luck. That said, a player may still view this sort of choice as being risk-based if she takes into account the probabilistic events that will precede future actions, and not just the ones that occurred before the current one. For example, choosing to move a pawn in *Shoot-Out* involves certainty—the action always results in the pawn moving one space forward. However, a player may view the decision to move as a calculated risk if he is focused on the probability of his opponent successfully shooting the pawn in the following turn.

Button Men

This is a clever little game for two players that was designed by James Ernest of Cheapass Games. Links to more information and additional fighters can be found at www.funmines.com/buttonmen.

Players:

■ Two players

Required Materials:

■ One fighter for each player (choose from the four that follow these rules).
■ An assortment of dice: the specific dice needed is determined by the fighters played. See "Dice setup" below.

Object of the Game:

■ To win three rounds of combat through the capture of the opponent's dice.

Dice Setup:

■ Each fighter uses several dice of different sizes, as specified by the numbers on that button. As a general rule, small dice mean speed, and large dice mean strength. An "X" is a variable die, or "Swing Die." You may use any die between 4 and 20 sides for this Swing Die, and you can change that die between rounds. If a fighter has more than one "X," (such as is the case for Ogi) each of those Swing Dice must have the same number of sides.
■ Non-standard sized dice (such as Fingle's 7-sided die, or a player's choice to use a non-standard Swing Die) can be had by using a larger sized die and re-rolling out-of-range values. For example, using the 7-sided die would involve rolling an 8-sided die and re-rolling any resulting "8s."
■ A coin can be used for Ogi's 2-sided die. A heads outcome equates to "1" and a tails to "2."

Rules:

■ A round begins by both players rolling their fighter's dice. Players arrange their dice in a row so they can be easily read. Whoever rolled the single lowest number takes the first turn. If the lowest dice are tied, compare the next lowest dice, and so on. If all the dice are matched, the round is a draw.
■ On each turn a player must make either a "Power Attack" or "Skill Attack."
  ■ Power Attack: Using one die to capture one of the opponent's dice. The number showing on the attacking die must be greater than or equal to the number showing on the captured die.

- Skill Attack: Using several dice to capture one of the opponent's dice. The attacking dice must add up *exactly* to the value showing on the captured die.
- The captured die is removed from play and the attacking die or dice are re-rolled.
- If neither a Power Attack nor a Skill Attack is possible, then the player's turn is passed. Players may not pass if an attack is possible.
- A round ends when one player's dice are all captured or neither player can make a legal attack. The round is scored as detailed below. The highest score wins the round (ties are disregarded), and the first player to win three rounds wins the game.

Scoring:

- Players earn a score equal to the cumulative number of sides for the dice they captured. For example, a player who captured a 20-sided die and an 8-sided die would earn 28 points.
- In addition to the points for capturing dice, players earn points for each of their dice that has not been captured. These dice earn a score equal to half their number of sides. For example, a player who has an 8-sided die that eluded capturing would earn 4 points. A die with an odd number of sides is still worth exactly half its number of sides when retained. For each die of your own which you kept, you score half its size. So, Fingle's 7-sided die would earn its player 3.5 points if it was not captured.

Example turn:

- Shown below are the starting rolls for two *Button Men* players. The size of each die is not important for the example, but the rolls are:

  Bill: 2 4 5 13 18
  Sarah: 2 2 6 9 13

- Sarah goes first because she rolled the lowest single number, not counting the first pair of 2s (which cancel out). Sarah cannot capture Bill's 18, because she does not have dice that add up to its value exactly (Skill Attack) nor does she have a single die showing a value equal or higher (Power Attack).
- Sarah decides to capture Bill's 13. She could do so with her rolled 13 or by using her added together 9, 2, and 2 values. She opts to use her 9, 2, and 2, so she re-rolls them and removes the captured 13.
- Now it is Bill's turn. Bill does not re-roll any dice to begin his turn. Dice are only rolled at the start of the round and when they are used in an attack.

These Button Men are courtesy of James Ernest (designer), Lee Moyer (artist), and *Sanctum* (the game whose characters appear on these buttons).

James Ernest

James Ernest is best known as the founder of Cheapass Games, a small game company in Seattle. He is an award-winning tabletop game designer with more than 150 published games, and is a member of the Origins Awards Hall of Fame. His better-known works include *Kill Doctor Lucky*, *Button Men*, **Lords of Vegas**, and *Pirates of the Spanish Main*. He has contributed to several game design books, including *Rules of Play*, *Hobby Games: the 100 Best*, and the *Kobold Guide to Board Game Design*. He is also an instructor at DigiPen Institute of Technology, where he teaches Introduction to Tabletop Game Design.

Information

A game of "perfect information" is one in which players are able to make their decisions with complete information about the current game state and all the changes that led up to it. *Chess* is a classic example of a game with perfect information—both players are completely aware of the game state throughout the game. Games of "imperfect information" hide some meaningful part of the game state from one or more of the players. *Sea Battle* has imperfect information because the players do not know the positions of each other's ships.

There is a lack of consensus regarding whether a game of perfect information can incorporate chance or whether it must be deterministic. *Backgammon* in particular tends to be used both as an example of perfect information (e.g., Salen & Zimmerman 2004, 204) and of imperfect information (e.g., Millington & Funge 2009, 669). For the purposes of this book, the dividing line between perfect and imperfect information is based upon whether players are able to make their decisions with certainty, that is, whether the player actions themselves have deterministic outcomes and the game state at the time of the decision is fully known. Games with simultaneous actions (such as *Rock Paper Scissors*) are not games of perfect information, however, because players must take their actions without being aware of the simultaneous game state changes being affected by their opponents' actions: players do not know the effect of their decision prior to making it.

By this definition, *Backgammon* is a game of perfect information. A player may not know the values of the dice prior to rolling them, but she does not need to make any decisions in the absence of that knowledge. When the player chooses her moves she is fully informed of the dice's values, the board's current state, and all the earlier moves in the game. The fact that a player does not know the values of future dice rolls does not make the game's information imperfect. An inability to see into the future is a characteristic of all games, both those with perfect information and those with imperfect.

A game that is deterministic is not necessarily a game of perfect information. The position of pieces in *Stratego* involves no randomness and the player making a move knows what affect it will have on the game state. Even so, the game has imperfect information because a player must make decisions without knowing the entire game state (the ranks of the opponent's pieces are hidden and unknown).

Deterministic games of perfect information lend themselves to logical challenges (Novak 2012, 196). The measure of skill in these games is often the ability to look farther ahead and see how various lines of play would resolve. Nondeterministic games of perfect information diminish players' ability to plan ahead, but still allow players to make choices whose impact on the game state is entirely informed. These games call for an ability to respond to changing circumstances and the game state as it currently stands as well as an understanding of probability so as to have some sense of the future game state changes that are likely to come. Games of imperfect information limit the players' ability to determine the best course of action by providing them with only a partial view of the game state (Novak 2012, 196) or of the effect their actions will have on it. These games can call for skills in deduction, working with probability, and mitigating the risks of the unknown.

Cathedral

Cathedral is a deterministic game of perfect information that was designed by Robert P. Moore in the late 1970s. The game's fiction involves two factions competing to dominate a medieval walled city.

Players:

■ Two players

Required Materials:

■ A 10 × 10 gridded board and building game pieces (on the pages that follow these rules)

Object of the Game:

■ Place as many game pieces (which represent buildings) as possible on the board.

Setup:

■ Divide the buildings into red and blue and determine who will place which.
■ The player with the blue buildings places the gray cathedral piece (which is neutral) on the board, aligned with the grid, in any location desired.

Rules:

■ Players take turns placing a building in any vacant space on the board's grid.
■ Players can claim sections of the town by "enclosing" it. See the enclosure rules below.

Enclosure:

■ Players can enclose a section of the board. Enclosing involves surrounding a section of the board with one's own pieces.
■ The edge of the board represents the walls of the city. These walls can be used as part of the enclosure, but the cathedral and the opponent's buildings cannot.
■ For the purposes of enclosure, a player's buildings must connect wall-to-wall. Corner-to-corner connection does not count.
■ To be considered enclosed, *the surrounded space can have no more than one building that does not belong to the player.* This means that the cathedral *or* one of the opponent's pieces can be enclosed. When this happens, the piece is captured (see capturing rules below).
■ A player who encloses a part of the board owns that section of the city and has exclusive rights to place buildings within it (the opponent may not place buildings in that part of the board).
■ Players are not allowed to enclose space on their first turn.
■ The game ends when no further moves can be made by either player. The player with the lowest score wins (see scoring rules below).

Capturing:

■ If the cathedral *or* one of the opponent's pieces is enclosed, it is captured and immediately removed from the board.
■ A captured cathedral is removed from the game.

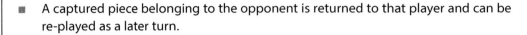

- A captured piece belonging to the opponent is returned to that player and can be re-played as a later turn.

Scoring:

- The player with the lowest score wins the game.
- The buildings that are not on the board and remain in the players' possession add to their scores.
- The number of points a building adds to the score is determined by counting how many grid squares it would fill if it had been played. A building that would occupy one square adds 1 point, a building that would occupy two squares adds 2 points, and so on.
- When a series of games is played, the players alternate placing the cathedral and taking the first turn. The winner of the series is the player who has accumulated the fewest points total.

Strategy:

- Concentrate on claiming space during the early stages of the game.
- Play your largest buildings first.
- Be careful not to let your buildings be captured.
- Never play buildings into your own enclosed space while unenclosed space remains on the board.

Although surrounded by blue buildings, these red pieces are not removed from the space due to the fact that more than one piece is surrounded. The space remaining is still available to both players.

This space is enclosed & claimed for the red pieces. Only red pieces can be played within it.

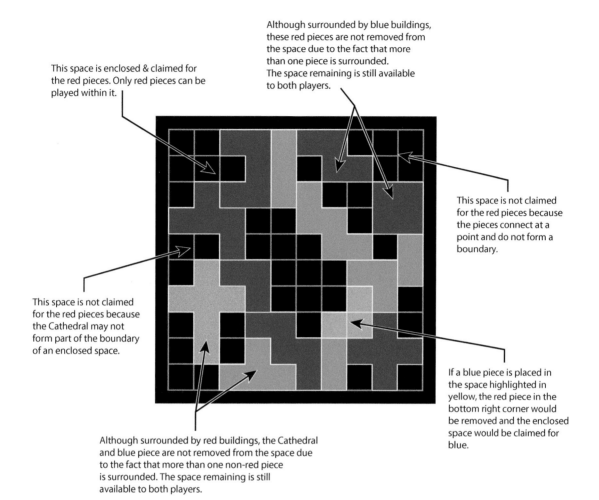

This space is not claimed for the red pieces because the pieces connect at a point and do not form a boundary.

This space is not claimed for the red pieces because the Cathedral may not form part of the boundary of an enclosed space.

If a blue piece is placed in the space highlighted in yellow, the red piece in the bottom right corner would be removed and the enclosed space would be claimed for blue.

Although surrounded by red buildings, the Cathedral and blue piece are not removed from the space due to the fact that more than one non-red piece is surrounded. The space remaining is still available to both players.

These pieces can be a bit frustrating when they are cut out of plain paper. The flimsiness can make them difficult to set down and keep in place. You may want to consider making them from foam core for a better playing experience – or perhaps purchasing the game at your local game store.

EXERCISE Expanding *Cathedral*

Cathedral is a deterministic game of perfect information. For this exercise you will change the game so that it incorporates both chance and imperfect information.

Before modifying the game, be sure to play it a few times using its original rules. As you do so, ask yourself what choices you are making when you select which building to place. See if you can make this choice more interesting in your version of the game.

As you think about the ways in which you can change and expand the game, consider some of the kinds of information that can be hidden. For example, a game piece's location could be hidden, or perhaps its special abilities, or the number of each kind of piece a player owns.

As you design the ways of hiding the game's information, consider whether it should be hidden from both players simultaneously or if it is something that should be "privileged information" that one player knows and the other does not.

Probability

An understanding of probability empowers game designers to shape their designs by helping them to anticipate the dynamics and consequences that might grow out of a game's nondeterministic mechanics. Our intuition about probabilities can be faulty, and even attempts to rigorously calculate probabilities can easily go astray.

While probability can be confusing and unintuitive, do not let the subject matter intimidate you. The remainder of this chapter is devoted to teaching you techniques for determining probabilities in such a way that you do not need to be a statistical genius or whiz at math.

To kick off the topic, try answering this surprising unintuitive probability question: When rolling two 6-sided dice, what is the probability of a "1" being rolled on at least one of them (Knizia 2010, 64)? The solution is later in the chapter, but rather than turning to it immediately, try waiting and see if you want to revise your answer after reading the techniques for determining probability that follow.

Dice Games Properly Explained

This book's explanation of dice and their probabilities is greatly indebted to Reiner Knizia's *Dice Games Properly Explained* (the "Theory of Dice" chapter, in particular). Knizia's book is filled with the rules and strategies of a large number of dice games. It is highly recommended reading.

Flipping Coins and Throwing Dice

What is the probability that a fair coin flip will come up heads? Flipping a coin has two possible outcomes (heads and tails), and it is unlikely to surprise you that heads will come up 50% of the time. Even though you probably require no explanation of why the probability is 50%, it is useful to understand how that number is determined so that the same techniques can be used in less obvious situations.

The probability of heads is calculated by creating a fraction whose numerator (the top) is the number of "heads" outcomes and whose divisor (the bottom) is the total number of possible outcomes. A coin has only one "heads," so the number of heads outcomes is 1. A coin has two possible outcomes ("heads" and "tails"), so the total number of possible outcomes is 2. Thus, our probability fraction for "heads" is 1/2. We can convert that to a decimal number by performing the division, which gives us 0.50. Multiplying that decimal representation of the probability by 100 gives us the percentile form of the probability, 50%. So, as expected, there is a 50% chance that a coin toss will result in heads.

Magicians (and cheaters) sometimes make use of a two-headed coin—a coin with heads on both sides. The two possible outcomes for this kind of coin are heads and heads again. So the number of outcomes yielding heads is 2 and the total number of outcomes are 2. Therefore, the probability of getting heads when flipping a two-headed coin is 2/2. When we perform the division and multiply it by 100, we see that (no surprise) there is 100% chance of heads with a two-headed coin.

We can apply this same approach to dice. By way of example, let us calculate the probability that a 6-sided die will roll a number higher than four. The die has two possible results that are larger than a four: 5 and 6. There are six total possible rolls: 1, 2, 3, 4, 5, 6. Therefore, the likelihood of a 6-sided die rolling a number larger than four is 2/6, or approximately 33%.

As you may remember from math class, determining the likelihood of multiple independent events is done by multiplying the probability of each individual event. For example, since the probability of rolling a number greater than 4 on a 6-sided die is 2/6, the probability of rolling *two* 6-sided dice and having both of them come up with a number greater than 4 is 2/6 * 2/6 = 4/36 = 0.1111 = 11.11%.

Likewise, the probability of getting heads for three coin flips in a row is 1/2 * 1/2 * 1/2 = 1/8 = 0.125 = 12.5%. Here is what is going on behind the coin probability multiplication:

1/2

a.

1. The first flip had two possibilities, one of which is heads. This gives us a 50% chance of a heads outcome (figure 10.1a).

1/4

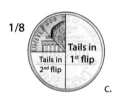

b.

2. When we attempt to get heads three times in a row, half the time we will be stymied with tails on our very first flip. If we did get heads in the first flip, we flip again. This second flip will result in tails half the time, which means only 1/4 of the time will we have gotten heads on the first two flips (figure 10.1b).

1/8

c.

3. If we have been lucky so far, we do one more flip. Half the time this third flip will result in tails (figure 10.1c).
4. So our chances of getting heads three times in a row is 1 in 8.

Figure 10.1 Odds of heads in one (a), two (b), and three (c), coin flips.

Note: While the scenario described above involves sequential coin tosses, the same math would apply to three coins flipped simultaneously.

When the number of potential outcomes is manageable, it can be useful to list them out. For example, Figure 10.2 shows all eight possible outcomes for three flipped coins.

Of the eight possible outcomes, only one results in heads for all three flips (re-confirming the 1/8 chance). If we were interested in knowing the likelihood of getting heads *at least* two times out of three flips, we could count up the number of outcomes that give such as result. There are four such outcomes (#1, #2, #3, and #4), indicating that there is a 4/8 (or 50%) probability of flipping two or more heads. Getting heads *exactly* two times (outcomes #2, #3, and #4) will happen 3 out of 8 times (or 37.5% of the time).

coin 1 coin 2 coin 3

When the author played *Dungeons & Dragons* in his teenage years, a common method of determining a character's statistics (such as "strength," "intelligence," and "dexterity") was to roll four 6-sided dice and use the highest three numbers. What is the probability of getting a maxed out stat of 18 by rolling 6 on at least three of the four dice?

Figure 10.2 Possible outcomes of three coin flips.

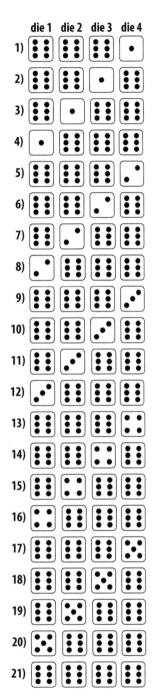

	die 1	die 2	die 3	die 4

1) ... 2) ... 3) ... 4) ... 5) ... 6) ... 7) ... 8) ... 9) ... 10) ... 11) ... 12) ... 13) ... 14) ... 15) ... 16) ... 17) ... 18) ... 19) ... 20) ... 21)

Figure 10.3 Outcomes yielding three or more "6's" when rolling 4D6.

There are 1,296 possible outcomes when rolling four 6-sided dice ($6 \times 6 \times 6 \times 6$), so it is not practical to write out all the possibilities. Instead, we can just focus on listing the outcomes that result in three 6's and divide that by 1,296:

This list shows that there are 21 different ways to achieve three (or more) sixes using 4D6. An alternative way of determining this would be by multiplying 4 * 5 and then adding 1. The 4 and 5 in that calculation come from the fact that each of the **four** dice can have **five** non-6 values when the other three dice roll a 6. The addition of 1 is because there is also the **one** outcome in which all four dice roll 6s.

Having determined that there are 21 ways to roll three 6s, we can then calculate that there is a 21/1,296 (or 1.62%) chance of rolling an 18 using the "4D6 drop lowest" method.

When determining the probability for two events (such as two dice rolls or two coin flips), it can be helpful to create a matrix chart. For example, figure 10.4 is a matrix showing all the possible outcomes for two coin flips.

Figure 10.4 Possible outcomes for two coin flips.

Using the chart, we can quickly see that there is a 1/4 chance of getting heads twice, a 1/4 chance of getting tails twice, and a 2/4 chance of getting one heads and one tails.

Matrices are particularly useful for analyzing situations in which one player is rolling dice against another. For example, imagine you are designing a mechanic in which one player rolls an 8-sided die and the other a 6-sided die. The eight-sider wins when it rolls higher and loses when it ties or rolls lower. What percentage of the time will the 8-sided die win? You might be able to calculate it out, but for many of us (the author included), it is easier and more reliable to determine the probability using a matrix (see figure 10.5):

6-sided die roll

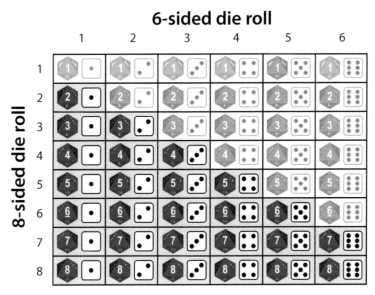

Figure 10.5 Outcomes in which an 8-sided die rolls higher than a 6-side die.

The cells that are highlighted with yellow show the cases in which the 8-sided die's roll beats the 6-sided die's roll. The other cells are ones in which the 6-sided die ties or beats the 8-sided die. By counting up the highlighted cells, we can determine that the 8-sided die will win in 27 out of the 48 outcomes, or 56.25% of the time.

Odds Versus Probability

Odds are used in betting to describe the stakes being put up by the bettors. For example, a horse might be at 1 to 10 odds for winning a race. This means that if the horse does win, the bettors backing it will win ten dollars (or whatever currency the bet is in) for every one that was bet. Often odds are represented using a colon and presented from the bookmaker's perspective. So a horse that has 1 to 10 odds for winning the race would be typically presented as having 10:1 odds against winning.

It is *very* easy to confuse odds with probability because they communicate the same thing, but express it in different ways. Odds are the ratio of the number of times the outcome is expected to happen compared to the number of times it does *not* happen. In contrast, probability is the ratio of the number of times the outcome happens compared to the total number of possible outcomes. Our 1 to 10 odds in the horse race means that for every one time the horse would win, it would lose 10 times. As a probability, the horse would be said to have 1 in 11 (or 1/11 or 0.09) chance of winning because the horse will win one time out of every 11 races. (It is worth noting that odds are usually spoken as being one number "to" another, while chances are one number "in" another.)

The odds that a randomly picked day is a weekend is 2:5, whereas the probability is 2/7. If the odds are mistakenly treated as a probability, then the chance of the day being a weekend would be calculated as a 2/5 (or 40%) chance, instead of the correct 28.6% chance, and we would have an extra four weekend days every month.

The odds of heads in a coin flip are 1:1, meaning there are "even" odds and the event is as likely to not happen as it is to happen. The probability of heads is 1/2 (or 50%) because on average heads will come up one time out of every two flips.

Odds are convenient for gambling because gamblers are primarily interested in the calculation of how much money they will potentially win for a given amount of money being bet. Game designers tend to use probability instead of odds because probability can describe not only the event's likelihood, but the method for determining it as well—the outcome of an event with a 2/6 chance can be determined by rolling a 6-sided die and having two of the numbers (say, 5 and 6) indicate success.

EXERCISE Broadsword Versus Longsword

NetHack is an open source fantasy game whose ongoing development dates back to 1987. While *NetHack*'s interface is crude, its gameplay is incredibly deep and detailed.

A broadsword in *NetHack* will deal 2D4 points of damage—meaning that when a sword successfully hits a monster, the amount of damage is determined by rolling two virtual 4-sided dice. A longsword will do 1D8 points of damage. Which sword offers the greater advantage?

A player's choice of which sword to use might be based upon calculating the "expected value" of the damage each sword inflicts. An expected value is the average result of a random event if the event was repeated an infinite number of times. On any given successful attack, the longsword has an equal chance of inflicting any of its possible damage amounts (1, 2, 3, 4, 5, 6, 7, or 8). The expected value of the sword is the average of those possible outcomes—that is, what the sword would inflict on average over the course of an infinite number of successful attacks.

The expected value of the longsword's damage is 4.5 points of damage. That was determined by taking the sum of all the possible outcomes (1 + 2 + 3 + 4 + 5 + 6 + 7 + 8 = 36) and dividing it 8 (the number of possible outcomes). The same method can be used to determine that the broadsword's 4-sided dice each averages 2.5 points of damage (1 + 2 + 3 + 4 = 10 divided by 4 sides = 2.5). Combining the averages of the two dice gives a total expected value of 5 points of damage for the broadsword.

When analyzed in terms of the expected value of damage, the broadsword is preferable. However, a longsword has a greater likelihood of dealing its maximum damage—it does 8 points of damage on average once every eight successful attacks (12.5% of the time).

How likely is the broadsword to inflict its maximum amount of damage? That is for you to calculate. Begin by determining the probabilities for the various amounts of damage the broadsword can inflict. You do this by filling out the matrix in figure 10.6. The vertical numbers 1–4 represent the outcome for one die and the horizontal numbers represent the outcome for the other die. Fill out the cells by adding the die outcome for the cell's column with the die outcome for its row. For example, the cell in the third column and fourth row is filled in with a 7 to indicate its combined dice outcome.

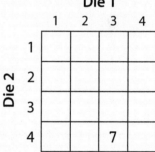

Figure 10.6 Fill in the summed values for every possible 2D4 outcome.

To determine the probability for each amount of damage, count the number of times it occurs in the matrix and divide that by the total number of outcomes. For example, you should find that there is a 2/16 chance of the broadsword dealing 7 points of damage. So what is its likelihood of dealing 8 points of damage?

Suppose that instead of dealing hit point damage, we have a mechanic in which combat is immediately resolved in favor of the person who has the higher roll. Your calculations should have determined that rolling an 8 is more likely on the 1D8 than it is on the 2D4, but does that mean that a longsword has an advantage when matched up against a broadsword?

This can be determined in the same manner as the 6-sided die versus 8-sided die matchup matrix shown in figure 10.5 (page 197). Start by filling in the grayed-out column (the one in

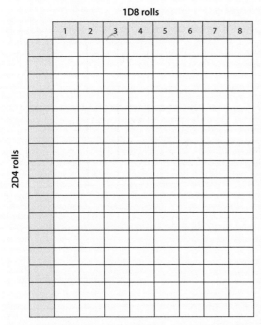

1D8 rolls

	1	2	3	4	5	6	7	8

2D4 rolls

Figure 10.7 Fill in this 2D4 versus 1D8 matchup matrix.

the far left) in figure 10.7 with the 16 possible outcomes for the 2D4. Put the lowest possible outcome in the field at the top, followed by the remaining outcomes in ascending order.

Next, determine how many match-ups result in the 1D8 winning and how many have the 2D4 winning. Note, because of ties, the number of 1D8 wins and 2D4 wins will not add up to 128 (the total number of possible match-ups).

To save yourself time, you can skip filling in every field in the table and just mark the ties. Assuming your 2D4 values in the first column are in ascending order, the fields to the upper-right of ties represent wins by the 8-sided die and the fields to the lower-left of the ties represent wins by the two 4-sided dice.

Based on your matrix, what is the probability that a longsword will win versus a broadsword? Your calculations should determine that a longsword will win 38.28% of the time, a broadsword will win 50% of the time, and that the two swords will tie 11.72% of the time.

If those ties are re-rolled until one sword or the other wins, what would be the total percentage of wins for the two swords?

Cumulative Probability

Knowing that a broadsword bests a longsword 56% of the time (the answer to the last question in the previous exercise) is clearly useful to a player deciding which sword to use. Why is it important for a designer to know? Understanding probability allows a designer to better understand and shape a game's dynamics. Suppose you were thinking of having a special event occur whenever a player rolls double-6s on 2D6. As a designer, you want to make sure that the event does not happen so frequently that it overpowers the game; and does not happen so rarely that its effect is negligible and is not worth the complexity it adds to the game. Probability allows you to determine the expected frequency of the event and immediately revise the mechanic if it is not what you desire.

The probability of rolling a 6 on a 6-sided die is 1/6. The cumulative probability of rolling 6s on two consecutive rolls is 1/36. This can be determined by multiplying the probability of each individual roll (1/6 * 1/6 = 1/36) or by creating a matrix of the possible outcomes (figure 10.8). Out of the 36 possibilities shown in figure 10.8, only one of them results in a 6 being rolled twice, hence the 1/36 chance.

This matrix can also be used to answer the earlier question, "When rolling two 6-sided dice, what is the probability of a 1 being rolled on at least one of them?" If you count the number of results that include a 1, you will find that there is a 11/36 chance of such a roll.

So if a 6 had just been rolled, what are the odds that the next roll will be a 6? The correct answer is 1/6 because past events do not affect future probabilities. Even if ten 6s had just been rolled in a row (a 1 in 60,466,176 occurrence), the probability that the next roll will be an eleventh six is still 1/6. This can seem strange and mystical. Getting 6s twice in a row happens 1 in 36 times, so why does rolling a second 6 (or an eleventh 6) have a 1/6 probability?

The reason is that everything that has occurred in the past has a 1/1 probability of having happened. If we combine the just-rolled 6 probability with the probability of the next roll being a six, we get 1/1 * 1/6 = 1/6. Figure 10.9 is a matrix which shows the six possible outcomes.

This matrix shows that since the first roll is a 6, the two rolls have six possible outcomes, one of which is double 6s. For similar reasons, rolling a 1 does not make rolling a 6 more likely on the following roll.

Die 2

	1	2	3	4	5	6
1	1 & 1	1 & 2	1 & 3	1 & 4	1 & 5	1 & 6
2	2 & 1	2 & 2	2 & 3	2 & 4	2 & 5	2 & 6
3	3 & 1	3 & 2	3 & 3	3 & 4	3 & 5	3 & 6
4	4 & 1	4 & 2	4 & 3	4 & 4	4 & 5	4 & 6
5	5 & 1	5 & 2	5 & 3	5 & 4	5 & 5	5 & 6
6	6 & 1	6 & 2	6 & 3	6 & 4	6 & 5	6 & 6

Die 1

Figure 10.8 Possible outcomes of rolling 2D6.

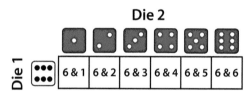

Die 2

	1	2	3	4	5	6
6	6 & 1	6 & 2	6 & 3	6 & 4	6 & 5	6 & 6

Die 1

Figure 10.9 The six possible outcomes for rolling 2D6 when one die has a value of 6.

EXERCISE 2D6 Probabilities

1. Using the information in figure 10.8's matrix, fill figure 10.10 with the probability for each of the possible outcomes that come from combining the result of two rolled six-sided dice. For example, there is one occurrence of rolling a 2 (which comes from rolling two 1s), so it has a 1 in 36 chance, which calculates to a 2.78% probability.

2D6 outcomes

	2	3	4	5	6	7	8	9	10	11	12
Number occurring	1										
Percentage chance	2.78%										

Figure 10.10 Probability of each possible 2D6 outcome.

2. Sicherman dice are a set of 2D6 that use a non-standard numbering. One die has the values 1, 2, 2, 3, 3, 4 and the other has 1, 3, 4, 5, 6, 8. These dice have an interesting characteristic. You can discover it yourself by filling out the matrix in figure 10.11 with the dice's summed values and then calculating each possible sum's probability using the matrix in figure 10.12. How do the Sicherman dice's probabilities compare to those of a standard 2D6?

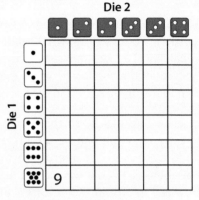

Figure 10.11 Possible outcomes of summed Sicherman dice rolls.

Sicherman dice outcomes

	2	3	4	5	6	7	8	9	10	11	12
Number occurring											
Percentage chance											

Figure 10.12 Probability of each possible Sicherman dice roll outcome.

EXERCISE Stone's Dice

Stone Librande teaches game design in addition to being a professional game designer. He uses the following two exercises to help his students gain a feeling for working with probability (Librande 2012).

Both exercises are based on a matchup between two 6-sided dice, higher roll wins. Using standard dice, both players have a 15/36 chance of winning and there is a 6/36 chance of there being a tie (figure 10.13).

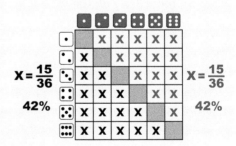

$X = \frac{15}{36}$

42%

$X = \frac{15}{36}$

42%

Figure 10.13 Possible win outcomes for standard 1D6 vs. standard 1D6 matchup.

Custom Dice Matchup

1. Instead of using typical dice, however, this exercise asks you to create your own non-standard numbering. Choose six integers, 0 and above, that add up to exactly 21. Twenty-one is the sum of a standard 6-sided die's values, so your die's rolls will have an expected value that is the same as a standard 6-side die: 21/6 = 3.5 average value per die face. Create your die by putting blank labels on a standard die and re-numbering it. Ideally, you will be able to play against someone who has created their own die—but if nobody is readily available, you can use your die against one that is randomly generated at www.funmines.com/custom-dice.

2. Roll the two dice against one another a few times. Once you have a feel for the dice, try to guess which one has the better chance of winning the matchup.

3. See if you guess correctly by creating a matchup matrix along the lines of the one shown in figure 10.14. In this example matchup, the blue die has a higher chance of winning than the black one, but in figure 10.15 the blue die will lose more often than not against the green die.

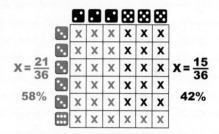

Figure 10.14 Win probabilities for two custom 6-sided dice.

How would the green die do against the black die? Interestingly, even though the blue die has a higher probability of winning when paired with the black die, and the green die has a higher probability against the blue die, the black die has a higher probability than the green die. The green die will (tend to) beat the blue die which will (tend to) beat the black die which will (tend to) beat the green die. This *Rock Paper Scissors* relationship means these are "intransitive" (or "non-transitive") dice. This particular set of intransitive dice is known as Grime dice.

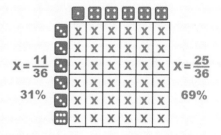

Figure 10.15 Win probabilities for two custom 6-sided dice.

An interesting characteristic of Grime dice is that if each of these dice is thrown as a pair (e.g., two green dice against two blue dice), the order of dominance flips so that two blue dice will (tend to) beat two green dice, two green will (tend to) beat two black dice, and two black dice will (tend to) beat two blue dice.

One-Shot Numbers

This second exercise also involves matching up numbers, but uses cards instead of dice (figure 10.16). A game consists of matchups. After each matchup, the

Figure 10.16 Card versus card.

numbers used are taken out of circulation for the remainder of the game (i.e., each number is used one time during the game).

1. Put together two sets of cards with numbers 1 through 6 by cannibalizing a standard playing card deck.
2. Create a matchup matrix for the game that shows which side wins each of the possible outcomes (figure 10.17).
3. You can play against yourself by shuffling the cards and turning them over one by one. Or you can play against another person and choose your cards one by one. If you do choose your cards, rather than select them randomly, does it affect the game's outcome?
4. After each number is played, update the matrix and recalculate the probability of victory for each player (such as is shown in figures 10.18 and 10.19).

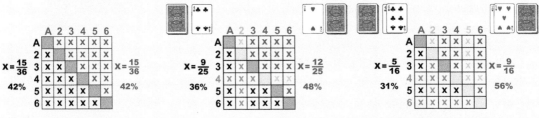

Figure 10.17 Card versus card probability matrix.

Figure 10.18 Probabilities recalculated after the first turn.

Figure 10.19 Probabilities recalculated after the second turn.

Yut Nori

Yut Nori is a Korean game that is often referred to as simply *Yut* ("nori" is the Korean word for "game"). It is an elegant circle & cross game (a class of racing games that take place on circular or cruciform-shaped tracks). The best known cross & circle game is the traditional Indian game *Pachisi* and its modern derivatives (*Ludo, Parcheesi, Trouble, Sorry!*).

Yut traditionally uses tossed sticks to determine the number of spaces the pieces can move. This version of the game substitutes coins for the sticks.

Players:

■ Two players

Required Materials:

■ *Yut* board (on the page following these rules)
■ 4 coins
■ 2 sets of 4 game pieces

Object of the Game:

- Be the first player to have four pieces complete a circuit around the board.

Setup:

- Place the eight game pieces on the start space.
- Determine who takes the first turn.

Rules:

- Players alternate taking turns.
- A turn begins by a player shaking the four coins in her hands and smacking them on the table.
- The player moves one of her pieces a number of spaces equal to the number of coins that landed heads up. If the coins are all tails, then the player moves a piece five spaces.
- A player can choose to either move a piece that is currently on the board or (if all four pieces are not currently in play) add a game piece to the board. When a game piece is added to the board, it lands on the space that corresponds to the toss. So a roll of 1 would be on the "start" space, a roll of 5 would have the piece enter the game on the space in the bottom-right corner.
- A coin toss of all heads or all tails gives the player an extra turn. There is no limit to the number of extra turns a player can take in a row.
- If a piece ends its movement on space occupied by any of the opponent's pieces, the opponent's pieces are returned home and the current player takes another turn.
- If a piece ends its movement on a space occupied by a friendly piece, they can join and be moved together in future coin tosses. More than two pieces cannot be joined into a single set. If the joined game pieces are landed upon and sent home, they become disconnected.
- The pieces move in only one direction: counter-clockwise.
- A game piece (or set of game pieces) that begins its move on one of the corner spaces or the center space can take a shortcut. Figure 10.20 shows the four routes a piece might take.

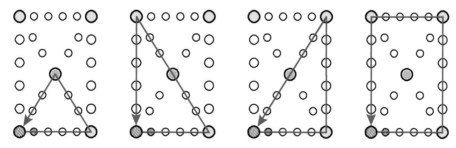

Figure 10.20 The four possible routes for pieces.

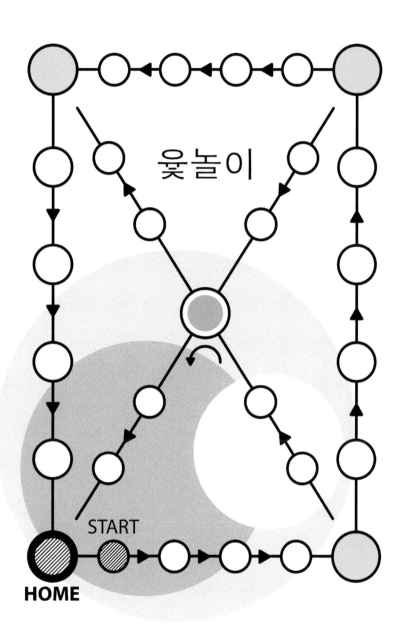

윷놀이

START

HOME

- To complete a circuit, a piece must complete one of the four paths in figure 10.20 and move *past* the home space. A piece that lands precisely on the home space will need to be moved an additional time for it to complete the circuit.
- The first player to have all four pieces complete the circuit wins the game.

Yut's Probabilities

Instead of dice, *Yut* traditionally uses four sticks that are flat on one side, and curved on the other (see figure 10.21). These sticks provide sixteen possible outcomes, of which there are five unique results (no flat sides, one flat side, two flat sides, three flat sides, all four flat sides). A player's turn involves tossing the sticks and moving a piece a number of spaces equal to the number of sticks that landed flat side up (if no sticks land flat side up, the lucky player gets to move a piece five spaces).

The rules to *Yut* on page 204 modify the game by having players use coins in place of binary sticks. The possible outcomes of tossing four fair coins are shown in table 10.1.

While coins are convenient, they do not really replicate the probabilities of *Yut* sticks. Unlike coins and dice, whose various outcomes are equally likely, the two possible outcomes for

Figure 10.21 *Yut Nori* using sticks.

Table 10.1 The probabilities of the possible outcomes when tossing four fair coins.

Result	Coin outcomes	Probability
One heads	1) heads, tails, tails, tails 2) tails, heads, tails, tails 3) tails, tails, heads, tails 4) tails, tails, tails, heads	4/16 = 0.25 = 25%
Two heads	1) heads, heads, tails, tails 2) heads, tails, heads, tails 3) heads, tails, tails, heads 4) tails, heads, heads, tails 5) tails, heads, tails, heads 6) tails, tails, heads, heads	6/16 = 0.375 = 37.5%
Three heads	1) heads, heads, heads, tails 2) heads, heads, tails, heads 3) heads, tails, heads, heads 4) tails, heads, heads, heads	4/16 = 0.25 = 25%
Four heads	1) heads, heads, heads, heads	1/16 = 0.0625 = 6.25%
No heads	1) tails, tails, tails, tails	1/16 = 0.0625 = 6.25%

a *Yut* stick (i.e., curved side up or flat side up) are *not* equally likely. Since *Yut* sticks are not all manufactured in precisely the same way, the probability varies, but in general there is an approximately 60% chance of a *Yut* stick landing flat side up (Park et al. 2013). The "4D10 *Yut*" exercise on pages 208–209 has you develop a method of generating random numbers that better simulates the probabilities provided by the sticks.

Combination

This math is a bit complicated, but worth taking the time to understand. Suppose we have a game that uses seven fair coins. We would like to know the probability of three of them landing heads up. To do that we start by figuring out the number of possible outcomes: $2^7 = 2 * 2 * 2 * 2 * 2 * 2 * 2 = 128$ possible outcomes.

However, it would be tedious (and possibly error prone) to list out all the possible outcome combinations for seven coins. A better way of determining the number of combinations would be to calculate it using the "*n* choose *k*" factorial function:

$$\frac{n!}{k!(n-k)!}$$

In this calculation, n = the number of total items, and k = the number of the smaller set. In our example case, n would be the seven total coins, and k would be the subset of three heads up coins. The ! in the function represents a factorial. A factorial is the multiplied set of all positive numbers less than or equal to the number next to the exclamation point. For example 3! is equal to 3 * 2 * 1. If you have a computer, it probably has a scientific calculator built in that can perform factorials for you (alternatively you can find one online by searching for "factorial calculator").

The 3-combination in the set of 7 is 7!/3!(7 – 3)! which is equal to 5,040/6 * 24 or 35. So the probability of getting three heads up when tossing seven coins is 35/128 or 27.34%.

EXERCISE 4D10 *Yut*

This exercise asks you to experiment with different ways (and probabilities) for determining the number of spaces moved in *Yut*.

1. If a *Yut* stick has a 60% chance of landing flat side up, what is the likelihood of each of the five possible outcomes? By way of example, the probability of only one of the four

sticks landing with one flat side up can be calculated by multiplying the probability of one stick landing flat side up (0.6) times the probability for each of the other three sticks landing curved side up (0.4) times the number of ways that this can happen (four, per table 10.1). Tossing one flat side has a 15.36% chance of happening (0.6 * 0.4 * 0.4 * 0.4 * 4). Based on that example, calculate the chances of tossing two flat sides, three flat sides, four flat sides, and no flat sides. Double-check your math by making sure all the probabilities add up to 100%.

2. Use four 10-sided dice to replicate the *Yut* sticks probabilities. Do this by using paint or tape to mark each die so that six of the D10's sides represent a *Yut* stick's flat side and four of the D10's sides represent a *Yut* stick's rounded side.

3. Roll the 4D10 twenty times, tracking the result of each roll. How closely did the outcomes match what you would expect based on the probabilities you calculated in Step 1? It would not be surprising if your results diverge significantly from the probabilities—the probabilistic behavior holds true for large numbers of dice rolls, but streaks are certainly possible in such a small set of rolls.

4. Try playing some games of *Yut* with coins and some with the 4D10. Also try playing the game so that each of the five outcomes has an equal chance of happening (this can be done by using a 6-sided die and re-rolling it whenever a 6 is rolled). How do the different probabilities affect the game?

Coin Age's Probabilities

You can find the rules and game board for Adam P. McIver's *Coin Age* on the following page. *Coin Age* tied (with *Tiny Epic Kingdoms*) for BoardGameGeek's 2013 Golden Geek "Best Print and Play Game" award. It is a microgame that can provide players a surprising amount of strategic play in a short amount of time.

Player actions in *Coin Age* are determined by flipping between one and four coins. A four-coin *Coin Age* flip involves the same probabilities as *Yut*'s possible outcomes when played with coins (table 10.1): a 37.5% chance of two matches, a 25% chance of one match, a 25% chance of three matches, a 6.25% chance of four matches, and a 6.25% chance of no matches.

Use the techniques covered in the previous exercise to determine the outcome probabilities for the situations in which a *Coin Age* player is flipping one, two, or three coins. What sorts of strategies might these varying probabilities encourage?

ADAM P MCIVER'S
COINAGE

GAME OVERVIEW:

Coin Age is a microgame for two players that is played with a single card and pocket change. Players take turns placing coins on a map to control spaces, outmaneuver their opponent, and score victory points.

SETUP:

Place the map card in the center of the table directly between the two players.

Each player begins the game with 4 dimes, 3 pennies, 2 nickels, and 1 quarter to the side of their play area as their "bank".

To determine which player will play the game as "heads" and "tails", one player flips a coin. The result of the flip is their "side". When placing a coin on the map, always make sure that your correct side is up.

The heads player takes the first turn.

FIGURE 1: ACTIONS

# of Matches	Actions (*optional, any order*)
✓✓✓	Place 2 *or* Pay 1 to Place 3
✓✓	Place 2
✓✓	Place 2
✓	Place 1 *and* Move
●	Capture *and* Move

TURN SEQUENCE:

At the beginning of your turn, take one of each different kind of your remaining coins from your bank into your hands.

Thoroughly shake up the coins in your hands and slap them down flat on the table.

You may perform actions based on how many of your slapped coins match each other's side.

Refer to Figure 1: Actions above.

All the actions are described on page 3/4.

Place:
Take one of your matching coins and place it on an empty map space. Ensure you place it your side up to indicate that it is your coin. You may also place on an occupied space if your coin can be stacked on top of any higher ranked coin.

Refer to Figure 2: Coin Rank on page 4/4.

Pay:
Transfer one of your matching coins to your opponent's bank.

Move:
Move all the coins in one space to an empty adjacent space.

Capture:
Remove any single coin from a space (or from the top of a stack) and place it in your bank.

GAME END:

The game ends immediately when a player places a coin in the last empty space or when a player runs out of coins in their bank (whichever comes first). The players then add up their victory points based on:

1) **Coin Values**
Coins that "control" spaces score victory points (VP) equal to their rank. A coin "controls" a space if it is either *a)* the only coin on the space or...

FIGURE 2: COIN RANK

- I — DIME
- II — PENNY
- III — NICKEL
- IV — QUARTER

b) the top of a stack of coins on the space.

2) **Region Bonuses**
If a player controls the majority of spaces in each color-coded region, the VP scored by their coins in that region is doubled. No region bonus is given in the case of a tie.

3) **Bank Bonuses**
Players score 1 bonus VP per coin remaining in their bank at the end of the game.

The player with the most VP wins! In the case of a tie, the player with the highest total value of coins (above) remaining in their bank is the winner.

COINAGE (THE COPPER PEAKS)

PLAINS OF KASHE

ADAM P MCIVER'S
COINAGE

Cut out rules and map along white lines.

#CoinAge — Game Design & Artwork: Adam P. McIver
Playtesting & Development: Alex Kevern, Levi Baer, & Pocket Earnhart
Coin Age © 2013 Adam P. McIver

PROJECT GAME
@PRGtweets
projectgame.net

CHAPTER ELEVEN

Economies

INTRODUCTION

A game's economy comprises the assets that are available to players and the mechanics that dictate how those assets move through the game's system. Economy mechanics can make up a game's core mechanic and provide the game's fundamental actions. Alternatively, economies can serve a secondary role that supports a non-economic core mechanic: for instance, reining in players' ability to perform certain actions by placing a cost on them. Either way, economic systems can offer you fertile ground for designing player actions and shaping interesting choices.

The learning objectives for this chapter are:

1   Understand the characteristics of game assets, resources, and victory points and how their use can lead to interesting choices.

2   Gain an awareness of how the flow of assets can affect a game's dynamics.

3   Be aware of auction and trading mechanics and the game experiences they can provide.

Assets and Resources

Assets are game elements that provide a benefit to the player who possesses them (or cause disadvantage due to their absence). Assets are not constant and static; in order for a game element to be an asset, it must not be always and unchangingly available to the player throughout the game. *Hive*'s game pieces are assets; *Button Men*'s dice are assets; and *Zombie in my Pocket*'s items, health points, and time of day are assets.

The term "resource" is often used interchangeably with asset, but it is worth reserving it for characterizing a particular type of asset; one that serves as a kind of currency that can be spent to change (or maintain) the game state. The characteristics of resources are:

1. Resources are generic and interchangeable with others of their type.
2. Resources are expendable.
3. Resource supplies can be impacted by player actions.

Resources are fungible, meaning that they are generic in quality. One unit of a particular resource type is indistinguishable and interchangeable with another. *Shoot-Out*'s revolver bullets all have the exact same impact on the game—it does not matter which particular revolver bullet a player uses when shooting. Resource fungibility allows game designers to have the goal of resource acquisition be ongoing throughout the game. A *Monopoly* player continually strives to acquire money (a resource), but the goal of obtaining a particular property asset (say, "Boardwalk") ends once the player purchases it (or it otherwise becomes unavailable).

Related to their fungibility, resources tend to be non-spatial once they come into a player's possession. *Shoot-Out*'s bullets can be represented by physical game pieces, but those physical pieces' positions are not part of the game state. It is not unusual for a resource (such as a clip of ammo in a video game) to enter the game with a physical location, but leave the game space upon being acquired and move into a dimensionless bank account (of sorts) from which the player can withdraw as needed.

Those withdrawn resources are spent in order to enact some game state change (or to prevent some game state change from happening). This expenditure might involve the resource being destroyed (removed entirely from the game), transferred out of the player's possession, or simply becoming unavailable to the player for a period of time. For example, *Shoot-Out*'s rifle bullets are destroyed, *Marrakech*'s coins are transferred, and an RPG's main character might heal lost hit points over time. The limited availability of these resources heightens the stakes for a player whose actions lead to them being spent.

The value of an asset is determined by the degree to which a player can leverage it into game advantage. When that advantage is particularly situational, then a player's decision to acquire, save, or spend an asset is most likely to be interesting. For example, the decision whether to use a bullet in *Shoot-Out* can involve the player assessing the value of the card at stake in the current duel, the values of the cards already won, the likelihood that using the bullet will make a difference in the current duel's outcome, and the likelihood that holding on to the bullet will make a difference to the game's ultimate outcome.

In contrast, *Marrakech*'s resource of Dirham coins have a value that is much more defined and static than *Shoot-Out*'s bullets. Certainly, a player who is about to be knocked out of the game by going bankrupt is likely to particularly cherish her last few Dirham, but overall the coins' value is defined and limited to their victory point role in determining the winner of the game (see sidebar). The influence the Dirham have on players' decision making is largely limited to motivating players to attempt to maximize their acquisition and minimize their loss.

Determining the Winner in *Marrakech*

Marrakech's winner is the player who has the largest number of rug halves visible on the board and Dirham, added together. The number of Dirham in a game is equal to thirty times the number of players and the board supports up to forty-nine rug halves, which means for a two-player game the maximum number of possible victory points is 109. Possessing a combined total of fifty-five Dirham and rug halves at the end of the game guarantees victory in a two-player game. Consequently, each Dirham can be considered to have a value of 1/55 of a victory in a two player game.

Victory Points

Shoot-Out's cards provide an asset whose nature is similar to that of a resource. Each card is distinct from the others in the number of points it provides, but the points themselves are interchangeable and fungible (possessing both the two-point and three-point cards is entirely equivalent to possessing the five-point card). However, the cards and their points are only collected and never spent. Their sole purpose is to help fulfill the game's victory condition. As such, rather than being a resource, they belong to a class of asset that is commonly referred to as "victory points."

It could be argued that winning the game involves spending the collected victory points. However, victory points create dynamics that are distinct from those typical of resources. Whereas resources are usually a means to an end, the victory points *are* the end (or closer to it, anyway).

Shoot-Out's use of victory points serves to differentiate the duels. The differing number of points at stake in the duels make some more worth winning than others. This makes the choice of spending a bullet more interesting ("Should I conserve my resources for higher point duel?").

Conversely, victory points can provide a shared, comparable trait for aspects of the game that are otherwise fundamentally different. For example, actions in *The Settlers of Catan* include building settlements and cities, establishing roads, collecting knight cards, and acquiring "development cards." What unifies these activities is the fact that they all can be a source of victory points.

Scrabble uses victory points both to differentiate and to create a comparable basis. Some letters provide more points than others—a hard-to-use 'X' is worth eight points, but an easily used 'E' is worth only one point. Certain word placement locations provide a point multiplier. A player who is able to use all seven letters in his rack gains a fifty point bonus. These point variations serve to present the player with conflicting goals and, consequently, a variety of strategies and interesting choices. A player might choose to save a valuable letter so that it can be used later in a more lucrative position; or forgo a high scoring move in order to deny a choice position to an opponent; or spend a turn trading-in letters in hopes that the new letters could lead to a fifty point bonus in the following turn. Each of these disparate actions are made comparable by the potential points they gain and sacrifice.

As this *Scrabble* example suggests, the abstraction of victory points can be a design tool for shaping a game's subgoals and motivating certain player behaviors. Consider how points are scored in *Basketball*. Making a basket from behind the three-point line rewards an extra point—just enough to motivate the occasional three-point-shot. Likewise, the potential point or two earned in a free throw is enough to discourage fouling, but not enough to altogether eliminate it. It would be easy to design a nearly foul-free version of *Basketball* by simply making free throws worth enough points that fouling intentionally would be unthinkable. The choice to foul is interesting because free throws are worth only one point per basket—sometimes fouling is a strategically sound decision, sometimes it is not.

Kramerleiste

Kramerleiste is the German word (named after Wolfgang Kramer, whose games introduced its usage) for a victory point scoring track that encircles a game board's periphery. A kramerleiste can be seen on *Ticket to Ride*'s board (page 157). The track is used as a bookkeeping device to record the points that players accumulate during a game. Prior to the innovation of the kramerleiste, the most common way of tracking the scores of players was to keep a running total using pencil and paper (as is still done in *Scrabble*). The kramerleiste is a marked improvement on this for a number a reasons:

1. The adjustment of a player's score can be seen by everyone, which reduces the likelihood of errors or cheating.
2. The current scores are always visible.
3. It is easy for any player to update the score, so no one person has to serve the role of "scorekeeper."
4. Updating a score by moving a piece is simpler and quicker than doing the calculation on paper.

Victory points are an almost ubiquitous mechanic in Eurogames (see page 19), but that was not the case prior to the introduction of the kramerleiste (Eggert 2006). It is very possible that the current widespread use of victory point mechanics is a result of how they have become more manageable (and perhaps even fun) to track. Effective interfaces can be that powerful.

EXERCISE *Coin Age*'s VPs

Coin Age's victory points are awarded for controlling a space, for controlling a region, and for having unused coins at the end of the game. What strategies do you think each of these varying ways of gaining victory points encourage? How do those strategies align and conflict?

Open and Closed Economies

As described earlier, assets are transitory game elements that provide a benefit to a player who possesses them (or a disadvantage to a player who does not). Resources are a particular kind of fungible asset.

A game's economy is composed of these assets and the mechanics that dictate how they move in and out of players' possession and through the game's various systems. The assets that populate *Shoot-Out*'s economy are rifle bullets, revolver bullets, and card points. *Shoot-Out*'s economic mechanisms involve bullets being discarded when shooting, bullets being recovered when conceding a duel, and cards being awarded when winning a duel.

Economies are sometimes described as being open or closed. The assets in a closed economy exist in the game state (not necessarily in the players' possession) from the start of the game. This means that no additional assets are introduced into the economy while the game is being played. If assets are added to the game state during play, then the game has an open economy. *Chess* might be described as having an open economy because pieces can be added to the board mid-game through the promotion of a pawn.

Coin Age has a closed economy. Its players start the game with 10 coins each, and though coins can move back and forth between the players' banks and the board, no new ones are added to the game over the course of play. The number of coins in *Coin Age* remains constant for the entire game, however, that is not required for an economy to be closed. A closed economy can have its assets decrease during play. For example, the stripped-down *Shoot-Out's Core* (which does not have the full-fledged game's "reload" mechanism) has a closed economy in which no bullets are added to the game state during play, but bullets are removed through the shooting action.

While it is standard to label an entire economy as being either open or closed, it is entirely possible for a game to have some of assets fixed at a certain number and others entirely unlimited. For example, *Monopoly* has twenty-eight purchasable properties, thirty-two houses, and twelve hotels. All these assets are available on a first-come basis and become unavailable once they are acquired by a player. When the buildings run out, no more can be had unless a player returns them to the bank. *Monopoly*'s money, however, is unlimited (the bank never goes broke, players are supposed to mint more money if it runs out). The game's economy has money added to it every time a player passes "Go" and receives $200 from the bank. Strictly speaking, the fact that *Monopoly* has one asset (its money) that can be added to the game state during play means that its economy is open. Even so, it is probably more meaningful to describe it as a "partially open economy" composed of both limited and unlimited assets.

Not every game's economy can be classified unequivocally as open or closed. Does *Checkers* have a closed economy? The answer depends on whether you consider "kinging" a checker to be introducing a new asset or to be simply an inherent state change of an existing asset. *Shoot-Out* might be described as having an open economy because players can "reload" two bullets by retreating from a duel. Yet the total number of reloads is tightly constrained—a player cannot lose more than three duels without losing the game so the maximum number of reloaded bullets is six. So it could be reasonably argued that *Shoot-Out* has a closed economy that consists of the bullets held by the players at the start of the game plus a limited reload reserve of six revolver bullets for each player.

Faucets and Drains

The mechanics that add resources to an open economy can be described as "faucets" (or "sources") and the ones which remove assets from an open or closed economy are "drains" (or "sinks").

Monopoly's faucets are the money gained from passing "Go" and from various Chance and Community Chest cards. The drains consist of the fines and penalties that the cards incur, the payments made from landing on the Income Tax space, and the interest charged when paying off a mortgaged property, and payment to the bank for purchasing a property or building.

Monopoly's drain from purchasing properties and buildings removes less money than it may appear at first glance. Buildings and properties are so easily converted back into cash that the amount that truly drains is the difference between purchase price and the amount that can be regained by mortgaging a property or selling a building back to the bank. Boardwalk's list price is $400 and it can be mortgaged for $200, so $200 drains out of the economy when the property is landed upon and purchased.

Many players of *Monopoly* eliminate the card and Income Tax drains by setting aside those payments in order to give them to players landing on "Free Parking." Even without the unofficial "Free Parking" rule, *Monopoly*'s faucets tend to pour much more money into the game's economy than its drains eliminate. This inflationary trend, combined with the victory condition of being the last player holding money, causes the game dynamic to stabilize and generally results in long, drawn out games. As the "Free Parking" example might suggest, a game's level of stability can be modified by adding and eliminating faucets and drains. Adjusting the flow of existing faucets and drains (i.e., the amount of resources they administer) can be just as impactful as adding and removing them.

The terms "faucet" and "drain" are most often applied to the economies of online persistent world games, such as *World of Warcraft*. They are intended to evoke an image of a bathtub's water level that will eventually either overflow or run dry if its faucet and drain are not perfectly set. For a game economy that persists indefinitely and is intended to be utilized by both veteran and newbie player alike, maintaining an even economic keel is both desirable and extremely difficult. There is an almost predestined tendency towards hyperinflation (see www.funmines. com/hyperinflation for more about this particular design problem). Outside the world of persistent massively multiplayer games, however, unbalanced faucets and drains are not necessarily a problem. *Shoot-Out*'s gameplay, for example, depends on the fact that the bullet resources drain away to nothing.

EXERCISE A Medieval Economy

Cathedral's assets consist entirely of the buildings players place to create a walled, medieval town. Your goal is to expand the game to incorporate at least two more assets and a victory point system. Design the game so that there are multiple ways (and strategies) for acquiring victory points. Experiment with various configurations of faucets and drains (including having one but not the other) and at various levels of flow. What settings provide the best playing experience and why?

Auctions

Auction mechanics can be particularly attractive to a game designer who is looking to add interesting choices to a game. By their nature, auctions require players to place a value on something whose value is not precisely calculable.

Auctions of items with calculable or set values do not work well. An auction's winning bid is very likely to be the item's precise value (or very near it). The true value of a used or classic car is harder to determine than the value of new car— that's why auctions are a common sales format for the former and rare for the latter. Likewise, unused retail items sold on eBay are likely to be sold at a set price via "buy it now" rather than through the site's auction mechanisms.

Monopoly's property auctions occur whenever a player lands on an unowned property and chooses not to purchase it and whenever a player goes bankrupt owing money to the bank. An auction gives players the opportunity to collectively determine the cost of the auction item and, consequently, handicap its ownership. This means that the disadvantage the auction winner incurs by having to pay the purchase price is more-or-less in balance with the advantage gained from the item won.

When a player is able to win an auction on the cheap (i.e., gains the auction item for less than its true game advantage value) it tends to because her opponents simply do not have the financial means to bid the cost up. This kind of situation can create a positive feedback loop in which a rich player's advantage snowballs (which is not necessarily a bad thing, especially in a game that may otherwise tend to drag on).

Auctions do not need to be limited to assets like *Monopoly*'s properties and buildings. Many Eurogames feature auctions of less tangible items such as turn order, special abilities, or (combining the two) the turn order for selecting special abilities. It can be difficult to design a special ability that does not over-advantage the player possessing it. By distributing special abilities through an auction, however, designers can reasonably hope that the advantages gained by the player possessing the special ability will be offset by the resources spent gaining it. This is not to suggest that auction mechanics are a way of avoiding the hard work of playtesting and balancing a game (the subject of the following chapter).

Auction Formats

Auctions in games are often a variant of an "English auction." This sort of auction has players making ever-higher bids of currency (or other game resource) in competition to acquire the item in question. The winner of the auction is the player who makes the highest bid and pays the price that no other player wants to top.

Monopoly's rulebook gives few details regarding how its auctions should be conducted, which may be one reason why auctions are so commonly dropped from the game. The details that do exist seem to suggest a standard asynchronous English auction where anyone can place a bid for any higher amount at any time. This can lead to a flurry of loud and nearly simultaneous bids; the resulting confusion is another likely reason that auctions are rarely played in the game.

A more tame (and common) form of game-based English auctions has players taking turns making bids. The bids might continue until all but one bidder drops out, or the auction might be structured so that there are a fixed number of bidding rounds, or (as in *Contract Bridge*) the bids might continue until all players "pass" in succession. It is worth noting that a small alteration to such a mechanic (such as whether or not one can pass and then subsequently re-enter the auction) can change the experience considerably.

While turn-based English auctions are the most prevalent in tabletop games, other auction types exist and these less common auction forms can offer interesting gameplay possibilities. A "sealed-bid" (or "blind bid") auction involves every bidder making a single hidden bid—the bids are made simultaneously so that no participant knows what the others are offering. Where an English auction can be hotly contested and lead players to make irrational choices, the choices made in sealed-bid auctions tend to be more coldly calculated.

A "Dutch auction" has no bidding; instead the item in question starts the auction with a high asking price that decreases until a participant decides to purchase it. Dutch auctions can have an edge-of-your-seat tension in which each player is

Bidding

Auction bids are usually in the form of resources, but other possibilities exist. A winning bid in a trick-taking playing card game such as *Spades* or *Contract Bridge* involves pledging to accomplish a task (i.e., winning a certain number of tricks)—failure to do so incurs a penalty. The tabletop game *Gauntlet of Fools* has an auction in which players bid for the characters they get to play by increasingly handicapping them with penalties: "I'll take the barbarian hopping on one leg, which lowers his defense by two," might be countered with, "I'll play him with that plus skipping breakfast, which doubles his first wound."

pushing his luck to get the best deal possible. This can be especially true when the price drop happens steadily, reinforcing the need to act decisively.

A "Japanese auction" is the opposite of a Dutch auction. A Japanese auction's prices start out low and rise until every bidder drops out but one. Bidding in this style of auction can feel like a contest to see who can bear the most pain.

"Reverse auctions" reverse the roles of buyer and seller. This sort of auction has multiple sellers who are competing (by dropping their price) to sell to a single buyer.

How an auction's payment is handled is just as important as the mechanics that determine the winner. Typically, the payment comes from the winner paying the amount she bid—but that is not the only possibility. An "all-pay auction" requires every bidder to pay their highest bid even though only the player with the highest bid of all wins the item in question. Such an auction can create a dynamic in which players are reluctant to start bidding and reluctant (once an initial bid is made) to stop bidding. Similar to the all-pay auction is one in which the top two bids pay, but only the highest one receives the item being bid upon—this sort of auction can provide a particularly intense dynamic.

The auction formats described above are a handy starting place, but they only touch the surface of what can be (and has been) done in games. Changing how an auction works can lead to any number of strange and interesting dynamics. When designing an auction mechanic, feel free to be creative in adapting it to whatever best serves your needs.

EXERCISE Adding an Auction

Choose an existing game for more than two players (such as *Marrakech*) and expand it to include an auction mechanic. In what ways does your auction mechanic improve the play experience? In what ways does it detract?

Trading

Trading and negotiation mechanics can serve a game role that is similar to an auction. In the same way that an auction works best when the item in question does not have a fixed value, a lively trading dynamic is encouraged when the items being exchanged provide a different level of benefit to the players involved. An exchange of *Monopoly*'s Reading and Pennsylvania Railroads might be made, but it will not elicit much excitement because the two properties are nearly identical in terms of their impact on the game. However, a trade which would allow one player to achieve a monopoly (i.e., complete a property set) is much more likely to engage and excite the players making the negotiation.

Trades differ from auctions in that what the two players consider "fair" can be given considerable weight in their decision making process. Auctions are framed as contests in which (typically) the highest bidder "wins." It is easy for auction participants to value the very act of winning the auction in addition to valuing the item won. It is not uncommon for an auction's winner to spend more than he would have done in a more straightforward purchase.

In contrast, trades tend to encourage players to be more conservative and stingy than they might otherwise be. Partly this is simply for strategic reasons. Paying too much in a trade costs a player double: the player is not only damaging his own position, but he is also improving his opponent's. In contrast, paying too much in an auction does not directly benefit opposing players if the payment is made to the "house" instead of an opponent.

Other, less conscious factors can influence this dynamic as well. Players often make an irrational choice to suffer a disadvantage rather than accept a trade which they think gives them the worst part of an uneven deal. This tendency has been studied with *The Ultimatum Game* (see page 224). Players of the game tend to reject divisions in which they receive less than 40% of the game's assets. If the game is being played as a series, the choice to reject may be strategic—the loss of assets in the current game might be suffered in order to incentivize the opponent to provide a more fair split in the future games. However, the tendency to reject unfair divisions happens even in single games despite the fact doing so is always the suboptimal choice—it is more advantageous to receive an unfairly tiny portion of something than nothing at all. Even chimpanzees who have been coaxed into playing the game display a similar behavior (Proctor et al. 2013). When given more time to consider their choice, however, human *Ultimatum Game* players become more likely to accept a lesser split.

The Ultimatum Game

This game was invented in 1970 by economic theorist Werner Güth when he was studying at the University of Münster (Grötker 2009). In the decades since, it has become a mainstay of game theory experiments.

Players:

- Two players

Required Materials:

- An asset in the form of a small amount of money, a pie, or other divisible and semi-desirable object. The asset should be provided by a third party (i.e., not either of the game's players). This is to ensure that the players do not feel that one of them has an inherently greater claim of ownership.

Rules:

1. One player is randomly selected to propose how to divide the asset between herself and the other player. The player is free to allocate as much of the asset to herself as she wishes.
2. The player who did not divide the money decides whether to accept or reject the division.
3. If the division is accepted, both players receive and can keep their share of the asset. If the division is rejected, neither player receives a share of the asset.

CHAPTER TWELVE

Balance

INTRODUCTION

Balance is an evocative term—it brings to mind not only the scales of justice, but also a precarious state in which one poor choice can tumble a tower of *Jenga* pieces. In game design, balance refers to how well the game mechanics are working. A game is out of balance when its mechanics encourage dynamics that are deemed to be undesirable by its designers or players. When a game's mechanics are so out of balance that they threaten to destroy the play experience entirely, the game is often said to be "broken."

The learning objectives for this chapter are:

1   Be able to identify and categorize game imbalances.

2   Be able to employ a variety of techniques for achieving game balance.

Balance in Games

The process of balancing a game begins early in the development cycle and continues until the game reaches its final form. Every change to a game's design, including changes intended to fix an imbalance, has the potential of introducing a new imbalance.

Game designer Ian Schreiber points out that while we often speak of game balance as if it were a single thing, there are actually any number of ways that a game can fall out of balance (Schreiber, *Game Balance* 2009). Drawing on Schreiber's list of the common kinds of game balance, we might categorize imbalances into five types:

1. **Action imbalance:** A player-driven mechanic is imbalanced if the benefit it provides is either too weak or too strong in comparison to its cost to the player.
2. **Event imbalance:** A systems-driven mechanic is imbalanced if it is too weak to factor into player decision making or so powerful that it overwhelms the impact of player actions. A too powerful event is liable to cause player choices to be either obvious or meaningless.
3. **Strategic imbalance:** A game is imbalanced if it supports a dominant strategy (see page 173).
4. **Asymmetric imbalance:** A multiplayer game is considered imbalanced if one player has an undesired systemic advantage at the onset of the game.
5. **Difficulty imbalance**: A single-player (or collaborative) game is imbalanced if its level of difficulty is not suited to its target audience.

Balancing Data

In the early stages of creating a game, designers often need to assign numbers to various aspects of the design. For example, expanding *Cathedral* to include an economy of assets (per the "A Medieval Economy" exercise on page 220), might involve adding a mechanic in which players must spend resources to bring a building into play. How much each building costs is something that a designer needs to specify.

So how does a game designer go about determining those building costs? She might choose to simply plug in numbers using her best guess. If the amount of the game's numeric data is small, the cost of guessing wrong can be minimal—it can be possible and practical to home in on the correct values through several rounds of playtesting and revising. With larger amounts of data, however, starting with off-target numbers can be much more detrimental to the development process. Every poorly chosen value adds noise to the game's system that makes it harder to determine which numbers are working and which need adjustment. In such a situation, trying to balance a game can feel like playing "Whack-A-Mole" in which each attempt to fix a problematic number results in unbalancing the seemingly correct ones.

Cathedral has eleven different building shapes, a number large enough that it is worth trying to price them using a more systematic and analytical method than just taking a stab in the dark. One approach is to try to quantify the benefit provided by each building in order to assign a cost that is proportional to it. In the case of *Cathedral*, the more squares a building covers, the more advantageous it is for the player to place it. So setting each building's price to be equal to its size in squares is a good starting place. Suppose, however, some of the building types provide special benefits to the player and we want the building costs to reflect that. In such situations, game designers strive to create a "comparable basis"—a way of relating the benefits provided by one thing to the benefits provided by another. This approach seeks to establish a "transitive relationship" between game elements (Schreiber, *Game Balance* 2009), which means that they can be ranked in terms of whatever aspect the designer is using to evaluate them.

Kingdom Rush is a "tower defense" video game whose tower types include three that can attack opponents at a distance (what is called a "range attack"). Each of these tower types ("archer," "mage," and "artillery") inflicts a different amount of damage and can fire at a different rate (see table 12.1). The towers can be upgraded to cause more damage and have longer ranges. The artillery tower attacks at a very slow rate, but the bombs it flings can cause damage to more than one opponent at a time ("splash damage"). The damage inflicted by mage towers is not reduced by armor, but it is reduced by creatures who have magical resistance.

Tower defense video games have a core mechanic that involves the player creating defensive fortifications (towers) to counter an onslaught of computer-controlled attackers.

Table 12.1 *Kingdom Rush* range-attack tower characteristics.

Tower Type	Level	Damage	Attack time in seconds	Range	Special
Archer	1	4–6	0.75	Short	None
	2	7–11	0.5	Medium	None
	3	10–16	0.5	Long	None
Mage	1	9–17	1.5	Short	Ignores armor
	2	23–46	1.5	Medium	Ignores armor
	3	40–74	1.5	Long	Ignores armor
Artillery	1	7–14	3	Short	Splash damage
	2	20–39	3	Medium	Splash damage
	3	33–66	3	Long	Splash damage

Suppose you were tasked with setting prices for *Kingdom Rush*'s towers and their upgrades. A good approach would be to do it through establishing a comparable basis. The towers' main purpose is to inflict damage, so it makes sense to use that for the cornerstone of the comparison. You would probably also want to take into account the fact that some towers have faster attack speeds and longer ranges.

A possible starting place is to establish a base cost for each tower and tower upgrade in terms of the amount of damage it inflicts per second on average—perhaps 10 gold per damage point. Where did that 10 number come from? To a degree it is arbitrary, but ultimately it needs to be in balance with the player's ability to acquire gold. If the towers seem too cheap, the solution might be to use a higher base cost (perhaps 15 gold per point of damage) or to reduce the speed at which players gather gold.

Having established how the towers' base costs are determined, you need to adjust those costs to take into account the other factors you think relevant. In this case you might decide to multiply the cost of artillery towers by 3.5, the cost of mage towers by 1.1, and the cost of towers with a long range by 1.3. Taken all together, each tower's price is calculated using a formula of:

10 * average damage per second * 1.3 [*if long range*] * 3.5 [*if artillery*] * 1.1 [*if mage*]

The prices generated in this manner are not too far off from the towers' actual cost in *Kingdom Rush* (see table 12.2).

Table 12.2 Calculated and actual *Kingdom Rush* costs.

Tower Type	Level	Calculated Cost	Actual Cost
Archer	1	66.7	70
	2	180.0	180
	3	338.0	340
Mage	1	95.3	100
	2	253.0	260
	3	543.4	500
Artillery	1	122.5	125
	2	344.2	345
	3	750.7	665

Note: The costs for towers above the first level is the sum of the price for a level 1 tower plus the price for each ensuing upgrade. For example, *Kingdom Rush*'s actual cost for a level 1 archer tower is 70 gold. Upgrading that tower to level 2 costs 110 gold, which results in a total of 180 gold for a level 2 archer tower.

You may wonder how one goes about coming up with the modifier numbers used in that calculation. A long range tower reaches about 30% further than a short range tower, thus the 1.3 multiplier. Based on an average grouping of enemies, an artillery shot can typically hit about three or four of them (let us say 3.5 on average), which determines its 3.5 multiplier. The 1.1 modifier for the mage towers could be established by setting up test cases and simply seeing how many more enemies a mage tower typically kills than an archer would in the same situation—10% more enemies killed would merit a 1.1 modifier in mage tower cost.

While there is logic behind all these numbers, establishing transitive relationships does not really eliminate the need to do guesswork. What it does is help you organize it and apply it consistently across the game's design to establish a starting place. In other words, it allows you to reduce the number of arbitrary factors in your game by having them correlate with one another. The hope is that the numbers that come out of this process are in the ballpark of being right, but the designer's expectation should be that there will be significant adjustments in response to the lessons learned in playtesting. For example, playtesting might suggest that the third level mage and artillery towers are overpriced—that the large amounts of damage they cause is not worth as much as the pricing formula calculates.

This kind of design process involves a lot of fiddling with numbers—adjustments to the way various aspects of the design are quantified and adjustments to the formula itself. This is work that really should be done in a spreadsheet. A spreadsheet allows the designer to easily play around with numbers and see how the pricing would be effective, for example, using a base multiplier of 15 (instead of 10) for each average point of damage per second. The spreadsheet the author used to generate this example can make such an adjustment by changing a single field. You can play around with the spreadsheet yourself at www.funmines.com/tower-spreadsheet.

This technique for designing numeric data is sometimes called creating a "cost curve" (Schreiber, *Game Balance* 2009) because of how it often results in a curved line when the relationship between the common basis and its result is graphed. For example, figure 12.1 is a chart of *Sid Meier's Civilization V*'s "social policy" improvement costs (Alpaca 2010). The cost of each ensuing improvement is greater than the previous ones and the more cities are owned by the player, the quicker the increase in price. This sort of inflationary rise in cost keeps a player's increasing ability to acquire game resources in check. This approach is a common difficulty balancing tool in video games.

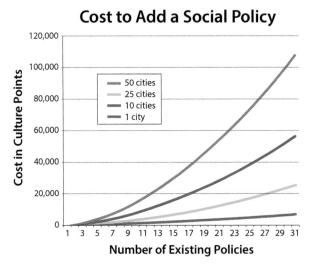

Figure 12.1 *Sid Meier's Civilization V* social policy costs.

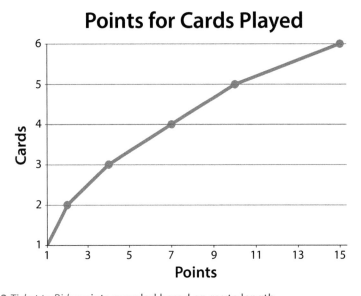

Figure 12.2 *Ticket to Ride* points awarded based on route length.

Other cost curves exist, however. For example, *Ticket to Ride* does the opposite of *Civ V*'s social policy curve and provides increasingly greater rewards per cost: the points gained for purchasing longer train routes increase faster than the cost of doing so (figure 12.2). Paying one card to claim a one-space route earns one point, but paying six cards to claim a six-space route gains 15 points.

Property Price to Rent

Property Price (y-axis): $75, $125, $175, $225, $275, $325

Rental Income (x-axis): $5, $10, $15, $20, $25, $30

Figure 12.3 *Monopoly* three-color group property price & rental income.

The relationship between a *Monopoly* property's purchase price and its rent is linear for its color sets of three (figure 12.3). Oriental Avenue has a purchase price of $100 and a rent of $6. As the properties increase in price around the board, each $20 of added cost results in a $2 increase rental income.

It is worth noting that just as a cost curve is not necessarily curved (per the *Monopoly* example), it also does not necessarily involve costs. A designer might use a comparable-basis/transitive-relationship technique to rate the relative strengths of the monsters she is designing and determine which and how many should inhabit each level of a video game.

Cost curve graphs (which are easily created using a spreadsheet) can be a visually appealing way of communicating a game's design, but keep in mind that they are usually ancillary to the actual work of making the design. Graphs are not typically used as a tool for making design choices, but rather as a way of communicating the design to others. It is also worth noting that what is being communicated by the line's curve very much depends on how the data is charted. For example, *Monopoly*'s linear relationship of property price to rent (figure 12.3) becomes curved when the rent is plotted as a percentile of the property value (figure 12.4), the curve becomes convex when the axes are flipped (figure 12.5), and curves yet another way when the property value is plotted as a multiple of the rent (figure 12.6).

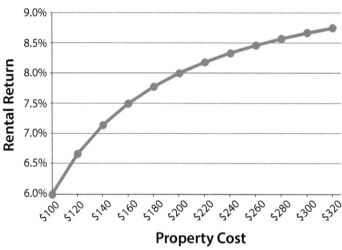

Property Cost

Figure 12.4 *Monopoly* three-color group property price & rental income as percentile of the price.

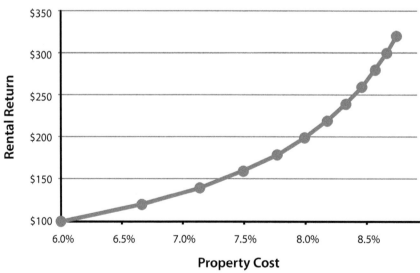

Property Cost

Figure 12.5 *Monopoly* three-color group property price based on rental return.

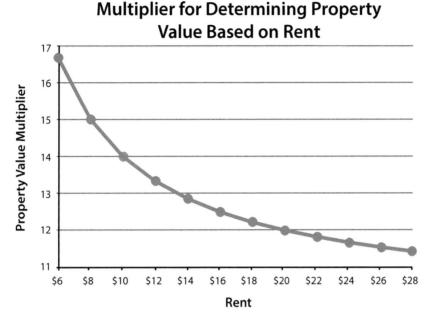

Multiplier for Determining Property Value Based on Rent

Figure 12.6 *Monopoly* three-color group rental income and multiplier for determining property price.

EXERCISE Fireball Spell

Design a formula for determining the damage inflicted by a fireball spell. The spell does not have a fixed casting cost, instead the player chooses how many "mana" points to devote to creating the spell. (Mana is a term that many games use for a resource that is required for casting magic spells). The player also determines the fireball's diameter and the location it centers upon. The damage caused by the fireball is based on those three factors (mana spent, fireball's diameter, and distance from the caster).

The wider the fireball's diameter and the farther it is from the spell caster, the weaker its damage should be. The more mana the player chooses to use in casting the spell, the stronger its damage should be. As a benchmark, the game's lightning bolt spell costs 4 points of mana, causes 1D6 points of damage, and has a range of 30'. A lightning bolt affects a single target, but the fireball deals damage to everything within its diameter. You may want to use the area of the fireball in your formulas for determining damage and cost. The formula for calculating it is: area $= \pi \times (\text{diameter}/2)^2$.

It is worth noting that there is no absolute correct answer to this exercise. The goal is to get used to thinking about balance and how to assign preliminary numbers to a game element. You want to make the fireball spell's costs and effect make sense when compared to the lightning bolt. If the fireball's effect is too powerful for the cost, then it risks making the lightning irrelevant. Conversely, if the fireball's effect is too weak, players may view it as a useless spell. Your design should support situations in which a lightning bolt is preferable, situations in which a fireball is preferable, and (ideally) situations in which it there is a tradeoff and the choice to cast one or the other is difficult (and, therefore, interesting).

Whatever solution you do come up with for this exercise will be based on some assumptions regarding the hypothetical game's mechanics and design (such as how many creatures could occupy a given targeted space). Can you identify what assumptions you made about the game?

Rankability

The fact that a design's data graphs nicely does not ensure that it is balanced. Are the property cost/rental benefit ratios for *Monopoly*'s properties balanced? Not in the sense that *Kingdom Rush*'s towers are. The towers are priced with the goal of having them provide a benefit that is in proportion to their cost—a tower that costs twice as much as another should provide twice the benefit. In *Monopoly* a $100 property generates a rental income of $6, whereas a $200 property provides an income of $16—a situation of 2 times the cost providing 2.66 times the benefit. Because the properties' benefit increases with cost, most players would prefer to own the more expensive monopolies given the choice. Yet this "imbalance" actually serves to make the game more interesting because it gives a reason for players to care about which properties they acquire. Similarly, it makes the game's trading more interesting because a one-to-one trade is rarely equitable, which causes player negotiations to be more complex and intense.

Kingdom Rush does provide players the freedom to choose which towers to purchase and upgrade, so their relative benefit must be proportional to their cost. If a tower's benefit is too high or low in comparison to its cost, then the decision to purchase it or not risks becoming obvious. However, if the different towers are too identical in terms of the benefit they provide, then the choice of which to purchase would be meaningless. What prevents this from being the case is the "intransitive relationship" between the towers.

In mathematics a relationship is transitive if the way that item A relates to item B and item B relates to item C can be applied to conclude that item A also relates that way to item C. For example, if Anne is taller than Brenda and Brenda is taller than Carol, then we know that Anne is also taller than Carol. An intransitive relationship is one in which A's relationship to C does not automatically follow from A's relationship to B and B's relationship to C. For example, the fact that Anne is Brenda's mother and Brenda is Carol's mother does not (and cannot) make Anne the mother of Carol.

Rock Paper Scissors offers a classic example of an intransitive relationship. Rock defeats scissors and scissors defeats paper, but rock does not defeat paper. In fact, rock not only does not defeat paper, but paper defeats rock (figure 12.7). This creates an "intransitive loop" relationship that defies being arranged in a set hierarchy (as we saw with intransitive Grime dice on page 203). Intransitive loops are often

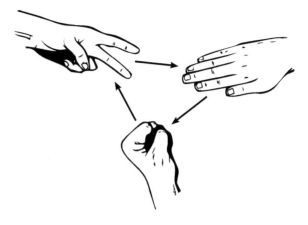

Figure 12.7 The intransitive loop in *Rock Paper Scissors*.

designed into real-time strategy video games. For example, infantry units in a game might be particularly effective against archers, archers particularly effective against mounted units, and mounted units particularly effective against infantry.

When game developers talk about intransitivity, they are almost always referring to intransitive loops. In fact, some game developers may not even realize that a non-looping relationship can still be described as intransitive. To avoid miscommunication, it may be best to use alternative terminology when referencing non-looping intransitive relationships. From a game designer's perspective, the fundamental difference between transitive and intransitive relationships is that a transitive set of items can be ranked in terms of the benefit they provide to a player, whereas an intransitive set cannot. So items in a transitive relationship could be described as being "rankable" and items in an intransitive relationship as "unrankable."

Unrankable (intransitive) relationships can create apples and oranges choices for players. Such choices are often more interesting than a rankable (transitive) choice between a bland apple and a tasty one. Unrankable relationships in games often incorporate several rankable relationships which combine to create a set of advantages and disadvantages. These combinations can make it difficult to definitively state how much benefit each composite of traits provides in comparison to the others. For example, suppose a game involves players managing a fleet of ships. Ships come in three types: fast ships with small cargo areas, slow ships with big cargo areas, and medium-speed ships with medium-sized cargo areas. The ships' speeds and cargo areas are rankable because we can sort and list them in order. Which ship is superior to the others in terms of benefit, however, is harder to rank. Even if all we care about is the profit a ship can generate, the game could easily be designed so each kind of ship yields better profits than the others in different situations.

We established a rankable relationship (in terms of price) for *Kingdom Rush*'s towers earlier as an example of creating a comparable basis. On its own, that relationship does not offer very interesting choices to the players. In fact, if the towers were perfectly priced in proportion to their benefit, one might wonder whether that renders meaningless the choice of which to purchase. What prevents that from being the case is an unrankable relationship between the towers in terms of their special abilities. Each of the towers offers a unique mix of three strengths and three weaknesses (table 12.3). This results in each tower type being best suited for some situations and worst suited for others (e.g., a mage tower is best against armored flying opponents). This enables a variety of synergies and strategies that players can explore and apply.

Table 12.3 *Kingdom Rush's* ranged-towers' special abilities.

	Strong damage	vs. armor	vs. magic	vs. flying	Speed	Multiple targets
Archer	No	No	Yes	Yes	Yes	No
Mage	Yes	Yes	No	Yes	No	No
Artillery	Yes	Yes	No	No	No	Yes

Creating a comparable basis for game elements and designing unrankable relationships can aid a designer in establishing a starting place for a game's data. As indicated earlier, however, the fact that data graphs nicely and has a systematic logic behind it does not assure that it is entirely in-balance. After creating an initial set of data for a game, a designer's next step is to test and tweak it into balance. This process is called "tuning" and is explained in the next section of the chapter.

EXERCISE *Shoot-Out* Shotgun

Shoot-Out arms the players with a revolver and a rifle. This exercise has you expand the arsenal to include a shotgun. A rifle offers more accuracy than a revolver, which is reflected in the +3 attack bonus provided by its bullets. Your shotgun should be designed with the idea that it is especially effective at close range, but quickly becomes less so as the distance between the shooter and the target increases.

Create a game setup mechanic in which players use a currency resource to purchase their rifle bullets, revolver bullets, and shotgun shells. The goal is to allow players to customize what ammunition they have in the game while maintaining balance through the assigned costs.

Tuning

Actions, assets, and events that are out of balance can often be fixed by "tuning" them. Tuning refers to a balance adjustment that involves changing some numeric trait of the game.

Tuning an action typically involves adjusting its benefits, drawbacks, accessibility, and/or cost. For example, an action in the form of a fireball spell might be tuned by changing its casting cost, how far it flies, the damage it inflicts, or how frequently it can be cast.

Events are tunable as well. For example, the fireball would be an event if it was triggered automatically by the game's system, instead of at a player's discretion. In such a case, the fireball probably would not have a casting cost, but the circumstances that cause it to manifest might be tunable. For example, if the fireball comes from a dragon's breath, it might be triggered when a player character comes within five hexes of the dragon and no fireball has been breathed in the previous three turns. The number of hexes and number of turns involved in that trigger are both tunable.

Assets often take the form of numerical attributes: health points, character level, gold pieces, victory points, and so on. An asset might be tuned by adjusting its starting value, the rate at which it increases, the rate at which it is expended, its maximum and minimum values, and so on. An asset might also be tuned indirectly by changing how its value is utilized by an action or event's algorithm.

Assets can also take more complex forms and encapsulate a set of connected sub-assets, statistics, actions, and/or events, each of which can be tuned in their own right. For example, an asset in the form of a gun might have a purchase price and resale value, the number of bullets it can hold, how much it encumbers the character, the rate at which it fires, and so on. Its actions might include shooting and reloading and it might have overheating or jamming events associated with it.

The term "tuning" is meant to evoke fiddling with a radio knob in order to get the reception as clear as possible. However, the need to manually tune a radio is rare these days, so perhaps a better analogy is the (slightly less rare) act of manually focusing a camera. A good technique for doing so is to turn the focus ring until the image sharpens *and then keep turning*. The idea is to overshoot and continue until the image begins to blur again. The photographer then turns the focus ring in the reverse direction until the image re-sharpens and then blurs again. By going back and forth, the photographer can center in on what setting provides the absolute crispest focus.

Because game dynamics can be hard to predict, a similar approach can be helpful when tuning a game. If playtesting suggests a value might need to be adjusted

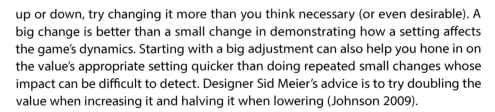

up or down, try changing it more than you think necessary (or even desirable). A big change is better than a small change in demonstrating how a setting affects the game's dynamics. Starting with a big adjustment can also help you hone in on the value's appropriate setting quicker than doing repeated small changes whose impact can be difficult to detect. Designer Sid Meier's advice is to try doubling the value when increasing it and halving it when lowering (Johnson 2009).

Making a big change can help you explore the dynamics of your game, but be careful about changing too many settings at once. It is often better to take the slower approach of changing and playtesting one value at a time so that you can clearly determine the effect it has.

Tuning is not the solution to every problem in balance. Balancing a game can also take the form of adding, removing, or changing mechanics (and not just the numeric data utilized by the mechanics). This might be done because an imbalance requires something more substantial than simply changing a number's value. Or perhaps the game designer sees an opportunity to add an interesting mechanic to the game (or eliminate one and streamline the game) and solve a balance issue simultaneously.

Imagine a game that is out-of-balance due to players being able to collect too much in-game currency once their characters reach a certain level of power. This could be addressed by decreasing the amount of currency awarded for higher level tasks (tuning), increasing the acquisition cost of higher level items (tuning), or creating additional mechanics to address the problem. For example, an "upkeep" mechanic might be instituted that requires players to spend resources to maintain their position in the game—perhaps in the form of paying guild fees based on the character's profession and level. Or perhaps expensive stays in luxury hotels are required to fully recover the higher levels of health points. Or perhaps higher level characters are provided the opportunity to purchase houses that create a continual drain on their excess capital through fees and maintenance costs.

Monster Hunter Spreadsheets

by Stone Librande

Stone Librande is the lead designer at Riot Games. Prior to joining Riot, Stone was the creative director at EA/Maxis where he has helped develop Spore *and* SimCity. *In addition to his work creating games, Stone teaches game design courses at Cogswell Polytechnic College and runs design seminars at the Game Developers Conference. Stone's game cabinet holds more than 300 tabletop games, including thirty of his own design.*

I have been designing video games for over a decade, first at Blizzard while working on *Diablo III* and then at Maxis on the games *Spore* and *SimCity*. In addition to my full-time job I also teach game design classes and give lectures at conferences and schools. After these talks I will frequently get asked the question, "How can I get a job designing video games?" The unfortunate answer is that most game companies will only hire candidates with previous experience designing games. For someone looking to get his or her foot in the door, this answer is far from satisfactory. Without experience you cannot get the job, and without the job you cannot get the experience. Or can you?

Although I was not aware of it at the time, my game design experience actually started many years before *Pong* was invented. At the age of seven I was already creating my own custom games using common objects found around the house: the backs of my father's business cards, glue and toothpicks, colored pencils and file folders. I continued making card and board games as a hobby all the way through college and after I had children of my own. I created these games for my own amusement and never attempted to publish them, as I had no interest in getting involved with the production, marketing, and distribution tasks associated with a commercial game.

Game design has been my lifelong passion, so after spending several years employed as a computer graphics programmer I decided to switch careers and attempted to get a job in the video games industry. The game studio Blizzard North (the creator of the *Diablo* series) was located nearby my home, so I decided to start there. I had no video game design experience at this point, but I took several of my tabletop games along with me. They were so interested in my collection of homemade games that we spent several hours playing a few of them as part of my interview.

The game that garnered the most attention was a card game called *Monster Hunter*. (This is not related to Capcom's video game series *Monster Hunter*, which was released several years after my card game.) Because this game is loosely based on Blizzard's *Diablo* game, many people in the studio were eager to try it out. The basic premise is that every player is a hero (a Sorcerer, Fighter, Rogue, Paladin, or Monk) and the cards in your hand represent items that are in the hero's town. These include armor, weapons, potions, and spells. In order to play cards from your hand you must purchase them by paying the item's gold cost. Gold is collected by hunting monsters and collecting a reward; the stronger the monster the more the gold it is worth.

We played the game for over an hour (by far, the most enjoyable interview I have ever had) and the next day I ended up getting a job offer. I assumed that the main reason they hired me was that they enjoyed the play session. But after talking with the hiring manager I found out that it was not the game itself, it was the supplementary material that I brought along. This included several detailed spreadsheets that I used to balance the *Monster Hunter* cards. As he explained to me, the spreadsheets showed them that I had

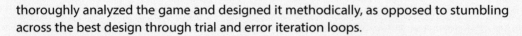

thoroughly analyzed the game and designed it methodically, as opposed to stumbling across the best design through trial and error iteration loops.

If I am working on simple tabletop games with only a few elements then a deep analysis of the game systems may not be necessary; trial and error may suffice. But for *Monster Hunter*, a game that has hundreds of unique cards, it was a necessity. There are three main uses for spreadsheets when developing a complex game: organization, probabilities, and balance. I will discuss each of these below and explain how they related to *Monster Hunter*. Try applying these techniques to your games to give you a better understanding of your underlying systems.

Organization

The simplest use of spreadsheets is to keep your game assets organized. Every component of your game should be listed out, with one item per row. This is not necessary for games with few components, but it is essential when making a game with a large number of unique cards.

Monster Hunter has 75 monster cards, 21 townsfolk, 14 events, 30 weapons, 15 pieces of armor, 9 potions, and 30 hero skills. Early in development I tried keeping track of everything in my head and when I needed to refer to the details of a specific card I would manually search through the deck looking for the card in question. It did not take me long to realize how much time I was wasting with this approach. At that point I decided it was time to use a spreadsheet.

It only took about an hour to transfer all the card values into a spreadsheet. After that, the design process became much simpler. Now when I needed to refer to a card I could find it in seconds. I could also re-sort the list at any time to see all the cards by alphabetic name order, or by cost, speed, damage, or any other variable. This made it easy to see patterns and distributions. I also recommend adding in a "Notes" field in order to keep track of your players' feedback and suggestions after each play session.

Instead of tracking your components in a flat list, you might consider organizing them into a matrix. The applicability of this technique will depend on the type of game you are making, but for *Monster Hunter* it was extremely helpful. For example, the game has five character types with six skills each. Instead of listing the heroes' skill cards in 30 separate rows, I created a 5 by 6 grid (figure 12.8).

The matrix makes it easy to compare cards across categories and will help you see where gaps exist in your design. I strongly recommend making the matrix first, and then creating the cards that will fit into the matrix as the second step in your design process. This forces a top-down approach to your design. It also keeps you focused on the key aspects of your game that are needed to fill out the table, which will prevent you from wasting time exploring non-critical paths. This is the first step towards keeping your design balanced.

	A	B	C	D	E	F	G	H	I	J	K
1		**Fighter**		**Paladin**		**Rogue**		**Sorcerer**		**Monk**	
2	**Movement**	Outdoor Survival		Faithful Steed		Wanderer		Town Portal		One with Nature	
3	**Close**	Deadly Aim		Day of Prayer	+	Back Stab	+	Shock	+	Fists of Fury	+
4	**combat**	Berserker's Rage	+	Divine Strength							
5	**Range**	Throwing Arm	+			Eagle Eye		Energy Bolt	+	Flying Kick	+
6	**Defense**			Guard Stance	+	Stealth		Force Shield	+	Expert Evasion	+
7	**Shopping**	Tough Talker	+	Charisma	+	Swipe	+	Alchemy		Constant Practice	+
8	**Other**	Battle Training		Alms to the Poor		Trap	+	Recharge	+	Master Tracking	
9											
10				"+" = skill increases as character levels							

Figure 12.8 *Monster Hunter* character skills.
By Stone Librande.

Probabilities

Another important use of spreadsheets is to calculate probabilities. This can be very helpful, especially in games that involve randomness. Instead of playing hundreds of games to get a feel for the odds, your spreadsheet can tell you the likelihood of a particular event happening with mathematical precision. While it is beyond the scope of this essay to teach probability theory, I did want to mention a few of the ways I used spreadsheets to calculate the odds for *Monster Hunter*.

There is a lot of combat in the game and I wanted to get a sense of how much damage a particular weapon would inflict. Because there are several random elements involved in each combat round the actual calculations were tricky. Fortunately, since I had already input a list of all of the weapon values, it was relatively simple to create a formula and then apply it to every row in the spreadsheet with only a few mouse clicks.

The first step, figuring out the average amount of damage caused by a given weapon when it hits, was trivial. Each weapon card has six numbers in a damage track along the bottom of the card. Whenever a weapon hits, the attacker rolls a 6-sided die and cross-references it to the numbers on the track. For instance, a Club has the numbers 0,1,1,1,2,3 in its damage track (figure12.9), meaning that if the attacker rolled a 1 then it would do 0

Figure 12.9 *Monster Hunter* "Club" card.
Illustration by Randall Mackey.

damage, while a roll a 6 would do 3 damage. By simply creating a new column called "Average Damage" and using the built-in "=AVERAGE()" function I could immediately see how powerful each weapon was.

The second step, calculating the odds that a given weapon hits, was more involved. In *Monster Hunter* each combat round begins with an "initiative roll" between the hero and the monster to determine who attacks and who defends. This is accomplished by rolling a 6-sided die and adding the result of this die roll to a "speed" trait. Whoever has the highest score attacks while the lower score defends. (In the case of a tie, both the hero and the monster hit each other simultaneously.) An added complication for the formula is that a natural 1 automatically misses and a natural 6 automatically hits, regardless of the speed modifiers. (This rule made the combat more exciting, since even a slow Rot Rat has a chance to attack a mighty warrior).

Figure 12.10 *Monster Hunter* "Rot Rat" and "Fighter" cards.
Illustration by Randall Mackey.

To determine the "chance to hit" percentages I created a spreadsheet that holds a number of probability tables, showing the range of speed differentials, from –4 to +4 (see figure 12.11). Each table is a simple 6 by 6 matrix that indexes the hero's roll in the top row and the monster's roll in the left column. The 36 cells in the table contain a formula that compares the two values (factoring in the speed differential) to determine who wins the

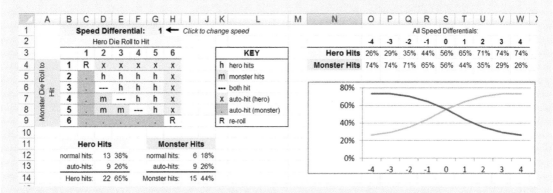

Figure 12.11 *Monster Hunter* "to hit" probabilities (left) and speed differentials (right).
By Stone Librande.

initiative and attacks. An "m" appears in the cell if the hero misses, while an "h" appears if the hero hits. A dashed line ("---") represents a tie.

Off to the side of each table a "=COUNTIF()" function is used to count up the number of hits and misses (with ties counting as both). The resulting number is divided by 36 to give the percentage chance that the hero will miss or hit. The values of the individual tables are stored into another table, making it easy to see how the hero's chances increase as the speed differential changes.

I strongly recommend making probability tables like these for all the random elements in your games. They are simple to create and let you see the entire space of your system at once. They are particularly good for showing you results of the extreme cases that may not appear that often in actual playtest sessions.

Balance

Trying to keep all of your components balanced against each other can be tricky, especially in games with many components. Fortunately, if you are already using a spreadsheet to organize your assets as described above then you are in a good place to start. In *Monster Hunter* I needed to make a wide spectrum of items with varying costs and strengths, but I didn't want any one item to dominate over the others. For example, there are five different types of bows in the game (figure 12.12), from a cheap common Short Bow to the expensive rare Spirit Bow. Each bow has a cost in gold, a speed (used to determine the chance to hit), and a damage track.

To help me understand the balance between the weapons I created a simple spreadsheet that contains all of the weapon data stored in rows. At the end of each row I added a column called, "Worth" that takes all of these numbers, runs them through a formula, and outputs a score. (The details of the formula are not important for this discussion, but

Figure 12.12 *Monster Hunter* bow cards.
Illustration by Randall Mackey.

generally speaking it calculates how much damage a given weapon does on average, divided by the amount of gold it costs.) The table is sorted by the Worth value which makes it easy to quickly see which weapons are too weak or too strong for their cost.

Since the Worth field is calculated dynamically it is a simple matter to adjust the overall balance. Just change any parameter value (speed, damage, or cost) and watch the weapon's Worth update. Deciding which parameter to change can be tricky, especially if you have many variables in your formula. My rule of thumb is to try to get the best distribution of values possible. For example, suppose a Hand Axe has a worth of 1.2 damage per gold coin and a Mace has a worth of 3.5. If both weapons cost the same amount then I would increase the gold coins required to buy the Mace. However, if both weapons already had different costs but the same speed, then I would decrease the Mace's speed. Having a wide range of values across all the parameters will make each of your components unique and it ultimately gives your player more interesting options.

In *Monster Hunter* I used this same technique for all the card types. Armor had its own table, as did potions and magic items. Of all the types, the monster spreadsheet is the most complex, as I needed to factor in special non-numerical abilities as well. For instance, the "Brak Mage" ignores armor with his magical attack, while the "Claw Fiend" gets a free attack at the start of combat due to his ability to ambush. In order to convert these abilities into numbers for the "Worth" formula (which, for monsters, determines if the gold reward is worth the effort it takes to kill the monster) I used a simple "weak-to-strong" ranking, where no special ability equals 0, a weak ability equals 1, an average ability equals 2, and a strong ability equals 3. These numbers are then inserted into the "Worth" formula.

Unfortunately, there is no correct way to determine these values and how they should affect the formulas. Usually a relative ranking of the abilities can be estimated through play testing. It should not take too many sessions before you get an intuitive sense of which abilities would be considered weak, average, or strong.

Although the spreadsheet makes it easy to tune every component of the game until it is perfectly balanced mathematically, I frequently put in a few components that have a slightly higher Worth than average. After playing a few games the players intuitively start to notice these anomalies. When this occurs these "power items" can add moments of excitement in the game as the players race to be the first to accumulate enough gold to buy them first. After all, if all your game components are perfectly balanced then the player would not need to make any decisions at all, since each choice would net exactly the same results as any other choice.

Conclusion

Developing a disciplined approach to design is an important skill, whether you are working on tabletop games or electronic games. Spreadsheets are excellent tools to track your game designs as they progress. Often you can learn more about your game from your spreadsheets than you can from your playtest sessions.

Of course, spreadsheets cannot replace human players. Players are fickle, emotional, and (with a few exceptions) are not too interested in calculating probabilities with mathematical precision. Ultimately, their entertainment and satisfaction is your primary goal. But a spreadsheet will help you gain a thorough understanding of all the

components in your game, along with the knowledge that you know the bounds of the play space. This will allow you to spend your playtest time focusing on the players themselves instead of the underlying systems and mechanics.

The *Monster Hunter* spreadsheets described in this essay can be downloaded at www.funmines.com/monster-hunter.

Asymmetry

An asymmetric game has gameplay that differs in some significant way for each of the players. Games can be asymmetric in terms of the players' starting positions or starting resources, what rules apply to the individual players, and/or victory conditions. Taking turns can also create asymmetry (see sidebar page 249), but generally that form of asymmetry is not what is being described when a game is characterized as being "asymmetric."

A game that starts its players in nonequivalent positions or unequal resources could be described as having an "initial game state" asymmetry. This kind of asymmetry appears in any playing card game that begins with players being dealt cards because each hand of cards is different from the others. War games often have asymmetric initial game states in which players occupy different positions on a map. While *Shoot-Out* as a whole is symmetric, the individual duels can have asymmetric initial game states if one player begins the duel with fewer bullet resources than the other player.

Ideally, an asymmetric initial game state adds interest to a game by encouraging players to employ different strategies of play in order to be competitive. The risk is that a player may start a game in such a disadvantaged position that it undermines the fairness and enjoyment of the game.

A game with asymmetric victory conditions is similar to one with multiple victory conditions in that both types of games have more than one criterion for winning. They differ in that the victory conditions are not applicable to everyone in the game; only some of the game's players can win by fulfilling a given victory condition's criteria. If a game has asymmetric victory conditions, it almost certainly has another form as asymmetry as well—most likely the rules are asymmetric or both the rules and the initial game state are asymmetric.

The ancient genre of hunt games typically has all three kinds of asymmetry. Hunt games present a scenario of hunter (or predator) and prey, with each player taking one of the two roles. The hunters try to capture the prey, the prey tries to escape (or sometimes tries to trap the hunters). Traditional hunt games include *Bagh Guti*, *Fox and Hounds*, *Brandub* (which casts the players' roles as king and guards versus attackers), and the ubiquitous playground game of *Hide and Seek*. *Three Musketeers* (page 249) is a modern addition to the hunt game tradition. When playing the game, one player controls three pieces that represent the Three Musketeers and the other player controls twenty-two pieces representing their enemies (Cardinal Richelieu's men). The two sides have different movement rules with only the Musketeers being able to capture pieces. The Musketeer side wins the game if it has no legal moves, the Cardinal's side wins if the Three Musketeers end up being positioned on the same row or column.

> The turn order in a tabletop game often provides some benefit for the player who is first (or sometimes the player who is last). Strictly speaking, it is correct to describe a game for which this is the case as being asymmetric. In practice, however, a game whose only form of asymmetry comes from taking turns (such as *Chess*) is still usually described as being symmetrical.

It is very difficult to ensure that asymmetric games are balanced and that the asymmetry does not favor any particular side. Probably the best a game designer can do is get the balance close. Some asymmetric games address this by having a match composed of two games, with the players trading off roles. This works if the victory can be measured so that if both players win there is a way to determine who had the greater margin of victory.

Try playing *Three Musketeers* and see what you think of the balance. Is one side favored over the other? Try to determine which side is favored. The answer is at the end of the chapter on page 251.

Three Musketeers

This game was designed by Haar Hoolim and first appeared in Sid Sackson's influential book, *A Gamut of Games*. Game designer Marc LeBlanc uses it for a design exercise in a workshop he has been teaching at the Game Developers Conference since 2001. (Visit www.funagain.com/leblanc for a link to LeBlanc's exercise.)

Three Musketeers is an asymmetric game: the players' resources, starting positions, and abilities differ. One player is cast in the role of the Three Musketeers and controls,

naturally enough, three game pieces. The other player controls 22 pieces that represent the Musketeers' nemeses, Cardinal Richelieu's men.

Players:

■ Two players

Required Materials:

■ 22 game pieces representing Cardinal Richelieu's forces
■ 3 game pieces representing the Musketeers
■ A 5 × 5 grid to serve as the game board

Object of the Game:

■ The Musketeer player's goal is to maneuver her three pieces so that none of them are orthogonally adjacent to any of the Cardinal pieces (see figure 12.14, left).
■ The Cardinal player's goal is to force all three Musketeer pieces to occupy the same row or column on the board (see figure 12.14, right).

Setup:

■ Two of the Musketeer pieces are placed in opposite corners of the board and the third in the center square. The Cardinal pieces occupy all the remaining squares. See figure 12.13.

Rules:

1. Starting with the Musketeers, players take turns moving one of their pieces. Players must move when possible; choosing to skip a turn is not allowed.
2. A move must be to an orthogonally adjacent square.
3. The Musketeer pieces must make a capture when they move; the square they move into must be occupied by a Cardinal piece.
4. The Cardinal pieces cannot capture and the square they move into must be vacant.
5. The Musketeer player wins if none of her pieces can move (i.e., none of them are orthogonally adjacent to a Cardinal piece). See figure 12.14 (left).
6. The Cardinal player wins if the three Musketeer pieces line up orthogonally (i.e., if the three pieces

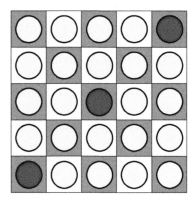

Figure 12.13 Setting up the game.

occupy the same row or column, though not necessarily in adjacent spaces). See figure 12.14 (right).

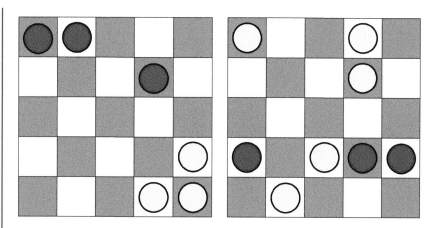

Figure 12.14 The Musketeers win (left), the Cardinal wins (right).

EXERCISE Expanding *ZimP*

Expand *Zombie in my Pocket* to be an asymmetric two-player game with the second player taking on the role of the zombies. Revise the core mechanic and add game pillars as necessary to support two-person competitive play.

Can you balance the game so that the zombie and human sides have an equal chance of winning? If not, is there a way of measuring the margin of victory so that players taking turns playing each side can see who had the larger victory?

Answer to the *Three Musketeers* Question on Page 249

While the Musketeer's capturing ability seems to give them the advantage, the *Three Musketeers* is actually imbalanced in favor of the Cardinal's men. The game has been "solved," which means that all of the game's possible outcomes have been calculated based on both players making the best possible choices. The solution shows that a player who controls the Cardinal's men will always win if she makes the optimal moves. Against this, the player who controls the Musketeers cannot win even if her moves are just as optimal.

CHAPTER THIRTEEN

Turns, Ticks, & Time

INTRODUCTION

One of the common stumbling blocks for novice video game designers is understanding how to design real-time games. This chapter aims to demystify " real-time" and show how the use of flowcharts can help a designer specify a design as a rigorous series of concrete steps.

The learning objectives for this chapter are:

1 Be able to describe how turn-based and real-time games are similar and how they differ.

2 Understand how a game's mechanics can be structured into a main game loop.

3 Become familiar with flowcharting as a game design tool.

Turns and Real-time

Most tabletop games are structured into turns and rounds, with players' actions unfolding one at a time. Much more unusual are tabletop games that utilize continuous time in which players' actions can overlap and occur at any time (see www.funmines.com/tag/continuous-time for some print-and-play continuous time games).

Video games are also often characterized as either being "turn-based" or having continuous "real-time." A turn-based video game typically has its game state remaining static while the player decides what actions to take. For example, the zombie apocalypse game *Rebuild 2* is structured into turns, each of which represents a day of in-game time. During each turn, the player assigns tasks to the people in his encampment and presses the "End Day" button to submit his choices. The game then presents the outcome of the player's actions, after which it is time to assign the next day's tasks. In contrast, *Tetris* and *Kingdom Rush* are real-time games—the play happens continuously and does not pause for the player to make a decision. The *Tetris* blocks keep falling and the *Kingdom Rush* baddies keep coming.

Continuous time is unusual in a tabletop game. Continuous time on the tabletop tends to create a frenetic dynamic—it is hard to have a relaxed game when players have to manage real-time game state changes. In contrast, a video game can utilize real-time without it necessarily putting pressure on the players because the computer can take over the task of managing the ongoing changes to game state. This is why continuous time is more common in video games than on the tabletop.

One way to make continuous time more manageable on the tabletop is to have it occur only in specific situations. For example, the standard playing card games *Egyptian Ratscrew*, *Slapjack*, and *Spoons* all have a suspenseful core mechanic that centers on switching from turn-based to continuous action when a certain criterion is met.

A "synchronous process" is one in which each step must finish before the next one commences; one thing happens at a time. An "asynchronous process" is one in which actions and events can overlap and happen simultaneously. The primary structure of a turn-based game's structure (a sequence of turns) is a "synchronous" process. This is not to say that a turn-based game cannot incorporate asynchronous elements. For example, *Magic: the Gathering* has "instant" spells which "you can cast . . . just about any time you want, even during your opponent's turn or in response to another spell" (Tabak 2013, 6). *Rebuild 2* provides another example of how synchronous and asynchronous processes can intermingle. While the game is turn-based, the fact that a player can have several actions ongoing simultaneously (figure 13.1) is more suggestive of an asynchronous process.

Real-time games have a primary structure (simultaneous gameplay) that is an asynchronous process. Real-time games can also incorporate synchronous structures. For example, *Kingdom Rush*'s main gameplay is asynchronous, but each level begins synchronously, allowing the player to place towers prior to starting the action. Another example can be seen in *Tetris*. It is a real-time game in which the player can take actions concurrent (asynchronously) with the falling motion of the game piece. But the series of falling game pieces itself is synchronous—there is only one falling piece at a time and the next piece does not appear until the current piece lands.

Figure 13.1 *Rebuild 2* circled icons showing the locations of player actions and the number of turns/days remaining until they are completed.

Tabletop game design skills are very applicable to designing turn-based video games, such as *Rebuild 2*. Tabletop games and turn-based video games both generally involve repeated cycles of the player (or players) deciding to take certain actions followed by the game state being updated. The primary difference between a tabletop game and a turn-based video game is that the video game automates the game state updating and the mediation of player actions. This gives a video game designer the option of hiding the exact underlying mechanics that determine how player actions impact the game state and have those mechanics be much more computationally intensive than is practical for a tabletop game.

For example, *Rebuild 2*'s interface communicates the idea that increasing the number of people in a zombie-clearing party increases the people's safety as well as the number of zombies that will be killed. However, how the safety is calculated is not presented to players (many of whom probably do not even notice the lack of information). Behind the scenes, Sarah Northway (*Rebuild 2*'s game designer) has the danger of a zombie-killing mission determined as a 15% base danger plus 10% * distance from the fort (less if you research Stealth) plus up to 78% based on the number of zombies on the square minus up to 25% per survivor in the mission based on their soldier and scavenger skills (Northway, email to author, 2013).

To the uninitiated, designing a real-time game like *Kingdom Rush* can seem a much more mysterious and daunting undertaking. Designing a real-time game becomes more manageable if it is treated as if it is turn-based. It may seem that doing so would

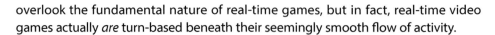

overlook the fundamental nature of real-time games, but in fact, real-time video games actually *are* turn-based beneath their seemingly smooth flow of activity.

Real-time games are turn-based in much the same way that the fluid motion of a movie (or game) character running across the screen is actually a series of still images. The illusion of smooth motion is created by the speed at which the images are shown. Similarly, the actions that a computer-controlled character takes in a real-time game are really a series of simple instructions.

Sarah Northway

Sarah Northway is the creator of the Rebuild *series. Here she describes how she has combined her love of travel with her work developing games.*

I grew up playing video games, first on a NES (Nintendo) that I saved a year's allowance for, then on PC where I lost myself in huge, open-ended strategy games (*SimCity, Civilization, Master of Orion, X-Com*) and RPGs (the *Elder Scrolls* series, *Might & Magic, Wizardry*). I toyed with making games in my spare time, but never imagined a career in game development since I assumed I would have to learn a lot of math and crunch nonstop, working through the

Photo 13.1 Sarah Northway working on her next game.

weekends. Instead I became a web developer and worked on tedious intranet projects and government databases, learning how to structure code and comment properly (a rare skill for indie game developers, I believe). My husband and I saved up and took a year off to travel through Southeast Asia, where I wrote a game for fun in my copious spare time—a huge, open-ended MMO, which of course I never finished. But it made me realize I could do this for a living, so when the year was up I took a job at the amazing indie games company, Three Rings in San Francisco. There I worked on games like *Puzzle Pirates* and *Whirled*. My husband Colin continued to write games in his spare time and when his game *Fantastic Contraption* took off, so did we. I wrote *Rebuild, Rebuild 2, Word Up Dog*, and *Incredipede* (with Colin) while living in countries like Turkey, France, Scotland, Honduras, Costa Rica, the Philippines, and Mexico. We stay for two or three months in each place and go back "home" to Vancouver every summer. Our plan is to keep traveling and writing games.

Ticks

Imagine you are playing a game of *Chess*. And you decide to impose a turn clock. Each player is given one minute to make a move. If the move is not made within that time, the turn is lost and the opponent can take a turn.

Now imagine you were playing a faster game with a turn length of 30 seconds. We can continue this thought experiment with turns as short as we like—we could even make the turns as inhumanly short as 0.05 seconds. At this point it becomes very difficult to take a turn within the time limit; you and your opponent will miss most of your turns. A move will take place only on a small number of the turns.

Your staid game of *Chess* has become a frantic series of moves—if you can move quick enough you can capture several of your opponent's pieces and put her king into check before she can react. At this point you are effectively playing a continuous time game.

This is how time works in video games like *Kingdom Rush*. The "turns" happen so quickly—perhaps one every 50 milliseconds (0.05 seconds)—that players are not even aware of their existence. From a player's perspective the game is continuous; but from a programmer's perspective the game is a series of discrete "ticks."

In the case of *Tetris*, at each tick the player has the opportunity to manipulate the falling block and the program checks and sees if it is time for the block to fall to

Figure 13.2 *Neptune's Pride II: Triton* detail showing that two ships are estimated to arrive at Propus in 4 hours, 39 minutes, and 25 seconds. Used with permission of Iron Helmet Games.

Turns & Ticks

Turns form an explicit part of the gameplay; players are aware of their existence. A tick is an internal part of the video game software; it happens behind the curtain and is generally imperceptible to players.

the next line. Most of these ticks go by with nothing happening—the player is not pressing a button and it is not yet time for the block to move. The game designer might have specified that the blocks should only fall every 0.5 seconds at the start of the game, so the programmer tracks how many ticks have passed since the last time the block fell—if it has been 10 ticks, then the block is moved down another line.

Speeding up a turn-based game creates the appearance of continual time. What happens if we slow down a real-time game so that its game ticks occur once every hour instead of every few milliseconds? That is exactly how the "real-time" strategy game of *Neptune's Pride II: Triton* works. The game slowly unfolds with player actions typically taking hours or even days to resolve. For example, figure 13.2 shows that a player's fleet of ships will take another 4 hours, 39 minutes, and 25 seconds to reach a relatively close destination. All actions begin on the hour, so if a player submits an order at 8:47am, the action does not actually commence until 9:00am. Similarly, player actions resolve and their outcomes are calculated on the hour, so fleets of ships always take an even number of hours to travel from one star system to another.

So while *Neptune's Pride II: Triton* is often described as being a real-time game, the game state is only updated once per hour. The game's ships glide smoothly (and slowly) towards their destinations, but their arrivals (and the action that follows) always coincide with a tick. The resulting gameplay does not differ significantly from that of an online turn-based game that is set up to have turns occurring every few days.

The Game Loop

What happens when a video game tick occurs? A tick is analogous to a round in a tabletop game. A round consists of each player taking a turn, so a round in *Marrakech* is made up of the following steps:

Marrakech Round

Starting with the first player, have each player take a turn as follows:

Marrakech turn:

1. Rotate Assam (if desired).
2. Throw the die.

---

3. Move Assam.
4. Pay an opponent (if necessary).
5. Place a rug.

Last player's turn is finished, start the next round.

In a similar manner, each tick in a video game involves the computer running through a series of steps. For example, a tick in *Kingdom Rush* might consist of the computer running through what is called the "main game loop":

Kingdom Rush Main Game Loop

1. Update enemy unit positions.
   a. Deduct player's life for each enemy who has successfully crossed the game's field.
2. Check to see if new enemy units should be spawned.
   a. If so, spawn enemy.
3. Check for player actions & handle.
4. Update in-flight missile locations.
   a. Handle missile impacts.
5. Update the locations of the player's units.
6. Handle melee combat.
7. Handle tower events.

After Step 7 is complete, return to Step 1 on the next tick and repeat.

Just as a tabletop game consists of one round after another until the game concludes, a video game's main game loop drives the game's core mechanics by repeating over and over throughout the game. Many games are actually programmed using a main game loop, but even when that is not the case, it is still often useful for the game designer to use a conceptual model of a game loop (see www.funmines.com/game-loops for more details about game loops from a programmer's point of view).

In addition to the main loop, a game may use "sub-routines" to run particular mechanics or game elements. A sub-routine is an algorithm that handles a secondary task, such as how Step 7 in the main game loop above manages the events associated with towers:

Tower Events Sub-Routine

If it is a missile tower:

1. Determine how long since the last missile was shot.
   a. End routine if it is not yet time for next shot.
2. Determine which enemies are in range.
   a. End routine if no enemies are in range.
3. Select an enemy to target.
4. Shoot a missile.

If it is a melee tower:

1. Check how many of the tower's soldiers are alive.
   a. End routine if three soldiers are alive.
2. Determine how long since the last soldier was spawned.
   a. End routine if not yet time to spawn a replacement soldier.
3. Spawn new soldier.

The main game loop calls upon each tower in turn to run through that sub-routine. In doing so, a special kind of loop is formed—a "for-each loop." Where the main game loop occurs over and over indefinitely (what might be called an "infinity loop"), a for-each loop involves running one time through a set of similar items and having the algorithm applied to each. So what Step 7 summarizes as "handle tower events" is (in more detail) "for each tower, run through the Tower Events sub-routine."

The Tower Events sub-routine could have sub-routines and for-each loops of its own. For example, Step 3 in the missile section of the Tower Events sub-routine might utilize a for-each loop that evaluates each enemy within range to prioritize who should be attacked.

The point of this is that the apparently seamless ongoing action of a real-time game can be broken down into a set of discrete steps. The steps in a real-time game loop are not all that different from the steps players go through when playing a tabletop game. A video game designer's job is to collaborate with the game's programmers in figuring out how to create a set of algorithmic steps from which the desired gameplay can emerge.

EXERCISE *The World's Most Boring Tower Defense Game*

The World's Most Boring Tower Defense Game (www.funmines.com/boring-tower-defense) allows you to experiment with the difference between turns and real-time. When "played" as a turn-based game, each press of the "Next Turn" button causes the main game loop to run once through. When played as a real-time strategy game, the main game loop is automatically executed at a rate set by the "turns per second" control. The main game loop consists of the following events:

1. Update the attacker's position.
2. Check and see if it is time for the attackers to attack.
   a. If so, initiate and resolve attack.
3. Check to see if the tower has run out of hit points.
   a. If so, tower collapses.
4. Check and see if it is time for the towers to attack.
   a. If so, initiate and resolve attack.
5. Check to see if the attacker has run out of hit points.
   a. If so, attacker dies.

You may wonder about the amount of space this book devotes to flowcharting. For many years I struggled to teach my students how to make the leap from designing tabletop games to designing video games. In particular, students without a programming background would consistently have problems defining a video game design as a series of concrete steps that do not leave gaping holes in the game algorithms.

Then one semester I taught my students flowcharting and had them create a flowchart that could play a simple game that I had designed. As if by magic, these students had no problem creating video game designs. Ever since that semester, I have always introduced students to video game design by starting with flowcharting. It has become my magical "turn you into a game designer" wand.

Flowcharting

The steps and processes in a game loop are often complicated and dynamic enough that a list does not capture or communicate them well. Flowchart diagrams can be better at documenting game mechanics because they make visible how the progression of the game changes based on the game state, events, and player actions.

Flowcharts tend to be filled with diamond and rectangle symbols that represent decision points and process activities, respectively. In addition to those two workhorses, dozens of other more specialized symbols exist, of which we will be looking at a couple (terminators and sub-routines). Arrows connect one symbol to the next to indicate the order in which the process's steps occur.

Diamond-shaped decision points represent places in a process where what step occurs next can vary and is determined by some condition. Diamonds pose questions, the answer to which determines which labeled, outgoing arrow is followed. Typically diamonds ask yes/no questions and have two exit arrows extending from them, but it is certainly okay to have multiple arrows extending from a diamond that has more

The *Kingdom Rush* algorithms and flowcharts presented in this chapter are hypothetical. They are intended as an example of what a designer *might* create—not what was actually created by the *Kingdom Rush* designers.

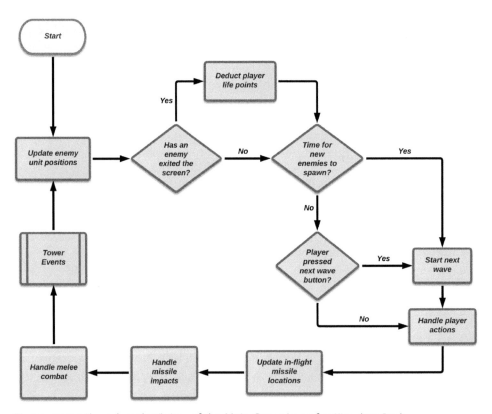

Figure 13.3 A "broad strokes" view of the Main Game Loop for *Kingdom Rush*.

than two possible answers. For example, if rolling a 1D6 had three possible outcomes based on the number rolled, a decision diamond that documents the roll mechanic might have three outgoing arrows, one for each outcome.

Rectangles represent an activity (often involving a change to the game state). Rectangles are where things get done. In figures 13.3 and 13.4, which chart

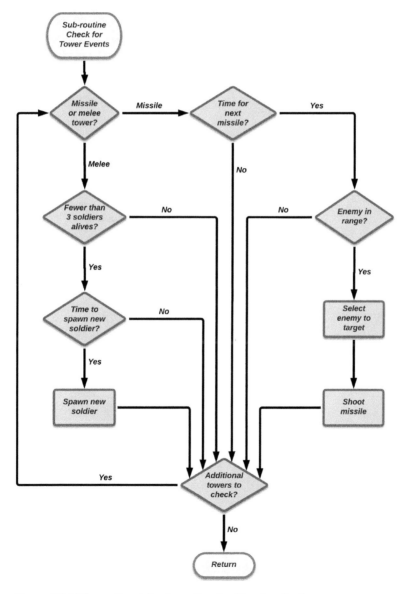

Figure 13.4 "Tower Events" sub-routine for *Kingdom Rush*.

Kingdom Rush, rectangle boxes are used to specify activities such as deducting points from the player and having new units appear on the playing field.

Terminators are usually lozenge (⬭) or oval shaped and represent the start and end points of the diagrammed process. There should only be one start terminator (located in the upper-left corner of the diagram), but multiple end terminators are possible and acceptable.

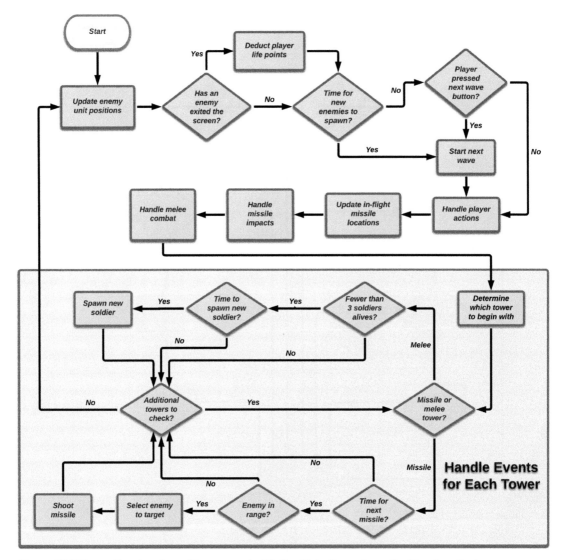

Figure 13.5 Tower Events sub-routine merged with the Main Game Loop for *Kingdom Rush*.

The main game loop flowchart (figure 13.3) does not include an end point—it documents what happens during the main game loop, but does not show how the loop is exited and the game is suspended or finished. Details such as the ways in which a player can save and exit a game can be important to programmers and user experience designers (who might create their own flowcharts that document those sorts of processes), but it is generally best for game designers to avoid bloating their own flowcharts with details that are not central to the game design.

Kingdom Rush's Tower Events sub-routine is represented by a special "sub-process" symbol: a rectangular box with double vertical lines (▯). This indicates that the sub-routine has been separated into its own secondary diagram (figure 13.4). When the sub-process symbol is encountered, the reader knows to jump to the secondary flowchart and follow its steps before returning to the main flowchart and advancing to its next step.

Sub-process flowcharts allow a complicated process to be broken up and organized into several flowcharts. If the steps in the Tower Events sub-routine were included in the Main Game Loop flowchart, it would nearly double in size (figure 13.5). Separating the sub-routine's steps into their own flowchart streamlines the main flowchart and makes understanding and updating the process more manageable. As further details are added to the Tower Events flowchart (such as how a missile tower determines who to target), it might end up having sub-process flowcharts of its own in order to keep the overall process easy to read, maintain, and expand.

Flowcharting Tools

Many document-creation software packages (such as *Word*, *Excel*, *OpenOffice Draw*, *Google Drive Drawing*, etc.) have shapes that can be used to create a flowchart. However, these tools are much clunkier and more tedious to use than software that is specifically designed for creating flowcharts. Quite a few free flowcharting-specific programs exist and a quick search can turn up a number of options for you. As a starting place, you might want to try *Lucidchart* (www.lucidchart.com) or *Gliffy* (www.gliffy.com). They are both free web-based programs—the former is what was used to create the flowcharts in this book.

Keep in mind that if you find yourself spending more energy grappling with a flowcharting tool than making actual progress, you can always opt for the straightforward simplicity of drawing out the diagram using pencil and paper.

EXERCISE Tower Flowchart

Chapter 2 included a flowchart (figure 2.6, page 36) that documents the process of determining whether the end condition for *The Tower* has been reached and, if so, who lost.

Create a similar flowchart that outlines the process for determining who won a game of *Marrakech*. The game's rules do not specify the outcome when multiple players are tied for the most points and have the exact same number of visible rug halves and possess the same number of Dirham. Determine how that situation should be handled and have the solution included in your flowchart.

EXERCISE *Shoot-Out* Flowchart

Create a flowchart based on the *Shoot-Out* turn outlined below.

Player performs one of the following three actions:

1. Advance 1 space
   a. At center of board?
      - Yes: Player wins the duel.
      - No: Opponent's turn.
2. Retreat
   a. Opponent on space 6 or higher?
      - Yes: Gain 2 revolver bullets.
   b. Opponent wins duel.
3. Shoot
   a. Player has bullets?
      - No: Cannot shoot, choose different action.
   b. Rifle or revolver?
      - Rifle:
         - Have rifle bullet?
            - No: Choose revolver or different action.

- Discard rifle bullet.
- Roll 20-sided die.
- Add 3 to the rolled value.
- >= Player's space?
    - No: Opponent's turn.
    - Yes:
        - Move opponent back 3 spaces (to maximum of 20).
        - Take another turn.
- Revolver:
    - Have revolver bullet?
        - No: Choose rifle or another action.
    - Discard revolver bullet.
    - Roll 20-sided die.
    - >= Player's space?
        - No: Opponent's turn.
        - Yes:
            - Move opponent back 3 spaces (to maximum of 20).
            - Take another turn.

Data Heavy Design

The flowchart in figure 13.3 includes a decision diamond that asks "Time for new enemies to spawn?" At some point, the game designer needs to provide further details for that step. The timing for when enemies spawn is data heavy and something which the designer might expect to tune extensively. Rather than try to capture the information in the flowchart, it would be better to keep it separate in a text or table format. Here is how *Kingdom Rush*'s enemy spawning mechanic might be documented:

The first group in each wave (see table 13.1) appears three seconds after the wave starts. For subsequent groups in a wave, there is a three-second interval before a goblin group appears and a seven-second interval before an orc group.

There is a one-second interval between the spawning of each enemy within a group. The enemies in Wave 7 are an exception to this rule: they have a half-second interval between each spawn.

Table 13.1 Enemy spawn timing.

Wave #	Enemy groupings	Elapsed time since start of previous wave
1	3 Goblins	N/A
2	3 Goblins 3 Goblins	31 seconds
3	3 Goblins 3 Goblins 3 Goblins	36 seconds
4	4 Goblins 1 Orc	41 seconds
5	3 Orcs	41 seconds
6	5 Goblins 2 Orcs 5 Goblins 2 Orcs	35 seconds
7	16 Goblins	58 seconds

Not only would it be cumbersome to put those design details into flowchart form, but it would be more difficult to read and revise as well. Flowcharts are useful for breaking down and presenting game mechanics, but they are not your only design documentation tool.

CHAPTER FOURTEEN

Designing Autonomy

INTRODUCTION

This chapter delves into designing autonomous behavior in games—what is often called "artificial intelligence." While the chapter does not shy away from using the term artificial intelligence (and its acronym, "AI"), the more expansive description of creating "autonomous behavior" is probably a better way of viewing the design task.

"Artificial intelligence" can be an apt description for the decision-making process of a computer-controlled soldier. Ascribing "intelligence" to how a computer-simulated ant navigates its surroundings is a bit of a stretch, but not entirely unreasonable. Intelligence seems entirely out of place however, when describing how a farming simulation's seed "decides" whether to sprout or not. Yet, the processes that determine the behavior of a simulated soldier, a simulated ant, and a simulated seed can be almost entirely identical.

The ability to devise such behaviors is a key one for a video game designer.

The learning objectives for this chapter are:

1 Be able to break down real-time autonomous events into discrete steps.

2 Understand what constitutes a finite state machine and how one can be used to create autonomous behavior.

3 Understand how a simple set of rules can result in emergent behaviors.

Artificial Intelligence in Games

In the world of game development, programmers and game designers often strive to create the illusion of intelligence. While artificial intelligence (AI) in games can be elaborate and complicated, the techniques involved are often surprisingly simple. The algorithm that controls a non-player character (NPC) soldier does not actually need to make reasoned decisions, it just needs to make the actions of the soldier *appear* reasonable. And because a typical NPC soldier has only one purpose (attack the human player), its decision-making does not need to be any more complicated than that of a brain-dead zombie.

It may seem odd to have the seemingly advanced topic of artificial intelligence precede the chapter that covers the broader, more general topic of paper prototyping video games. But the ability to design autonomous behavior is one of the main characteristics of video game design that differentiates it from tabletop game design. As such, it is a fundamental skill that a designer needs to develop prior to tackling the creation of paper prototypes of video games.

This chapter will get you started, but there is a lot more to artificial intelligence and game autonomous behaviors than can be covered here. If you would like to dive deeper into the topic, Ian Millington and John Funge's *Artificial Intelligence for Games* book is a good place to start.

An NPC's game AI would typically consist of a set of rules that direct its behavior. For example, the rules for a soldier NPC might be:

- If the NPC has a line-of-sight view of the player character, then advance towards her.
- If the player character is in attack range, shoot at her.
- If the player is not in view or attack range, patrol the area.

A slightly more sophisticated AI might add the appearance of self-preservation by having the NPC flee after receiving a certain amount of damage (and perhaps yell, "Medic, medic!"). Describing this as intelligence (even artificial intelligence) may seem an overstatement. And in fact, what game developers call AI is much more modest than what computer scientists mean by the term. Computer scientists are generally not interested in illusions—they are trying to create actual intelligent behavior. For a computer scientist, an AI is something that can react to changing circumstances and goals, make appropriate choices based upon those goals, and possibly learn from experience (Poole and Mackworth 2010, 4).

A game developer can give a soldier AI access to perfect knowledge of its position relative to the player, so determining when to start shooting is a trivial calculation. In contrast, on a real battlefield it would be an incredibly difficult task for an AI to determine whether a moving object is an enemy combatant. Computer scientists need their AIs to be able to work with the real world's imperfect knowledge and, within the constraints of reality, perform as perfectly as possible. In video games, however, there are many situations in which it is easy to create an AI that performs perfectly—in fact, too perfectly. Because game developers are trying to create the illusion of reality, they need to give their AIs a real-world tendency to err. Giving an NPC soldier perfect aim is easier than making it realistically inaccurate. In a way, the ideal for programmers is not artificial intelligence, it is artificial stupidity. Game AIs are often intended to put up a good fight and then lose, whereas a classic computer science AI would be designed to make optimal decisions.

Mick West (Neversoft's co-founder) describes an AI opponent he designed for a pocket billiards video game: "The AI I created was very simple. The computer just picked the highest value ball that could be potted, and then potted it. Since it knew the precise positions of all the balls, it was very easy for it to pot the ball every time" (West 2009). To make the game playable, inaccuracy was added to the AI's shots by adding a random adjustment to the angles it calculates. This design made the creation of difficulty levels easy—a small range of adjustment to the AI's otherwise perfect aim was used for "Hard" play (so that it would make most shots) and a wider range of adjustment for "Easy" play (so that it would miss a lot of shots). Even though West was able to provide a frequency of missed shots that his playtesters liked, they still thought that the AI was playing too well. Playtesters felt that the AI's positional play (where the cue ball and other struck balls came to rest after a shot) was too expert—that it was strategic in making sure that the cue ball ended up in a position that did not give the human player a good shot. In actuality, the AI's positional play was entirely random—when making its shots it did not take the cue ball's ending position into account. But every time a playtester was left with a difficult shot, the tester assumed that her predicament was the result of the AI's skill rather than chance. All it takes is a few randomly difficult shots in a game to make a player believe that the AI's positional play is unfairly strong. West's solution was to have the "easy" mode of the AI not only miss shots, but do so in a way that sets up the human player for an easy shot.

A poker playing AI could take a similar approach of having its easy mode secretly aid the human opponent. Towards that end, it might tend to play hands that a wiser player would fold, and bet more than it should. But what if the designer took it a bit further? What if the AI's decision-making utilized information that is not supposed to be available to players of the game, such as the order of the deck, and the cards that are in each player's hand? Having access to that kind of hidden information would allow the designer to more directly control the flow of the

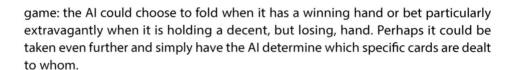

game: the AI could choose to fold when it has a winning hand or bet particularly extravagantly when it is holding a decent, but losing, hand. Perhaps it could be taken even further and simply have the AI determine which specific cards are dealt to whom.

Designing an "easy" AI can require more finesse than having it simply play poorly. A case in point is the AI for a *Scrabble* video game that the author used to play. *Scrabble* is a game in which an AI has a huge advantage over a human player—it is a relatively trivial matter for the AI to play the optimal, highest possible scoring word every turn. The designer of this particular *Scrabble* AI reined in its abilities for the easier levels by having it tend to play shorter length words (shorter words score fewer points). This did result in a very beatable artificial opponent, but even so the AI's style of play was unsatisfying. While the AI would play short words, it was still able to utilize the entire dictionary within that constraint. As a result, the AI had an inhuman vocabulary and turn after turn it would play incredibly obscure (albeit short and low scoring) words. Playing against an opponent (even one who loses) who continually plays unfamiliar words lessens the enjoyment of the game.

Does it ruin the game to have an AI "cheat"? If so, at what point was the line crossed: when the AI played poorly, when the AI gained access to private information, or when the AI took control of the aspects of the game that are supposed to be random? What about the reverse? Is it wrong to have an AI cheat in order to play stronger so as to provide a skilled human player a more satisfying challenge? How about a mix of cheating-to-win and cheating-to-lose in order to create edge-of-your-seat games in which the human player runs perilously low on chips before hitting a hot streak that bankrupts all the AI players?

Assuming there is no real money at stake, it might seem that whatever provides the most exciting experience for players should be a designer's goal. Yet in practice, this sort of game manipulation alienates players, especially when the AI takes the form of an anthropomorphized opponent. Manipulating the cards in poker may be particularly egregious since it undermines the statistical nature of the game's core gameplay. Someone who plays the poker video game in order to sharpen his poker skills might be very unpleasantly surprised when he plays the game in the real-world and is not constantly dealt choice hands from a stacked deck.

How an AI is designed depends greatly on the particular design goals and there are certainly times in which the AI needs to "cheat" in order to play at an appropriate level. When designing such an AI, it is worth asking yourself how your players would feel if they knew the ways in which the AI's abilities are enhanced or diminished.

EXERCISE *Shoot-Out* Bot

Many AIs exist as part of a game's content, such as the algorithms that dictate the behaviors of a computer-controlled character or the game's environmental systems. Artificial intelligence can also be used to create a "bot," a computer-controlled player that can take the place of a human opponent.

For this exercise you will create a flowchart that determines the actions of a *Shoot-Out* playing bot. As a starting place, you may want to play the game several times, keeping notes on what you take into consideration when deciding what action to take. How are your choices affected by your pawn's position, the position of your opponent's pawn, the number of bullets you and your opponent possess, the points at stake in the current duel, and the points won in early duels?

Analyzing your decision making process can help you develop "heuristics." A heuristic is a rule of thumb that aims to describe a course of action that is generally good, even if it is not necessarily always optimal. For example, here is a simple American football AI that uses heuristics (adapted from Patek & Bertsekas, 1998) to select offensive plays:

1. On a first down, pass the ball.
2. On a second down:
   a. If the number of yards to the next first down is less than three, then run the ball;
   b. Otherwise, pass the ball.
3. On a third down, randomly choose between running or passing.
4. On a fourth down:
   a. If the end zone is less than 41 yards away, then randomly choose between running, passing, or kicking (attempting a field goal).
   b. If the end zone is 41 or more yards away, then randomly choose between running, passing, or punting.

Along these lines, create a *Shoot-Out* AI in the form of a flowchart that determines whether to shoot, move, or retreat using only a few decision diamonds. Once you have a flowchart that can reliably direct the bot's behavior for an entire game, you can begin adding more diamonds to the flowchart and, consequently, complexity to the bot's decision-making process. For example, The heuristic of retreating when the opponent's pawn is on 6 might be further refined by only doing so if the bot's pawn is on 9 or above and conceding the duel will not lose the game (i.e., the opponent will not gain a total of 14 or more points by winning the duel).

The goal is to create the strongest bot possible. Try playing several games against the bot, expanding it whenever it runs into a situation that it cannot handle or when the choices it makes are obviously flawed.

If you would like to experiment with an AI that "cheats" and can alter the dice roll outcomes, feel free. But make sure that you do create at least one version of your *Shoot-Out* AI that plays "honestly."

As you develop your bot, continue playing games against it to ensure that the flowchart is working correctly (i.e, there are no dead-ends or places where the next step is ambiguous) and to look for ways to make it a stronger player (without cheating). See if you can find someone else to develop a *Shoot-Out* bot and pit the two non-cheating bots against one another. If doing this exercise in the context of a class, perhaps have an AI tournament.

Finite State Machines

The enemy soldier NPC described in the previous section has a limited number of activities it can perform: advance, attack, or patrol. The NPC will continue doing one of these activities until a change in the game results in the AI shifting to a different activity. For example, if the NPC is patrolling and spots the player character, it will shift to attack mode. If the NPC is in attack mode and the player is out of range, the NPC will determine a good firing position and move towards it. When the NPC reaches the firing position it will shift back to attack mode if the player is in sight, otherwise it will return to patrol mode.

Game programmers call this sort of AI structure a "finite state machine" (FSM). A finite state machine consists of a set of states (such as the NPC's "patrol," "attack," and "advance" states) and the behaviors associated with each state (Millington & Funge 2009, 309) as well as the possible transitions between states, and the conditions for each transition.

In the case of our NPC, the patrol state is associated with walking along a pre-defined route; the attack state is associated with shooting at the player character and taking cover; and the advance state involves the NPC running to be within firing range of the player, with preference given to a location that offers cover.

Figure 14.1 is a "state chart" diagram of the NPC's state machine. Its layout is based on the conventions of UML (Unified Modeling Language), a flowchart-like system for creating a visual model of a program's behavior. The black circle points to the FSM's initial state. The boxes represent the various states and the arrows indicate how the states transition from one to another. The arrows' bracketed text specifies what condition triggers the state change.

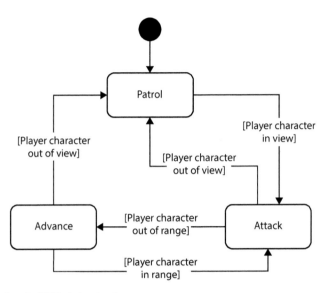

Figure 14.1 A simple NPC state chart.

A slightly more elaborate version of the NPC's AI can be seen in the state chart shown in figure 14.2. This version moves the Advance state to reside within the Attack state. This results in a "hierarchal state machine" in which Attack is a "composite state" that contains the nested "substates" of Advance and Shoot.

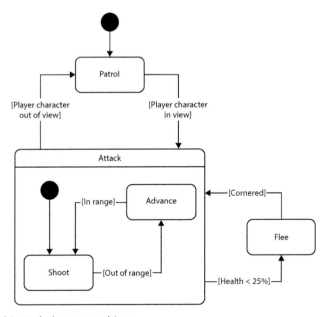

Figure 14.2 A hierarchal state machine.

Essentially, the Attack state is a state machine in itself and an NPC that is in an Attack state is consequently in one of its substates, either Advance or Shoot.

A Flee state has also been added to the state machine. Flee is intended to simulate a sense of self-preservation. Fleeing is triggered when the NPC's health falls below 25%. If cornered while in the Flee state, the NPC returns to an Attack state.

Game designer Raph Koster describes using finite state machines for the creature AIs in an early version of the pioneering persistent world game, *Ultima Online* (Koster, *UO's resource system, part 2* 2006):

The basic AI behavior of a creature was

- If I'm hungry, search for items that produce stuff on my FOOD list, and attack or eat them. Wander as far as needed to accomplish this.
- If I am not hungry, then start looking for a home base. If I already have one, then go there. If I get hungry while doing this, go back to hunting for food.
- If I am sheltered and not hungry, then look around for stuff that I just like. If I can pick it up, bring it to my shelter. If not, just hang around there—until I get hungry.

For a real-world example of a finite state machine in *Splinter Cell: Chaos Theory*, see Clint Hocking's 2006 Game Developers Conference talk "Designing to Promote Intentional Play" at www.funmines.com/hocking.

A finite state machine, such as the one described by Koster, can create behaviors that seem compellingly life-like (at least within a limited context) with a few simple states. The choice to use this sort of artificial intelligence, however, is something that needs to be done in consultation with the game's programmers. If a game engine is being used, it will likely determine how the game AIs are structured—and even when a game is being created from scratch, the programmers may have other ideas regarding how to create the AIs.

Video Game Designers and Programmers

Game designers who are inexperienced in software development can have a tendency to create overly vague designs. The prospect of breaking down a desired behavior into specific programmable details can seem overwhelming. For example, when designing a zombie apocalypse game, a game designer might be tempted to simply state that "zombies attack when they detect a human" and not work out exactly how the zombies' senses work. In such situations, a programmer might work out the design details—which may or may not be appropriate depending on how your development team wants to work.

How might those zombies be designed to sense a human? Here is one possible design:

1. The percentage chance that a zombie detects a human is equal to 100 minus the distance in meters between the human and the zombie.
2. The chance of detection increases 25% when a gun is fired. This means, for example, that a zombie 110 meters away from a human who has just fired a gun, has a 15% chance of sensing the human.
3. The chance of detection increases 10% for any humans who are running.

There is nothing about that design that requires programming knowledge. That said, it would not be at all unusual for a game programmer to come back to the designer with questions, change requests, and ideas. For example, the programmer might suggest an increased chance of detection when a human is bleeding, and might ask whether there are multiple checks for a group of humans.

The relationship between designers and programmers is complicated. It is not always easy to specify what parts of a video game are the designer's responsibility and what belong to the programmers. Ultimately, it is important for designers and programmers to be in communication and open to collaboration.

Emergent Behavior

In his book *Game Design: Theory & Practice*, Richard Rouse III describes a puzzle in an RPG that utilizes pressure plates. In the game there is a section of the floor that, when stepped upon, causes a locked door to open. The player needs her character to go through the door, but as soon as she steps off the pressure plate, the door closes and re-locks. Nearby there is a pile of rocks. Placing several of the rocks on the pressure plate triggers the door and holds it open so the character can go through it.

Liz England is a game designer at Insomniac Games. Her design background encompasses a diverse range of game genres, game systems, and designer roles. England has worked on first-person shooters, third-person shooters, puzzle-platformers, and open world games that have been published on Nintendo DS, 3DS, and Wii; PlayStation 3; Xbox 360 and Xbox One, and iOS systems. Her designs have included puzzles, systems, economies, skill trees/ progressions, missions, scripting, combat, and levels.

Liz likes to explain what a game designer does in terms of "The Door Problem." After reading her list below, you may find yourself taking a moment to appreciate all the work that went into designing a door the next time you encounter one in a game.

The Door Problem

by Liz England

Adding doors to your game? Here are some of the questions you might ask yourself as a designer:

- Can the player open them?
- Can the player open every door in the game?
- Or are some doors for decoration?
- How does the player know the difference?
- Are doors you can open green and ones you can't red? Is there trash piled up in front of doors you can't use? Did you just remove the doorknobs and call it a day?
- Can doors be locked and unlocked?
- What tells a player a door is locked and will open, as opposed to a door that they will never open?
- Does a player know how to unlock a door? Do they need a key? To hack a console? To solve a puzzle? To wait until a story moment passes?
- Are there doors that can open but the player can never enter them?
- Where do enemies come from? Do they run in from doors? Do those doors lock afterwards?
- How does the player open a door? Do they just walk up to it and it slides open? Does it swing open? Does the player have to press a button to open it?
- Do doors lock behind the player?
- What happens if there are two players? Does it only lock after both players pass through the door?
- What if the level is REALLY BIG and can't all exist at the same time? If one player stays behind, the floor might disappear from under them. What do you do?

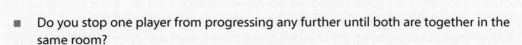

- Do you stop one player from progressing any further until both are together in the same room?
- Do you teleport the player that stayed behind?
- What size is a door?
- Does it have to be big enough for a player to get through?
- What about co-op players? What if player 1 is standing in the doorway—does that block player 2?
- What about allies following you? How many of them need to get through the door without getting stuck?
- What about enemies? Do mini-bosses that are larger than a person also need to fit through the door?

© 2014 Liz England.

You can see how programmers, art directors, and QA testers view doors at Liz England's blog, www.lizengland.com/blog/2014/04/the-door-problem.

One approach to creating this puzzle would be to test for the specific situations in which the player's character or the rocks are on top of the pressure plate. This allows the puzzle to be solved, but rigidity of that solution may reveal the game world to be more little more than a thinly constructed set piece by not allowing any alternative solutions that might occur to the player. Another approach to designing the puzzle would be to create a "weight" trait for the objects in the game. Rather than having the pressure plate trigger when the player character or rocks are on it specifically, it could be designed more generally to trigger when a certain amount of weight is placed upon it. Suddenly there are multiple solutions to the puzzle—perhaps ones even the designers did not anticipate (Rouse 2005, 116). A "create food" spell might be used to open the door because the rations it instantiates have weight. Or perhaps the body of a dead monster could be put on the plate—or a live one tricked into stepping on it. Or the player might have his character remove her armor and use it to trigger the pressure plate (a choice that might later be regretted if there is a monster on the other side of the door).

This second approach, in which the puzzle is more open-ended and allows multiple solutions, is an example of a game that supports emergent behaviors. The concept of emergent behaviors in games has generated a lot of excitement (as well as eye-rolling due to over-hype) among game designers and players. The experience that emergence can offer is one of a rich variety of choice for players and a game world that takes on a life of its own. Towards this end, the concept of "weight" in the example needs to be an intrinsic part of the general game to truly constitute emergent play. If weight was only used for the one specific puzzle, then it is just an elaborate special case that requires much more design work than it is worth.

Emergent gameplay comes from game mechanics and events that are designed to be as responsive to one another as they are to the actions of the player. They involve simple systems that interact in complex ways. Any game can have emergent qualities, but "sandbox" games/toys such as *Conway's Game of Life* and *The Sims* have it almost by definition.

A sandbox game emphasizes play that centers on exploratory changes to the game state rather than a dogged pursuit of a victory condition. *Conway's Game of Life* provided a particularly early and influential example of emergence. It was first played on a *Go* board and was later implemented on computers (Gardner 1970). The game is played on a grid whose squares are either blank (empty) or filled in (representing a living cell). Each game turn, squares are filled and cleared to represent cells being born and dying. Each cell's life and death is determined by four simple rules that evaluate its neighbors (cells in the eight surrounding squares):

1. Birth: An empty square with exactly three neighbors becomes populated with a cell.
2. Survival: A cell with two or three neighbors lives on to the next turn.
3. Death: A cell with fewer than two neighbors dies from loneliness.
4. Death: A cell with more than three neighbors dies from overcrowding.

The game is turn-based (each turn is referred to as a "generation"), and between each turn all the cells in the grid are updated simultaneously based upon the above four rules. Complex behaviors can arise despite the simplicity of the game's rules. For example, there is a five-cell group called a "glider" that repeats its shape, shifted one square on the diagonal, every fourth generation (see figure 14.3).

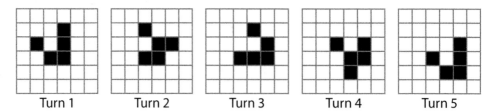

Turn 1 Turn 2 Turn 3 Turn 4 Turn 5

Figure 14.3 *Conway's Game of Life* glider movement over five turns.

Gliders are so-called because they seem to fly across the screen (or board, if using *Go* pieces).

The glider shape can be manually set up prior to starting the game and running through its generations. But even when it is not specifically created by the player, glider shapes often arise unexpectedly as the game's cells grow and die.

Emergence supports gameplay that is more complex than the rules' complexity (Juul 2005, 191), but this does not require that the rules be as streamlined as the ones in *Conway's Game of Life*. The alpha version of *Ultima Online* offers a more complex example of emergence:

Much more goes on behind the scenes than most players will ever notice. Nearly everything in the world, from grass to goblins, has a purpose, and not just as cannon fodder either. The "virtual ecology," as Starr Long, the game's associate producer calls it, affects nearly every aspect of the game world, from the very small to the very large. If the rabbit population suddenly drops (because some gung-ho adventurer was trying out his new mace) then wolves may have to find different food sources—say, deer. When the deer population drops as a result, the local dragon, unable to find the food he's accustomed to, may head into a local village and attack. Since all of this happens automatically, it generates numerous adventure possibilities.

(GameSpot 1996)

Ultima Online's emergent system (which included the creature finite state machines described earlier) was abandoned before the beta version of the game. The reasons for the change include issues of game balance, the strain it put on the game's servers, and development team members who preferred a more hard-coded implementation (Koster 2006). This might also be a situation in which the underlying complexity of the game's mechanics muddies the players' understanding of the system's dynamics. A dragon's attack might be so far removed from the player actions that triggered it, that it would seem like a random event. Given that, actually designing it as a random event might be preferable because it would allow the designer to better anticipate and shape how the players experience the game. The more straightforward version of *Ultima Online* was probably better able to adhere to Sid Meier's principle that "the player should have the fun, not the designer or the computer" (Soren 2009).

Open World Games

Games such as *NetHack* and the *Grand Theft Auto* series are sometimes referred to as sandbox games, but they are more frequently described as "open world" or "free-roaming" games. Open world games are similar to sandbox games, but differ in that they tend to have a storyline and fixed tasks for the player to perform. What makes an open world game "open" is that it is designed to allow players to go off-the-rails and abandon the story in favor of exploring the game's world.

EXERCISE Herding

This is a paper prototyping exercise in which you create emergent gameplay using a simple set of AI rules. Taking inspiration from *Conway's Game of Life*, you will create a herding simulator that gives flocking behavior to a group of creatures (which can be sheep, pigs, cows, wolves, chickens, cats, goblins, or any other animal you fancy). The purpose of the prototype is to help develop and test the AI movement rules.

1. Use hex paper for the game space, which will provide the game's creatures six possible directions of travel, plus the option of standing still. A link to printable hex paper can be found at www.funmines.com/resources.
2. You should determine the set of states that form the creature AI (such as lonely, startled, scared, hungry, angry, etc.).
3. For each state, create a set of rules to specify the creature's behavior (especially movement behavior) while in that state and what causes it to switch to another state. The rules can take into account the terrain, the surrounding animals, food sources, or anything else you want to make relevant. It is important to note that every creature in the flock will utilize the same set of AI rules, though at any given time they may be in different states and exhibiting different behaviors.
4. Devise a way to track the creatures' states. One possibility is to use dice for the creature game pieces. This would allow you to have each side of a die represent a different state—so a change in state would simply entail a rotation of the dice.
5. Design the game to be turn-based. You will probably want to treat the changes to the creatures' states and behaviors as happening sequentially. This means that you update the game state for each creature in turn and simply reference the game state as it stands rather than attempt to use it as it was at the start of the turn.

Strive to create complex interactions that arise out of a few simple rules. Start modestly with just a few states, playtest, and add from there if necessary. Resist the temptation to use an existing flocking algorithm (such as "Boids"). These kinds of algorithms are much more complicated than is practical for a paper prototype. Also keep in mind that the flocking behavior does not necessarily need to involve traditional flocking. For example, a group of cats might frequently move independently and only occasionally come together in small groups to interact in the form of playing, fighting, grooming, or sleeping together.

When you are ready to test your simulation, you can do it by placing a number of creatures on your playing field, varying their starting states, and see what sort of behavior results. If you are using dice as game pieces, you could establish the creatures' starting positions and states by simply rolling the dice so that they scatter across the game board. Continue playtesting and adjusting your AI rules until you achieve a flocking behavior that you are satisfied with.

The game's bookkeeping may be tedious, but try to focus on whether the changes to the game state are satisfying (even if the series of calculations and time to update it is not). Strive to make your design as simple as possible in order to keep the state changing manageable.

Once you have the flocking behavior you want, design an avatar to be controlled by the player—it could be a shepherd, a herding dog, a predator, prey, or anything else you like. Create rules for how its position and actions affect the creatures around it.

CHAPTER FIFTEEN

Prototyping Video Games

INTRODUCTION

This chapter deals with the creation of discardable video game mock-ups. These prototypes can be created on a computer (digital prototypes) or take a non-digital form that is reminiscent of tabletop games (paper prototypes).

The learning objectives for this chapter are:

1 Understand the benefits and drawbacks of prototyping digitally and on paper.

2 Learn techniques for translating video game mechanics into a tabletop form.

3 Gain experience from paper and digitally prototyping video games.

Why Prototype on Paper?

A paper prototype (or a "physical prototype") is a manually driven video game mock-up that exists outside of a computer. Paper prototypes range from a simple sketch of a screen layout created in seconds to an elaborate tabletop game that was days in the making.

Paper prototypes are more limited than digital prototypes in their ability to capture and present the action of a video game. So why prototype on paper?

The Briggs/Chase Law

The Briggs/Chase Law of Program Development is a tongue-in-cheek method for estimating how long it will take to write and debug a program. The "law" says to take your best estimate, multiply it by two, add one, and convert to the next higher unit type (i.e., hours become days, days become weeks, etc.). So a digital prototype that you think will take two days to complete would (according to the Briggs/Chase Law) actually require five weeks to finish.

A common answer is the speed in which a paper prototype can be created makes it particularly well-suited to an iterative design process. Paper prototypes are easy to make and easy to change. A mechanic can be modified instantly by the players simply agreeing to a rule change. The easy immediacy of paper prototypes can open up the design process and shift it from a back-and-forth between a designer and programmer to something in which the entire development team can take part.

A working paper prototype of *Tetris* can be made in well under an hour and revised almost instantaneously while playtesting. Creating a rough digital *Tetris* prototype would take quite a bit longer. Exactly how much more time is difficult to say. Programming-time estimates are notoriously inaccurate, but it is usually safe to assume that a programming task will take several times longer to do than predicted (see sidebar).

Paper prototyping's speed offers an additional benefit. Human nature leads us to become invested in the outcome of our efforts (and the efforts of our teammates). The more time we spend creating something, the less willing we are to toss away a not entirely satisfactory result. Because creating a paper prototype is simpler and less time consuming than a digital prototype, there is less psychological resistance to modifying the initial design it expresses. The reluctance to change can be even greater when the prototype is actually an early version of the game and there is no intention of discarding it.

Paper prototyping's pliability and speed provide major benefits. Yet there is another one that may be even more important to a game designer. Paper prototyping enables a designer to experience her design (or at least a semblance of it) prior to handing it over to a programmer. Tabletop game designers have the luxury of working in their game's actual medium. In contrast, video game designers depend on others to translate their ideas into the game's digital medium. An analogy might be drawn to how a playwright's words are brought to life by actors. A playwright who has never spoken his dialogue out loud and hears it for the first time in rehearsal risks embarrassment and wasting time. Paper prototypes are a way for video game designers to experience their creations prior to having them expressed by someone else.

So while paper prototypes are limited in the insight they can provide, they are the best that is available for game designers who cannot program. And even for designers who *can* program, prototyping on paper still offers substantial rewards. Towards this end, it is worth noting that paper prototyping does not preclude digital prototypes. Rapid iterations on paper can help developers shape and gain confidence in their initial design, which is then realized as a digital prototype in order to deal with the issues that are better explored in the game's target medium.

The Limits of Paper Prototyping

Small games, such as mobile game apps (and game student projects) can often be realized in a single, unified paper prototype. For larger games, however, trying to incorporate everything into one prototype quickly becomes unwieldy. In such cases, a designer is usually better off targeting the areas of the design that merit deeper inquiry and breaking them into separate prototypes.

For example, a designer might decide to create three prototypes for a single game: an economy prototype, a combat system prototype, and a prototype of the game's puzzles. Each of those prototypes would be made with an eye towards answering specific questions. Is the economic system balanced? How does the player character fare when fighting various monsters? Do the puzzles present an appropriate level of difficulty?

Playtesting a video game prototype should always focus on the specific questions that it was created to answer. If the prototype was not designed to mock-up the game's balance, then any balance issues that arise during playtesting do not necessarily shed any light on how balanced the actual game would be.

Devising a paper prototype that can answer a given question is not always easy. Video game mechanics involving continuous space and time are difficult to translate verbatim onto the tabletop. In such situations, you must ask yourself whether adjusting the mechanic to work on paper will provide any useful information. If not, then perhaps the mechanic would be better explored in a digital prototype.

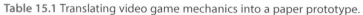

Table 15.1 Translating video game mechanics into a paper prototype.

Video game mechanic	Paper prototype implementation
Continuous space.	Convert to discrete units and use grid or hex paper to represent the game space. Alternatively, retain the game's continuous space and use rulers to measure it during playtesting.
Real-time gameplay.	Convert to a turn-based mechanic.
Three-dimensional game space.	Convert to two dimensions.
Physics of movement is core to the gameplay.	Create simple heuristics for the motion if possible, otherwise consider a digital prototype.
Heavy use of data and/or intensive calculations.	Simplify the algorithms and data for the prototype. Alternatively, create a paper/digital hybrid prototype that is paper-based where possible, but uses a spreadsheet for the more elaborate calculations.
Twitch skills (such as firing a gun at moving targets) are a core part of the gameplay.	Convert to a non-twitch mechanic. For example, establish the probability of a player accomplishing a task and then randomly determine whether it was successful. Alternatively, substitute a real-world feat of dexterity for the in-game twitch mechanic. For example, shooting an in-game target might require the player to successfully toss a wad of paper into a trash can.
Artificial intelligence.	Use flowcharts and state charts to determine the behavior of game AIs. Alternatively, add another player to the game who takes the place of the AIs. Or the designer can take on the role of "game master" and determine the behavior of the AIs during play.
The game has information that is hidden from the players, but requires updating during play.	Have someone who is not playing the game take on the role of maintaining the hidden game state.
The gameplay involves players gaining an intuitive understanding of the game's algorithms, rather than having a complete understanding of them.	Where applicable, do not inform the players about the rules that drive the prototype. A game master (who is aware of the game's rules) updates the game state in situations where the players are unable to determine the outcome of their actions.

Table 15.1 provides a list of video game mechanics that are challenging to implement in a paper prototype along with possible approaches for dealing with them.

Perhaps paper prototyping's greatest limitation is in providing a sense of whether the design will result in a fun game. This is particularly true when one of the

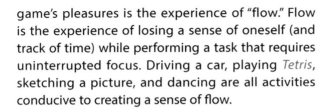

game's pleasures is the experience of "flow." Flow is the experience of losing a sense of oneself (and track of time) while performing a task that requires uninterrupted focus. Driving a car, playing *Tetris*, sketching a picture, and dancing are all activities conducive to creating a sense of flow.

Flow

See www.funmines.com/flow for further information about flow, including a link to the TED talk by the psychologist who originated the concept of flow, Mihály Csíkszentmihályi.

While flow is not entirely impossible in tabletop games, the turn-based nature of most tabletop games prevents it due to constantly interrupting the players' engagement with the game. Paper prototypes are especially prone to providing a clunky game-playing experience, and a mechanic that might provide flow in a video game probably will not in a paper prototype.

Capturing the Experience

Even though paper prototypes are often ill-equipped to test how fun a game will be, it is possible for them to aid designers in exploring the player experience. In the same way that the prototype of a mechanic does not have to capture the experience of playing the game, a prototype of the player experience can focus more on simulating the dynamics of the game rather than replicating its actual mechanics.

Brenda Laurel, designer and co-founder of Purple Moon, describes using such a prototype while conducting user research:

> During the prototype testing for the *Secret Paths* series at Purple Moon, we gave kids paper dolls that represented animals, plants, and other outdoor objects and asked them to make us a play about them. We were expecting *Secret Garden*-type stuff where kids would have magical adventures together. But the girls surprised us; they consistently felt that a place "in nature" would be a place where they would go alone. They wouldn't be taking care of the animals . . . they expected animals and magical creatures to take care of them.
>
> (in Novak 2012, 355)

Rules and mechanics were entirely absent in this paper prototype—it was simply a collection of the game's elements rendered on paper and a direction to create a narrative using them. Yet the exercise enabled the development team to revise their basic assumptions about the game. This saved the company a significant

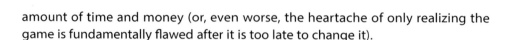

amount of time and money (or, even worse, the heartache of only realizing the game is fundamentally flawed after it is too late to change it).

EXERCISE Rebuilding *Rebuild 2*

Create a paper prototype based on *Rebuild 2*. The goal for the prototype is to develop algorithms that provide the feel of the original game's mechanics for clearing and reclaiming territory. Determine what aspects of the game are relevant to the prototype and determine how to incorporate them.

Normally a prototype comes before the finished game exists, but working in the other direction is a good way of practicing and developing paper prototyping skills.

The prototype should utilize a 3 × 3 game board (nine squares total). The player starts the game possessing the middle square and has the goal of reclaiming the surrounding eight spaces.

EXERCISE Making a GOB

The Sims is a sandbox game in which the player oversees a household of semi-autonomous simulated humans (sims). Each sim has a set of needs (such as bladder, energy, fun, hunger, and social) that it attempts to maintain. Fulfilling one need generally happens at the expense of the others. Eating decreases hunger, but increases the need to relieve one's bladder. Dancing can fulfill fun and social needs, but also causes the sim's energy to drop.

The sims are programmed to have AIs in the form of "goal oriented behaviors" (GOBs). Various objects in *The Sims* broadcast their ability to help fulfill a need (Millington & Funge 2009, 426). For example, a toilet object would broadcast that it can relieve the bladder need. Different objects broadcast at different strengths, and the signal weakens as it travels further from the object. So while a toilet would broadcast a strong "helps bladder" signal, a tree might be set to broadcast a weak "helps bladder" signal. When a sim decides to address a need, it follows the strongest relevant signal to its source. A sim would only choose to relieve itself on the tree if it was right next to it and the closest toilet was far enough away that its signal was dampened significantly.

This goal oriented approach results in sims that take care of their needs to a degree, but are not entirely self-sufficient and regularly require the player to intercede and guide them.

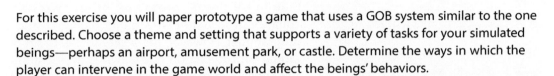

For this exercise you will paper prototype a game that uses a GOB system similar to the one described. Choose a theme and setting that supports a variety of tasks for your simulated beings—perhaps an airport, amusement park, or castle. Determine the ways in which the player can intervene in the game world and affect the beings' behaviors.

Design a set of needs that motivate the behavior of the game's AIs as well as game objects that can alleviate and exacerbate those needs. It may be helpful to view the task as designing an economy in which the needs are resources that are gained and lost.

You may want to create specialized beings (e.g., carnies for your amusement park), but resist the temptation to become overly elaborate and detailed. The prototype is a proof-of-concept; it does not need to (in fact, should not) incorporate every feature that you might envision for a finished video game.

Prototype your design and adjust it until it is working the way you wish and seems reasonably balanced.

Digital Prototypes

A "digital prototype" is a computer-based mock-up of a video game. Digital prototypes are intended to provide some insight into a game's design or technology. After the development team has learned as much as they can from the prototype, it is abandoned. What was learned from creating and playing it, helps inform the development of the game's "production code"—the work-in-progress software that will eventually evolve into the finished game. As you might expect, digital prototypes have some advantages over paper prototypes, due to the fact that they exist in the same medium as the game they are mocking-up.

Depending on what design (or technical) question a digital prototype is intended to answer, it may or may not visually resemble the finished product. When the goal is to evaluate the game's usability or to present the visual, aural, or haptic (touch) aesthetics that are intended for the game, the prototype will probably have a more polished look. If a digital prototype's primary purpose is to investigate game mechanics or balance, then the prototype may not look like a video game at all. Even so, the fact that the prototype exists on a computer allows it to perform calculations, process data, and respond to user input much more efficiently than is possible in a paper prototype.

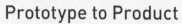

Prototype to Product

Some video game developers refer to an alpha or other early version of a video game as being a prototype. This kind of prototype will continue to be honed and expanded upon until it eventually develops into the finished product that is sold (or otherwise made available) to players.

This chapter deals with a different kind of digital prototype—discardable mock-ups that allow the development team to explore or test some aspect of the game's design, interface, or technology.

Prototyping in Excel

The original version of *World's Most Boring Tower Defense Game* runs in Javascript. An Excel-based version that demonstrates the prototyping capabilities of a spreadsheet is also available. Both versions can be found at www.funmines.com/boring-tower-defense

Building a digital prototype often involves a collaboration between a game designer and a programmer. However, the ability to create simple digital prototypes on one's own is an incredibly useful skill for a game designer. If you do not already know a programming language, you may want to try learning one. Almost any scripting language (such as Python, Javascript, Processing, or even the VBA language built into Excel) is capable of creating useful text-based prototypes.

A text-based prototype (or one with very simple graphics) can be a surprisingly effective design tool. The *World's Most Boring Tower Defense Game*, for example, allows a game designer to see how different tower and attacker configurations lead to different combat outcomes.

There are also visual languages that are programmed by setting up flowchart-like structures (see figure 6.4 on page 125). Visual programming languages have (relatively) simple tools for creating game graphics. Including graphics in a prototype can be useful when mocking up a twitch-based mechanic that would not be easily conveyed in a more text-oriented prototype. See www.funmines.com/visual-programming for a list of some of the more popular and useful visual programming languages.

EXERCISE Digital Herding

The herding paper-prototype exercise (page 284) had the goal of establishing the preliminary creature-movement rules. Building the prototype enabled you to determine what behaviors arise out of the various sets of rules you tried. Your paper prototype's ability to provide you insight into the player experience, however, is limited. Playing the paper

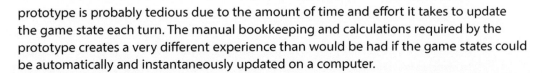

prototype is probably tedious due to the amount of time and effort it takes to update the game state each turn. The manual bookkeeping and calculations required by the prototype creates a very different experience than would be had if the game states could be automatically and instantaneously updated on a computer.

This exercise calls for you to further develop your design by creating a digital prototype. The goal of the digital prototype is to better emulate the game's actual user experience. The prototype will help you evaluate whether the actions a player can take provide a sense of player agency and create engaging play.

Player agency means providing the player a sense of control over her fate. Towards this end, the player's choices must be able to impact the game state in a meaningful (and reasonably foreseeable) way. By speeding up the interaction between the player's actions and the AI creatures' behaviors, you will be better able to determine whether players have that sense of control and whether the interaction engages them. If that proves not to be the case, revise the rules regarding the AI movement and/or the player actions until a satisfactory play experience is achieved.

Creating this digital prototype will be a challenge if you do not already know how to program. If that is the case, consider this as a call to begin learning a skill that will be invaluable to you as a game designer. You might aim to create something (perhaps a spreadsheet) that requires the game state and player actions to be manually entered and updated. The prototype would use the information to calculate and output how the paper prototype's game board should be updated for the next turn. While this digital prototype is limited in its ability to fully achieve the goals of the exercise, it could make the paper prototype less onerous and faster to play.

If you have strong programming skills, you might have the digital prototype encompass the entire design as prototyped on paper. This would involve tracking and visually presenting the game state and its changes on the computer as well as providing an interface for the player to directly enter her moves each turn. When you have finished this digital prototype, you will have taken a "build the toy first" approach (as described on page 70). Having created a satisfying interactive system, you might want to take on the challenge of adding player goals to the game (such as attempting herding the creatures out a door).

Demos and Vertical Slices

The dreaded "dog & pony show" is a demo intended to convince an audience of game reviewers, executives, potential investors, and so on that a game in development will be a runaway success.

Such demos often involve presenting an early version of the game or a prototype of the game's core mechanics. Showing a work-in-progress may seem advantageous because it not only demonstrates the concept of the game, but also the fact that there has been actual progress in getting it done. Showing a work-in-progress, however, risks making a disastrous impression. If the audience is not accustomed to seeing games in unfinished states, they will have a hard time focusing on anything but the obvious ways in which it is incomplete and unpolished. It is like showing dinner guests a bowl of raw eggs and telling them it is going to be dinner—they are going to gag if they have never seen eggs in anything but a cooked form.

Because of this, production teams are sometimes asked to create a "vertical slice" of their game. What precisely is meant by vertical slice varies, but generally it indicates that a small section of an in-development game is brought to a state that is meant to showcase the look and feel of the finished product. To draw an analogy, a vertical slice of cake might involve cutting a section of the baked cake so that it can be used for experimenting with icing flavors and decorations. This does not save the baker the work of making the cake, but does provide him (or potential customers) the chance to sample the final product prior to actually frosting an entire cake. Similarly, a vertical slice of a game requires that the underlying game systems are largely functional and that the development is far enough along that the team has a fairly solid idea of how the game's interfaces will work and what its content will look like.

Vertical slices generally have a bad reputation because they are often requested too early in the development cycle. Attempting to create a vertical slice when the project is not ready for it can completely derail the development effort. Undertaking a vertical slice at the right time, however, can provide benefits to the development team that go beyond simply pleasing game executives and having something to show outsiders. The creation of a vertical slice creates a milestone that drives the integration of the game's systems. It forces the team to fully think through and agree upon what they are in the midst of creating and allows the evaluation of the game's content prior to it being fully realized.

Further Reading

If you finish this book hungry to know more, please stop by www.funmines.com, the website that accompanies this book, to read more about game design and to access links to games, useful websites, and sources for design materials.

You may also be interested in seeking out additional books on games and game design. There are many admirable books on the topic, below is a short list of ones that the author has found particularly insightful.

Game Production

Jesse Schell's *The Art of Game Design* provides a unique perspective on game design. The book is built around 100 sets of questions for designers to consider while working on a game. It is a great book for anyone who has a grasp of the fundamentals of game design and is looking to improve further.

Brenda Brathwaite and Ian Schreiber's *Challenges for Game Designers* shares this book's philosophy that tabletop game development is an ideal way of learning and honing the skills necessary for video game design. If you want to continue working through the kinds of exercises that this book provides, then *Challenges* is the book that you want.

The Kobold Guide to Board Game Design is a very readable book filled with essays by professional tabletop game developers. Among its contents is an informative set of essays about the tabletop game industry and getting a tabletop game published.

Tabletop: Analog Game Design is a collection of essays by designers and academics about making and analyzing tabletop games. Best of all, it is available as a free download at press.etc.cmu.edu/content/tabletop-analog-game-design.

Game Design Workshop by Tracy Fullerton provides a nice view into how the video game industry's development processes and culture works. It is particularly well suited for aspiring video game producers. The video game industry's role of producer was modeled on producers in the music industry. Game producers are tasked with overseeing the process of developing the game and, towards that end, generally have a fair amount of authority over the technical and creative decisions made along the way.

John Ferrara's *Playful Design* is written from a user experience designer's point of view. Among its topics are gamification, games for learning, and games for persuasion.

If you want to dive deeper into the topic of autonomous behaviors and artificial intelligence, *Artificial Intelligence for Games* by Ian Millington and John Funge is highly recommended.

Tabletop Games

Reiner Knizia's *Dice Games Properly Explained* and David Parlett's *Oxford History of Board Games* are compendiums of abstract games, most of which can easily be played based upon the authors' descriptions. Parlett's book is out of print and is hard to find. Your best bet may be purchasing an electronic version of the text directly from the author (www.davidparlett.co.uk).

Game Studies

"Game studies" refers to a diverse academic discipline which analyzes games in terms of (among other things) their social, aesthetic, and historical meanings. While game studies texts generally do not tackle the topic of "how to make good games," their academic perspective can provide an awareness of games that can be useful to the practice of making them.

The seminal book in game studies is *Rules of Play* by Katie Salen and Eric Zimmerman. If your interest in games has an academic bent, then this book is required reading.

Jesper Juul's *Half-Real* is another game studies book that is well worth reading. Its title refers to Juul's thesis that video games are a hybrid of a real experience and a fictional world. While that idea serves as the touchstone, the book provides a broad overview of video game studies and can serve as a general text. It is a quicker read than *Rules of Play*, so if your time is limited and you do not mind bypassing the "go to" book for the field, you may find Juul's book the better choice.

Game Narrative

Anyone interested in game narratives should seek out Tom Bissell's *Extra Lives*. Bissell is an accomplished fiction writer and journalist. He is also an avid video game player. His writings about video games have a unique, penetrating perspective that is simultaneously insider and outsider. He is able to both appreciate the greatness in a game while at the same time being fully aware of the shortcomings that seem to inevitably come hand-in-hand with the medium.

See also the list of books about game writing and game narrative on page 133.

Ludography

This "ludography" lists the games that are discussed in the book. The games whose titles are printed in *blue text* can be played at no cost to you. Links and downloads to these games can be found by visiting the book's accompanying website at funmines.com/games.

Apologies to the many game developers who worked on the video games in this list, but were not credited with authorship. More comprehensive video game credits can be seen at mobygames.com.

Abbot, Scott and Chris Haney, *Trivial Pursuit* (Horn Abbot, 1981).

Abbott, Eleanor, *Candy Land* (Milton Bradley, 1949).

Abbott, Robert, *Switch* (*Abbott's New Card Games*, 1963).

Adams, Sherid, *Monopoly Inner Board* (unpublished).

Alexander, Whit and Richard Tait, *Cranium* (Cranium, 1998).

Almes, Scott, *Tiny Epic Kingdoms* (web published, 2013).

Anderson, Jake, John Murphy, and Brian O'Donnell, *OctoDad* (freeware, 2010).

Andromedus Software, *Blueprint Billiards* (Turbo NUKE, 2011).

Anthropy, Anna, *Town* (web published, 2009).

Asperheim, Mark and Cris Van Oosterum, *Ultimate Tic-Tac-Toe* (originally *Tic-Tac-Ku*) (Mad Cave Bird Games, 2008).

Azofra, Alvaro, Pablo Realini, and Gonzalo Sande, *Kingdom Rush* (Ironhide Game Studio, 2011).

Bissell, Rebekah, *Fairy Tale in my Pocket* (web published, 2009).

Braun, Jeff, Robert Strobel, and Will Wright, *SimCity* (Maxis, 1989).

Burm, Kris, *TAMSK* (Schmidt Spiele, 1998).

Butts, Alfred Mosher, *Scrabble* (Production and Marketing Company, 1948).

Calhammer, Alan B., *Diplomacy* (Games Research, 1959).

Camp, Walter, *American Football* (1880).

Capuano, Gregory, *Zamboni Doodle* (Google, 2013).

Chalcraft, Adam and Michael Greene, *Penultima* (public domain, 1994).

Conrad, Christwart, *Vino* (Goldsieber Spiele, 1999).

Conway, John H., *Conway's Game of Life* (*Scientific American*, October 1970).

Conway, John H. and Michael S. Paterson, *Sprouts* (public domain, 1967).

Crawford, Chris, *Balance of Power* (Mindscape, 1986).

Darrow, Charles, *Monopoly* (Parker Brothers, 1933).

Dutyfarm, *Deluxe Pool* (Miniclip and Gamesload, 2010).

Edan, Hermance, *Stratego* (originally *L'attaque*) (Au Jeu Retrouvé, 1910).

Ehrhard, Dominique, *Marrakech* (Gigamic, 2007).

Engström, Tomas, *Dungeonquest in my Pocket* (web published, 2008).

Ernest, James, *Button Men* (Cheapass Games, 1999).

———, *Kill Doctor Lucky* (Cheapass Games, 1996).

———, *Mapple* (Cheapass Games, 2011).

Fischer, Bobby, *Chess960* (originally *Fischer Random Chess*) (public domain, 1996).

Gabrel, Gary, *Pente* (Pente Games Company, 1977).

Garfield, Richard, *Magic: the Gathering* (Wizards of the Coast, 1993).

Garriott, Richard, Raph Koster, Starr Long, and Rick Delashmit, *Ultima Online* (Origin Systems, 1997).

Gottschalk, John, Yhorik Aarsen, and Jeroen Wimmers, *Westerado* (Ostrich Banditos, 2013).

Green, Ernest, *Patent-Mine* (unpublished, 2014).

Güth, Werner, *The Ultimatum Game* (public domain, 1970).

Gygax, Gary and David Arneson, *Dungeons & Dragons* (TSR, 1974).

Ham, Ethan, Jamey Harvey, Lee Moyer, John Mueller, and Benjamin Rosenbaum, *Sanctum* (Digital Addiction, 1998).

Hamilton, Keith R., *Grand Theft Auto* (DMA Design, 1997).

Haskell, Paul T., Jr. and William Henry Storey, *Sorry!* (1929).

Hason, Simon, *Tactical Assassin 3* (Simon Hason Design, 2011).

Hayes, Geoffrey, *Duell* (Lakeside, 1975).

Hersch, Brian, *Taboo* (Hasbro, 1989).

Hewison, C.B., *Stock Exchange* (Capitol Novelty Company, 1936).

Hoolim, Haar, *Three Musketeers* (*A Gamut of Games*, 1969).

Hudson, Casey and Preston Watamaniuk, *Mass Effect* (Bioware Corporation, 2007).

Iwatani, Toru, *Pac-Man* (Namco, 1980).

Joris, Walter, *Tabletop Billiards* (originally *Billiards*) (*100 Strategic Games for Pen and Paper*, 2002).

Kirby, Matthew and Mark A. Osterhaus, *Apples to Apples* (Out of the Box Publishing, 1999).

Klamer, Reuben, *LIFE* (Milton Bradley, 1960).

Knizia, Reiner, *Shoot-Out* (*Games Unplugged*, June 2002).

Koster, Raph, Richard Vogel, and John Donham, *Star Wars Galaxies: An Empire Divided* (LucasArts, 2003).

Kyburz, Jay, *Neptune's Pride II: Triton* (Iron Helmet Games, 2013).

Lambert, Richard, Andrew Rilstone, and James Wallis, *Once Upon a Time* (Atlas Games, 1994).

Lamorisse, Albert, *Risk* (originally *La Conquête du Monde*) (Miro Company, 1957).

Laurel, Brenda, *Secret Paths in the Forest* (Purple Moon Media, 1997).

Leacock, Matt, *Pandemic* (Z-Man Games, 2008).

Leacock, Matt and Thomas Lehmann, *Pandemic: On the Brink* (Z-Man Games, 2009).

LeBlanc, Marc, *3-to-15* (n.d.).

Lee, Jeremiah, *Zombie in my Pocket* (web published, 2007).

Looney, Andrew, *Nanofictionary* (Looney Labs, 2002).

McIver, Adam P., *Coin Age* (Project Game, 2013).

Meier, Sid and Bruce Campbell Shelley, *Sid Meier's Civilization* (MicroProse Software, 1991).

Metzen, Chris, Robert Pardo, and Ayman Adham, *World of Warcraft* (Blizzard Entertainment, 2004).

Mollett, John W. and Lewis Waterman, *Reversi* (also published as *Othello*) (*The Queen* magazine, 1880).

Moon, Alan R., *Ticket to Ride* (Days of Wonder, 2004).

Moore, Robert, *Cathedral* (Robert P. Moore Games, 1978).

Muscat, Luke, *Jetpack Joyride* (Halfbrick Studios, 2011).

Naismith, James, *Basketball* (public domain, 1891).

Northway, Sarah, *Rebuild* (Northway Games, 2011).

———, *Rebuild 2* (Northway Games, 2011).

Opus Corporation, *Surfing H3O* (Rockstar Games, 2000).

Pajitnov, Alexey, *Tetris* (Spectrum Holobyte, 1987).

Pardo, Robert and Ayman Adham, *World of Warcraft* (Blizzard Entertainment, 2004).

Pratt, Anthony E., *Clue* (originally *Cluedo*) (John Waddington Ltd, 1948).

Reynolds, Brian, Douglas Kaufman, and Jeffery L. Briggs, *Sid Meier's Civilization II* (MicroProse Software, 1996).

Robbins, Merle, *Uno* (International Games Inc., 1971).

Rotberg, Ed, *Battlezone* (Atari, 1980).

Saltsman, Adam, *Canabalt* (Semi Secret Software, 2009).

Schafer, Tim, *Full Throttle* (LucasArts, 1995).

Shafer, Jon, *Sid Meier's Civilization V* (Firaxis Games, 2010).

Scott, Leslie, *Jenga* (Oxford Games, 1983).

Skaggs, Mark, *Farmville* (Zynga, 2009).

Stephenson, Mike, *NetHack* (freeware, 1987).

Straley, Bruce and Neil Druckmann, *The Last of Us* (Naughty Dog, 2013).

Suckling, John, *Cribbage* (public domain, 1630).

Sweeney, Tim, *ZZT* (Epic MegaGames, 1991).

Tahta, Rikki, *Coup* (La Mame Games, 2012).

Teuber, Klaus, *The Settlers of Catan* (originally *Die Siedler von Catan*) (Kosmos, 1995).

Traditional, *Agon* (late 18th century).

Traditional, *Alquerque* (twelfth century).

Traditional, *Backgammon* (modern incarnation, seventeenth century).

Traditional, *Bagh Guti* (unknown date).

Traditional, *Brandub* (ninth or tenth century).

Traditional, *Checkers* (modern incarnation, sixteenth century).

Traditional, *Chess* (modern incarnation, fifteenth century).

Traditional, *Five Card Draw* (modern incarnation, 1820s).

Traditional, *Fox and Hounds* (unknown date).

Traditional, *Go* (earliest reference, fourteenth century bc).

Traditional, *Janggi* (modern incarnation, sixteenth century or earlier).

Traditional, *Misère Chess* (unknown date).

Traditional, *Nine Men's Morris* (circa 0 ad).

Traditional, *Pachisi* (unknown date).

Traditional, *Rock Paper Scissors* (unknown date).

Traditional, *Slapjack* (unknown date).

Traditional, *Snakes & Ladders* (200 bc).

Traditional, *Soccer* (modern incarnation, 1863).

Traditional, *Spoons* (unknown date).

Traditional, *Tic-Tac-Toe* (1 bc).

Traditional, *Xiangqi* (modern incarnation, circa twelfth century).

Traditional, *Yut Nori* (sixth century).

Tweet, Jonathan, Monte Cook, and Skip Williams, *d20 System* (Wizards of the Coast, 2000).

Uncredited, *Egyptian Ratscrew* (public domain, circa 1975).

Uncredited, *Hut* (public domain, date unknown).

Uncredited, *Old Maid* (public domain, circa 1875).

Uncredited, *Sea Battle* (public domain, circa 1917).

Uncredited, *Spades* (public domain, circa 1938).

Uncredited, *The Tower* (public domain, date unknown).

Vaccarino, Donald X., *Dominion* (Rio Grande Games, 2008).

———, *Gauntlet of Fools* (Indie Boards and Cards, 2012).

Vanderbilt, Harold Stirling, *Contract Bridge* (public domain, 1925).

Von Wickler, Clifford, *Battleship* (Milton Bradley Company, 1967).

Wrede, Klaus-Jürgen, *Carcassonne* (Hans im Glück, 2000).

Wright, Will, *The Sims* (Electronic Arts, 2000).

Yianni, John, *Hive* (Gen42 Games, 2001).

Bibliography

Academy of Art University. *School of Game Design: BFA Degree in Game Design.* 2006. www. academyart.edu/game-design-school/bfa-program.html (accessed August 9, 2012).

Alpaca. *Mathematics of Civilization V.* October 24, 2010. www.civilization.wikia.com/wiki/ Mathematics_of_Civilization_V (accessed January 28, 2014).

Bell, R.C. *Board and Table Games from Many Civilizations.* New York: Dover, 1979.

Brathwaite, Brenda and Ian Schreiber. *Challenges for Game Designers.* Boston, MA: Cengage Learning, 2008.

Burgun, Keith. *Game Design Theory: A New Philosophy for Understanding Games.* Boca Raton, FL: CRC Press, 2012.

Costikyan, Greg. *Uncertainty in Games.* Cambridge, MA: The MIT Press, 2013.

Costikyan, Greg and Drew Davidson, eds. *Tabletop: Analog Game Design.* Pittsburgh, PA: ETC Press, 2011.

Crawford, Chris. *Balance of Power: International Politics as the Ultimate Global Game.* Redmond, WA: Microsoft Press, 1986.

Daviau, Rob. "Design Intuitively." In *The Kobold Guide to Board Game Design*, by Mike Selinker, 42–49. Kirkland, WA: Wolfgang Baur, 2011.

Eggert, Moritz. *The "Kramer Leiste"?* May 20, 2006. www.westpark-gamers.de/index.html?/ transcripts/ggn15.html (accessed September 12, 2013).

Elias, George, Richard Garfield, and K. Robert Gutschera. *Characteristics of Games.* Cambridge, MA: The MIT Press, 2012.

Ernest, James. "Caribbean Star." In *Rules of Play: Game Design Fundamentals*, by Katie Salen and Eric Zimmerman, 592–601. Cambridge, MA: The MIT Press, 2004.

———. *Kill Doctor Lucky Free Edition Rules.* Cheapass Games, 2011.

Extra Credits. "Choice and Conflict." *Extra Credits.* December 30, 2010. www.extra-credits.net/ episodes/choice-and-conflict (accessed January 14, 2013).

———. "Playtesting." *Extra Credits.* December 14, 2011. www.extra-credits.net/episodes/ playtesting (accessed September 22, 2013).

Fisher, Robert. *Diagonal Movement on a Square Grid.* August 3, 2011. www.malirath.blogspot. com/2011/08/diagonal-movement-on-square-grid.html (accessed May 30, 2013).

GameSpot. *Ultima Online Preview.* May 1, 1996. www.gamespot.com/ultima-online/previews/ ultima-online-preview-2559974/ (accessed September 24, 2012).

Gardner, Martin. "Mathematical Games: The Fantastic Combinations of John Conway's New Solitaire Game 'Life.'" *Scientific American*, October 1970: 120–123.

Garfield, Richard. "Play More Games." In *The Kobold Guide to Board Game Design*, by Mike Selinker, 8. Kirkland, WA: Wolfgang Baur, 2011.

Grötker, Ralf. "A Game for Life." *Max Planck Research*, February 2009: 80–85.

Howell, Dave. "Stealing the Fun." In *The Kobold Guide to Board Game Design*, by Mike Selinker, 84–89. Kirkland, WA: Wolfgang Bauer, 2011.

Hunicke, Robin, Marc LeBlanc, and Robert Zubek. "MDA: A Formal Approach to Game Design and Game Research." In *Proceedings of the Challenges in Games AI Workshop*. San Jose, CA: AAAI Press, 2004. www.cs.northwestern.edu/~hunicke/MDA.pdf (accessed August 6, 2014).

Järvinen, Aki. *Games without Frontiers: Theories and Methods for Game Studies and Design*. Tampere: PhD diss., University of Tampere, 2008.

Jacklin, Kevin. "Simply Knizia: The Art in Keeping Game Design Simple." In *Tabletop: Analog Game Design*, by Greg Costikyan and Drew Davidson, 55–59. ETC Press, 2011.

Johnson, Soren. *Analysis: Sid Meier's Key Design Lessons*. May 5, 2009. www.gamasutra.com/view/news/23458/Analysis_Sid_Meiers_Key_Design_Lessons.php (accessed April 1, 2014).

Jones, M. Tim. *Artificial Intelligence: A Systems Approach*. Hingham, MA: Infinity Science Press, 2008.

Joris, Walter. *100 Strategic Games for Pen and Paper*. London: Carlton Books, 2002.

Juul, Jesper. *Half-Real: Video Games between Real Rules and Fictional Worlds*. Cambridge, MA: MIT Press, 2005.

———. "A Certain Level of Abstraction." *Paper Presented at the DiGRA 2007 Conference*. Tokyo, September 24–28, 2007.

———. "The Game, the Player, the World: Looking for a Heart of Gameness." In *Level Up: Digital Games Research Conference Proceedings*, edited by Marinka Copier and Joost Raessens, 30–45. Utrecht: Utrecht University, 2003.

Kent, Steven L. *The First Quarter: A 25-year History of Video Games*. Bothell, WA: BWD Press, 2001.

Kierkegaard, Alex. *The Stupidest Word in Videogames*. April 20, 2007. insomnia.ac/commentary/gameplay (accessed November 5, 2012).

Klibanoff, Peter. "Uncertainty, Decision, and Normal Form Games." mimeo, Northwestern University, July 1996.

Knizia, Reiner. *Dice Games Properly Explained*. Surrey, United Kingdom: Elliot Right Way Books, 2000 (reprinted 2010).

Koster, Raph. *A Theory of Fun for Game Design*. Scottsdale, AZ: Paraglyph Press, 2004.

———. *UO's Resource System, Part 2*. July 4, 2006. www.raphkoster.com/2006/06/04/uos-resource-system-part-2/ (accessed September 26, 2012).

———. *The Fundamentals of Game Design*. October 12, 2010. www.raphkoster.com/2010/10/12/the-fundamentals-of-game-design/ (accessed September 10, 2013).

Leacock, Matt. "Cooperation and Engagement: What Can Board Games Teach Us?" *YouTube*. April 30, 2008. www.youtube.com/watch?v=cdTVcFo2EQw (accessed April 3, 2014).

———. *Pandemic Version .1*. February 22, 2008. www.boardgamegeek.com/image/303842/pandemic (accessed April 4, 2014).

LeBlanc, Marc. *The Collected Game Design Rants of Marc "MAHK" LeBlanc*. www.8kindsoffun.com.

Librande, Stone. "Designing Games for Game Designers." Game Designer Conference, San Francisco, CA. March 8, 2012. www.stonetronix.com/gdc-2012/GDC2012-GamesForDesigners.pptx.

Millington, Ian and John Funge. *Artificial Intelligence for Games*. 2nd Edition. Burlington, MA: Morgan Kaufmann Publishers, 2009.

Morehead, Albert H. and Geoffrey Mott-Smith. *Hoyle's Rules of Games*. 3rd Edition. New York: Signet, 2001.

Novak, Jeannie. *Game Development Essentials: An Introduction*. 3rd Edition. Clifton Park, NY: Delmar, 2012.

Osborne, Martin J. and Ariel Rubinstein. *A Course in Game Theory.* Cambridge, MA: The MIT Press, 1994.

Park, Hye Jin, Hasung Sim, Hang-Hyun Jo, and Beom Jun Kim. "Analysis of One-Dimensional Yut-Nori Game: Winning Strategy and Avalanche-Size Distribution." *Journal of the Korean Physical Society* 63, no. 8 (October 2013): 1497–1502.

Patek, Stephen D. and Dimitri P. Bertsekas. "Play Selection in American Football: A Case Study in Neuro-Dynamic Programming." *Advances in Computational and Stochastic Optimization, Logic Programming, and Heuristic Search Operations Research/Computer Science Interfaces Series* 9 (1998): 189–213.

Poole, David L., and Alan K. Mackworth. *Artificial Intelligence: Foundations of Computational Agents.* New York: Cambridge University Press, 2010.

Proctor, Darby, Rebecca A. Williamson, Frans B.M. de Waal, and Sarah F. Brosnan. "Chimpanzees Play the Ultimatum Game." *Proceedings of the National Academy of Sciences of the United States of America* 110, no. 6 (February 2013): 2070–2075.

Rasmusen, Eric. *Games and Information: An Introduction to Game Theory.* 4th Edition. Malden, MA: Blackwell Publishing, 2007.

Rogers, Scott. *Level Up!: The Guide to Great Video Game Design.* West Sussex: John Wiley & Sons, 2010.

Rollings, Andrew and Dave Morris. *Game Architecture and Design: A New Edition.* San Francisco, CA: New Riders, 2003.

Rouse, Richard, III. *Game Design: Theory & Practice.* 2nd ed. Sudbury, MA: Wordware Publishing, 2005.

Salen, Katie and Eric Zimmerman. *Rules of Play: Game Design Fundamentals.* Cambridge, MA: The MIT Press, 2004.

Schell, Jesse. *The Art of Game Design: A Book of Lenses.* Burlington, MA: Morgan Kaufmann Publishers, 2008.

Schreiber, Ian. *Decision-Making and Flow Theory.* July 20, 2009. www.gamedesignconcepts. wordpress.com/2009/07/20/level-7-decision-making-and-flow-theory (accessed May 29, 2014).

———. *Game Balance.* August 20, 2009. www.gamedesignconcepts.wordpress.com/2009/08/20/ level-16-game-balance (accessed January 10, 2013).

———. *Kinds of Fun, Kinds of Players.* July 23, 2009. www.gamedesignconcepts.wordpress. com/2009/07/23/level-8-kinds-of-fun-kinds-of-players (accessed April 9, 2014).

———. *Level 2: Game Design / Iteration and Rapid Prototyping.* July 2, 2009. www. gamedesignconcepts.wordpress.com/2009/07/02/level-2-game-design-iteration-and-rapid-prototyping (accessed July 21, 2013).

———. *Mechanics and Dynamics.* July 13, 2009. www.gamedesignconcepts.wordpress. com/2009/07/13/level-5-mechanics-and-dynamics (accessed April 1, 2014).

———. *The Early Stages of the Design Process.* July 9, 2009. www.gamedesignconcepts.wordpress. com/2009/07/09/level-4-the-early-stages-of-the-design-process (accessed September 13, 2013).

Sicart, Miguel. "Defining Game Mechanics." *Game Studies* 8, no. 2 (December 2008). www. gamestudies.org/0802/articles/sicart (accessed August 6, 2014).

Suits, Bernard. *The Grasshopper: Games, Life and Utopia.* Toronto: University of Toronto Press, 1978 (reprinted 2005).

Tabak, Matt. *Magic: the Gathering Basic Rulebook.* Renton, WA: Wizards of the Coast, 2013.

West, Mick. *Intelligent Mistakes: How to Incorporate Stupidity Into Your AI Code.* March 18, 2009. www.gamasutra.com/view/feature/132339/intelligent_mistakes_how_to_.php (accessed July 15, 2014).

Wizards of the Coast. "Revised (v.3.5) System Reference Document." *Wizards of the Coast.* July 1, 2003. www.wizards.com/d20/files/v35/CombatII.rtf (accessed May 30, 2013).

Woodruff, Teeuwynn. "It's Not Done Till They Say It's Done." In *The Kobold Guide to Board Game Design*, by Mike Selinker, 99–105. Kirkland, WA: Wolfgang Baur, 2011.

Woods, Stewart. *Eurogames: The Design, Culture and Play of Modern European Board Games.* Jefferson, NC: McFarland & Company, 2012.

World Chess Federation. *Laws of Chess.* www.fide.com/component/handbook/?id=171&view=article (accessed May 28, 2014).

Yu, Dale. "Developing Dominion: What Game Development Is All About." In *The Kobold Guide to Board Game Design*, by Mike Selinker, 74–79. Kirkland, WA: Open Design, 2011.

Zimmerman, Eric. "Play as Research: The Iterative Design Process." In *Design Research: Methods and Perspectives*, edited by Brenda Laurel, 176–184. Cambridge, MA: The MIT Press, 2003.

Index